The Grateful Dead's 100 Essential Songs

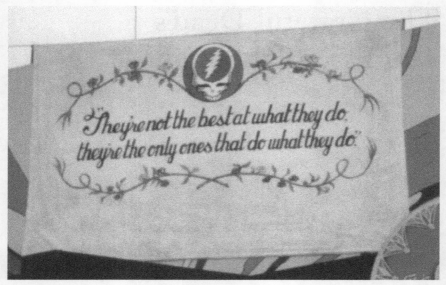

Bill Graham's Quote at Cal-Expo, May 1992

The Grateful Dead's 100 Essential Songs

The Music Never Stops

Barry Barnes
Bob Trudeau

ROWMAN & LITTLEFIELD
Lanham • Boulder • New York • London

Published by Rowman & Littlefield
An imprint of The Rowman & Littlefield Publishing Group, Inc.
4501 Forbes Boulevard, Suite 200, Lanham, Maryland 20706
www.rowman.com

Unit A, Whitacre Mews, 26-34 Stannary Street, London SE11 4AB

British Library Cataloguing in Publication Information Available

Library of Congress Cataloging-in-Publication Data

Names: Trudeau, Bob, 1940– author. | Barnes, Barry, 1944– author.
Title: The Grateful Dead's 100 essential songs : the music never stops / Bob Trudeau, Barry Barnes.
Description: Lanham : Rowman & Littlefield, [2018] | Includes bibliographical references and index.
Identifiers: LCCN 2018012686 (print) | LCCN 2018013483 (ebook) | ISBN 9781538110584 (electronic) | ISBN 9781538110577 (cloth : alk. paper)
Subjects: LCSH: Grateful Dead (Musical group) | Grateful Dead (Musical group)—Discography.
Classification: LCC ML421.G72 (ebook) | LCC ML421.G72 T78 2018 (print) | DDC 782.42166092/2—dc23
LC record available at https://lccn.loc.gov/2018012686

∞™ The paper used in this publication meets the minimum requirements of American National Standard for Information Sciences—Permanence of Paper for Printed Library Materials, ANSI/NISO Z39.48-1992.

Printed in the United States of America

Bob Trudeau "deadicates" this book to his granddaughter, Cleo, in the hopes that she will enjoy this music as she grows into adulthood, and to his wife, Pat: what a long, great trip it's been.

Barry Barnes "deadicates" this book to Bart Biechele, who insisted Barry attend his first Grateful Dead performance in Des Moines, Iowa, on June 16, 1974, and to his wife, Chris, who was adventurous enough to see 150 shows with him.

Contents

Preface

This book project began informally in February 2017, at the twentieth annual meeting of the Grateful Dead Scholars Caucus, a section of the Southwest Popular/ American Culture Association conference in Albuquerque. At a preconference workshop led by Stephen Ryan of Rowman & Littlefield publishers, Bob Trudeau on the spur of the moment decided to pursue a project documenting 100 essential Grateful Dead songs. Soon after, Barry Barnes joined the project, and together we've been engaged in a labor of love, focusing on songs we think are the most essential for a serious appreciation of the music of the Grateful Dead.

It takes a village to write a book, and this project has been nurtured by the spirit of the Grateful Dead Scholars Caucus, most of whom are academics studying the Dead from various disciplinary perspectives. Barry has been involved with the Caucus since 1999, almost from its beginning in 1998. Bob discovered the Caucus while attending the Unbroken Chain conference at the University of Massachusetts in Amherst in November 2007, which was his introduction to scholarly analysis of the Dead's music and its impact on society. We have enjoyed the support of many of our colleagues in the Caucus. They are also part of the genesis of this project.

Both of us have been fans of the Grateful Dead—that is, Deadheads—since the early 1970s, and we both feel our lives literally were changed by our involvement with this music. The major goal of this project is to share the significance of this special music with our readers—those who might be familiar with the Dead, those who might not be as involved as we have been, and hopefully even with newbies to the Grateful Dead. We want this music never to stop.

OUR STORIES

Barry's Story

In grade school I took piano lessons for a while and played the trumpet in junior high, but I'm certainly not a musician. What I am, however, is a passionate music listener and have been as far back as I can remember. That passion for listening to music increased as I got older and led me to open a record store from 1973 to 1976 and to become a DJ on the first progressive FM rock station in Kansas City during that time. It was during this period that I first began to appreciate the Grateful Dead. Although I bought their first album in 1968, I didn't care for it and still find it the least enjoyable of all their subsequent releases. I saw the Dead for the first time in Des Moines, Iowa, on June 16, 1974.

I continued to see the Dead about once a year when they played in Kansas City. There were a few years when they didn't come to town, but my appreciation of their music continued to grow as I began to listen to bootleg LPs and a few cassettes. In 1985, after having seen them twelve times, I scored tickets to their twentieth anniversary shows in Berkeley, and that was when I really "got it." I understood that their music was all about dance—perhaps even the cosmic dance of the universe! And the combination of the delightful community of Deadhead listeners dancing to the unique improvisation of the Dead's music made it clear to me that I needed to see more—much, much more of the Grateful Dead.

I had completed my MBA in 1984, and at the Berkeley shows in 1985, it became clear to me that not only was the Dead's music improvisational, but their behind-the-scenes business organization must also be improvisational in order to have successfully navigated the challenges of the music industry for twenty years. So I knew then that there were business lessons from the Grateful Dead that needed to be studied and shared, and I was the one to do that. I realized I needed to see more Dead performances, not only to feed my passion, but also to gain a better understanding of the lessons I intuitively knew were there. This was really the beginning of my own "long strange trip," during which I taped 189 of the 194 Grateful Dead shows I saw.

My epiphany at the Berkeley shows led me to quit my job, go back to school, and earn a PhD in business so I could gain a deeper understanding of business theory and terminology, all to be able to explain what was unique about the Dead's business. And of course, I increased the frequency of seeing the Dead to about fifteen shows a year . . . as part of my research! I also began to connect with Dead insiders and knowledgeable outsiders, and I started interviewing them. When I finished my PhD, I began teaching and continued seeing the Dead. I also began to incorporate what I had seen in the Dead into my teaching and scholarly writing, and all of this was aimed at writing a business book about the Dead, which ultimately became *Everything I Know about Business I Learned from the Grateful Dead: The Ten Most Innovative Lessons from a Long Strange Trip*, published in November 2011. Since then

I've continued to expand my thoughts and beliefs about the Dead's business side. I've written more articles, and since 1999, I've met annually in Albuquerque with the multidisciplinary Caucus group.

Bob's Story

Like Barry, I took piano lessons as a child but focused much more on listening to music than on playing it. I grew up in a household that continually had music in the background, either classical music or standards from the American songbook. In college I followed fellow students and now-famous musicians Buffy Sainte-Marie and Taj Mahal when they were starting out, not to mention a capella singing groups, square dancing music, and so on.

After college my wife and I lived in Choluteca, Honduras, as Peace Corps volunteers. Even there local teenagers exposed us to the early Beatles albums; the teens needed translations of the lyrics, so we listened. In 1967, we moved to Chapel Hill, and I completed a PhD in political science in 1971 at the University of North Carolina. My first real day job started in the fall of 1970 at Providence College.

When you read our review of "Bertha," you'll see that the Grateful Dead made a sudden and powerful leap into my life a year later in late 1971. I became hooked on their music immediately. After my first show on March 28, 1973, in Springfield, Massachusetts, I happily repeated to anyone who would listen what appears on many Deadhead bumper stickers: "There's nothing like a Grateful Dead concert!"

I saw many concerts during the northeast tours in the mid- and late 1970s. About the same time I learned to play the electric bass and even sat in a couple times over the years with an Athens, Georgia, Grateful Dead tribute band. Needless to say, I quickly developed an immense amount of respect for what Phil Lesh did with the Dead. I saw fewer shows in the early 1980s but continued to listen to the Dead via albums and bootleg tapes. Later in the 1980s, I began attending more shows, particularly enjoying the three-night run at the Providence Civic Center on September 7, 8, and 9, 1987. I approached that run with an empirical question: how many consecutive shows would it take before I tired of the experience? It turns out that I still don't know the answer to that question, but I do know that it's more than three. I attended several more shows in the late 1980s and 1990s, some of which were less than wonderful musically, but all of which were great dance parties.

Since 1995, I've continued to listen to the Dead continually thanks to official album releases and friends with access to the tape-trading network. Who knows—I might have been listening to Barry's tapes well before we met at the Caucus meetings. It wasn't until twelve years after the Dead stopped performing that I paid any serious scholarly attention to the phenomenon of the Dead, Deadheads, and so forth. As mentioned earlier, that started at the Unbroken Chain conference in 2007, which took place in the same building in which my wife and I had first started dating. That seemed like a good omen.

At that point, early 2008, I started attending the Grateful Dead Scholars Caucus meetings in Albuquerque. The Caucus has connected me with many fine people over the years, ranging from widely published authors and experts on the Grateful Dead to colleagues too young to have seen the Dead in person. I've learned much and am still learning from these colleagues.

WRAPPING IT UP

As much as both of us know about the Dead and their music—which isn't much compared to many others in our Grateful Dead Scholars Caucus—this book project has been a special and illuminating experience. Our appreciation for the Dead's music and performance history has increased dramatically. Focusing on a particular song from its debut to final performance and studying its lyrics has been far more exciting and heartwarming than we ever expected when we started. This band, about which we've felt passionate since the 1970s, has shown us an even deeper level of musicianship, songwriting skill, and brilliant improvisational performance ability in performance after performance after performance.

We spent a year working together via the internet and the telephone, having a "real good time," as Jerry Garcia sang. We are grateful for this opportunity to share our work with you. What we've both deeply reinforced in ourselves is that the Grateful Dead are amazing! We hope you'll gain some of the appreciation for them that we share.

Bob has a more musical background that will be apparent in his musical insight and commentary. Barry's focus in reviews relates to the concert experience of listening to and taping almost 200 Dead concerts. What we've both deeply reinforced for ourselves is that these guys are fucking amazing! We hope you'll gain some of the appreciation for them that we both share.

Acknowledgments and Thanks

In addition to those we acknowledge in the introduction to this book, we add the following.

Bob acknowledges and thanks:

- The late "Tex" Reynolds for bringing the Grateful Dead's music to our home;
- Paul and Tobie for their encouragement;
- Floyd Meadows and Michael Wegner for lots of music over the years;
- thoughts and ideas from Leon Harris, Dean and Lizzie Weinberg, Thad Russell, and David Spitzman;
- David Gans for early support for this project;
- Natalie Mandziuk at Rowman & Littlefield for tolerating early bloviating about the Dead and for taking a chance on us in spite of it;
- the editorial crew at Rowman & Littlefield, who provided welcome assistance throughout this project;
- Rowman & Littlefield's reviewers who remain anonymous to us and who provided interesting and provocative suggestions;
- the more than 300 people who responded to Rowman & Littlefield's marketing survey—you helped make this book possible; and
- Nick Meriwether of the Grateful Dead Scholars Caucus for the work he does for the Caucus and for inviting me in.

Barry acknowledges and thanks:

- Chris Barnes, who took a chance and saw her first show with me on April 9, 1987, subsequently watching 148 more shows with me, marrying me along the way, and always supporting my Grateful Dead passion;

- Ted Carleton for trading tapes, sharing the hosting of the Grateful Dead Hour on occasion, introducing me to Dennis McNally, and giving me the chance to interview Dan Healy backstage at Sandstone;
- David Gans for being a longtime friend and supporter of my writing efforts;
- Nick Meriwether for being my writing muse and grand supporter;
- Michael Marlitt for sharing the Portland "Fire on the Mountain" story;
- Alan Trist for sharing an insider's understanding of how the Grateful Dead's business organization worked;
- Bob Trudeau for inviting me to work on this book and being a great colleague;
- and, of course, the Grateful Dead and their extended family—we *love* you!

Finally, we both want to thank Michael Parrish for his feedback and Kay Alexander for her early comments.

Introduction

There is a line, often attributed to the comedian Martin Mull, to the effect of "Writing about music is like dancing about architecture." This . . . is to say that music touches aspects of the human condition in ways that cannot be limited to words, [which are] simultaneously the refuge and prison cell of our intellect. (McNally, 2015a, 142)

Welcome to this interactive guide to *The Grateful Dead's 100 Essential Songs*. Because this book is aimed at newer listeners to the Grateful Dead's music as well as at veteran Deadheads, we begin with some basic information about the Grateful Dead before looking at—and listening to—the songs. Following this first section, we outline some of the decisions we made in choosing material for this book.

THE GRATEFUL DEAD

The Grateful Dead performed for thirty years, from 1965 to 1995, when lead guitarist Jerry Garcia died at the age of fifty-three. During that thirty-year run, besides Garcia, Phil Lesh (bass), Bill Kreutzmann (drums), and Bob Weir (rhythm guitar) were continuous members of the band. Ron McKernan (aka "Pigpen" on keyboard) was also a founding member of the band. Mickey Hart (drums) joined the band in 1967 and was a member for the rest of the thirty-year run, except for a three-and-a-half-year hiatus from February 1971 until October 1974.

The keyboard position for the Dead was not nearly as stable as the rest of the band. Pigpen played until June 1972, when he stepped down due to ill health. His strength was blues and R & B. Tom Constanten played as a second keyboardist from 1968 to 1970 and is identified more with the Dead's full-speed-ahead jams during that period, as well as with their more psychedelic and avant-garde music.

Keith Godchaux handled keyboards from 1971 to 1979, and his wife Donna Jean provided vocal backup support for most of those years. After the Godchauxes left the band, Brent Mydland played the keyboards from April 1979 until his death in July 1990. He added fine vocals to the band as well as renewed interest in blues and slower ballads. Vince Welnick took over keyboards after Mydland and remained for the rest of the Dead's career. Bruce Hornsby, already independently well-known with his band the Range, also played keyboards temporarily, beginning when Welnick did, and the two overlapped for some 100 Dead shows until March 1992.

The various members of the band brought different emphases to the music. As mentioned, Pigpen was a blues musician, adept at the harmonica as well as the keyboard. Garcia came from a folk background and had played bluegrass but was widely known for his eclectic taste in music: he was interested in the entire American songbook. Weir was also interested in a broad range of music and jazz, and Lesh was into avant-garde classical music, having originally played jazz trumpet before joining the Dead on electric bass. Kreutzmann was a fan of R & B, and Hart was a master military drummer with an interest in jazz and world music. In many bands, such variety might produce personnel ruptures, but the Dead were able to draw from these many roots and styles to produce their own distinctive sound. Phil Lesh, in the 2017 documentary *Long Strange Trip*, uses the metaphor of separate fingers of a hand to describe the musical development of the Grateful Dead.

That is not to say the Grateful Dead always played the same music over and over. Quite the contrary: 1965 and 1966 Grateful Dead does not sound a lot like 1969 Dead, which in turn does not sound like 1972 Dead, and which does not sound like post-1980 Dead. In fact, the Grateful Dead transitioned from one style to another over the years. For example, from around 1969 into the early 1970s, they shifted from their early emphasis on blues and psychedelic jamming to include some country style of rock as well. The amazing trove of new songs that band members composed during that period later enabled the band to play an amazing variety of musical styles in a single show. We discuss this in more detail in our reviews of these songs and in the Quick Start Guide that follows this introduction.

By 1970 or so, the band had shifted from all-out psychedelic jams to a style in which many jams occurred either within individual songs or as a bridge between two individual songs. As part of the same style transition, the Dead began to emphasize vocals and lyrics more than they had in the first four or five years of their run. The structure of shows varied as well: in the early years, the Dead might play only one three-hour set of music or two shorter sets. After about 1970, a standard two-set format became the norm, which continued through 1995.

With this as basic background, we now look more closely at what you can expect in the pages that follow. As we hinted at the beginning of this introduction, we are well aware that we are using mere words to describe awesome music, a difficult task at best. We believe you will not be disappointed. Obviously, the proof is in the listening, not the reading.

WHY SONGS?

There's a serious quandary that faces anybody doing what we are doing: at a certain level, you can't really appreciate Grateful Dead music one song at a time—you have to listen to entire concerts or at least try to see how one song leads to another, usually via a seamless jam or segue. Ultimately we agree with that point of view, but there is much to be learned from a focus on individual songs. For newer listeners, be aware that it takes some time and attention to really appreciate this music. You start with the songs, but if you like the songs, you're likely to move on to a more expansive style of listening. We're here to get you started but trust us when we say that many new vistas await you if you make an investment in this music.

THE MUSIC

One unique and special quality of the Grateful Dead's live performances was their "jams" or improvisation. Grateful Dead improvisation is music that is spontaneous, in-the-moment, one-time-only, collective creativity that reveals itself simultaneously to the musicians and the listeners. And Deadheads like it a *lot*. Their style gave rise to "jam bands" in the 1990s.

Another unusual thing about the Grateful Dead's music is that it remains extremely popular more than twenty years after the Dead stopped performing, one reason why we are able to write this book. How can we explain this ongoing appeal? One way to answer this question, which has always been a little suspect to us, is that you just have to "get it." But there are other, more tractable reasons. For example, the Dead performed more than 2,300 shows, and except for many shows from their first three or four years, almost all of these performances were recorded by audience members, the Grateful Dead's crew, or both. Just about all of these recordings are available to listeners today, either on the internet—especially at Archive.org (Intro #1)—or on albums issued by the Dead. There is plenty of easily accessible music to listen to, and this helps keep their music popular.

Second, the Grateful Dead *continue* to issue new releases of music from their now-historical live performances. Since 1995 the band has officially released more than 100 albums, most of which are complete shows. If you want to own Grateful Dead music, there is no shortage of options, for sure. Deaddisc.com (Intro #2), a site we link to frequently in this book, provides a complete discography as of 2016.

This gets us to a third reason for the Grateful Dead's continuing popularity. At first, the band tolerated "tapers"—individuals who smuggled in recording devices and taped the shows. Coauthor Barry Barnes personally recorded nearly 200 shows. In this book, you can link to some of his recordings. In 1984, the Dead "officially recognized" taping by setting up a separate section for the tapers with special "taper tickets." Long before the internet gave us access to an incredible trove of the Dead's music, there were "bootleg" recordings circulating via informal networks since as early as 1967. All of this has contributed to the enthusiasm and size of the Dead's fan base and helped to ensure that the music endures.

Fourth, the surviving core members of the Grateful Dead—Bob Weir, Phil Lesh, Bill Kreutzmann, and Mickey Hart—continue to perform mostly Grateful Dead music, both together and separately as well as with other musicians. They have appeared with bands such as the Other Ones, the Dead, Furthur, Ratdog, Phil and Friends, the Rhythm Devils, and most recently, Dead and Company. Moreover, there are countless cover and tribute bands playing the Dead's music around the country. In short, the music remains popular because live performances of Grateful Dead music are still easily accessible for those, like us, who want to hear the Dead's music live, not just on recordings.

Finally, perhaps the most important reason the Dead's music remains popular is that it is absolutely great music with great lyrics. That brings us back to this book. If you are a newbie, introducing you to this music and these lyrics is what we are about, and it's a thrill to be able to do it. If you're a veteran Deadhead, we hope you'll find some new insights into the music you already love.

ESSENTIAL SONGS

We start by acknowledging that there is no objective list, nor can there be, of the Grateful Dead's 100 essential songs—this is our personal list, no more, no less. Deadheads will agree with most of our choices, we're sure, but some probably will elicit, um, feedback, to put it pleasantly.

We've prepared short review pieces on each of the 100 essential songs, listing them in alphabetical order. In each review, we discuss lyrics as well as music and offer suggestions for listening. This is an interactive book: for each of these songs, we provide links to performances, to the song's lyrics, and to other information about the song. You've already seen above two samples of these hyperlinks. With these links, you can interact with the music and perhaps form a basis for further listening. If you are reading a hard copy of the book, you can access the links by connecting to Rowman & Littlefield's dedicated webpage under the features tab, which is found at this link: (Intro #3). If you are reading an e-copy of the book, the links in each review are "hot," allowing you to read and listen at the same time. We provide links to several performances of each song so you can decide how many or few versions to listen to. We don't necessarily recommend listening to all the links provided; this may be particularly true for the debut performance of a song that may have been undeveloped.

COVERS: WHAT'S IN, WHAT'S OUT

We've made some decisions you should know about before you begin reading, particularly about how we chose the songs to include or exclude. During their career, the Grateful Dead performed 484 different songs at least once. There are more than 100 original songs by the Grateful Dead composed either by musicians in the band or by one of them with a lyricist. The most well-known composer teams are those of Jerry Garcia with lyricist Robert Hunter and Bob Weir with lyricist John Perry Barlow. Hunter, in particular, was considered a full member of the band from the time he appeared in the late 1960s, and Barlow was almost as close to the core group, even acting as tour manager for a short time.

There are fewer original Dead songs than cover songs, songs the Dead performed that were composed by other artists. There probably are Deadheads who feel that only songs composed by the Grateful Dead should be included in a book like this. Our view is that many cover songs are integral to the Grateful Dead experience, so we have included some cover songs, though not many, at the risk of some controversy.

Some of the cover songs the Dead performed remained so closely identified with their original artists or performers that we cannot call them "Grateful Dead" songs, even though the Dead may have performed them dozens of times. Consequently, we've left out many songs performed by the Dead but written by Bob Dylan, the Beatles, and the Who. Along the same lines, we've excluded songs like Chuck Berry's "Johnny B. Goode," Johnny Cash's "Big River," and Merle Haggard's "Sing Me Back Home," though these are great tunes that we love to hear the Dead perform—and we offer a list of bonus tracks at the end of the book.

Other "cover songs" are not easily traced to their original composers. For example, the Dead performed traditional songs, such as "Going Down the Road Feelin' Bad" and "I Know You Rider," songs for which there may exist recordings by other artists but no clear authorship. The Dead also played "old-timey" songs, such as "Cold Rain and Snow" and "Beat It on Down the Line," which do have recognized composers. These oral tradition songs started to be recorded in the 1920s and represented blues, folk music, and bluegrass. The Dead borrowed many of these songs, updated lyrics, created their own arrangements, and made the songs their own. Some of these cover songs are included in our list.

Finally, there are songs with clear authorship that remain identified with their original composers to varying degrees but that became so central to the Grateful Dead's repertoire that they simply could not be excluded. The most obvious of these is Bonnie Dobson's "Morning Dew." Other songs are more complicated: songs that are clearly major parts of the Grateful Dead's *persona* but that also remain identified with their original composers. Among these is Buddy Holly's "Not Fade Away," for example, and perhaps Bobby Bland's "(Turn on Your) Lovelight." The Dead's performances of these songs and other covers, show how they made these songs their own. We believe that any list of essential Grateful Dead music should include those songs.

MEDLEYS AND PAIRS

We also made decisions about song medleys. For example, after about 1966, "I Know You Rider" was almost never heard without being preceded by "China Cat Sunflower," with a jam between the two songs. Consequently, "China > Rider," as

Deadheads refer to it, has to be considered as one unit for purposes of this book, even though two songs are involved. The good news is that this encourages readers to listen to the segues between songs that we mentioned earlier, which we think is critically important. On the other hand, it means there may be a few songs included in this book that are not really "essential," but we leave that to readers to decide.

There are other medleys in the book besides "China > Rider." Some song "pairs," such as "Estimated Prophet" and "Eyes of the World," were played together on many occasions, but they were also played separately many times. In these situations, we've usually treated them as separate songs. On the other hand, "Scarlet Begonias" enjoyed its own independent spot in the repertoire for a few years, but when the Dead introduced "Fire on the Mountain," the two songs (aka "Scarlet > Fire") were nearly always paired for the rest of the Dead's run. So we treat these as a pair, allowing newer listeners to hear some of the continuity of songs as they transitioned in a live concert environment.

Veteran Deadheads will notice that we have *not* included "Drums," "Drumz," or "Space" in this book. The most obvious reason for this is that none of these musical pieces is a "song," although it might be good music. Newbies in particular might need to develop a better sense of the Dead's music before tackling the long drum solos and otherworldly space music that usually appeared in the second set of a Dead show. We hope they develop an appreciation for that dimension of the Dead's music after they become more invested in the songs we've include here.

Finally, some Grateful Dead songs evolved and developed over the years so that later versions were quite different from earlier versions. Some songs were restructured to include longer jams, became parts of regular pairings, or changed their tempo. An example of the latter is "Friend of the Devil," which started out as a peppy folk song and became a slow tempo, rather heavy song by the end of the Dead's thirty-year run. We have not allowed these changes to keep any song off the list. Indeed, the fact that songs evolved over time is one of the great qualities of Grateful Dead music. We hope you agree.

CODES AND CONVENTIONS

Throughout this book, we use annotations familiar to Deadheads, including the ">" symbol to indicate that one song flows into another without a break in the music. You've already seen examples above. When describing songs you might listen to, we use its official title and (usually) a nickname familiar to Deadheads. For example, in our review of "They Love Each Other," we usually refer to the song as TLEO but only *after* the full title has been used. This is both to save space and to inculcate basic knowledge about the Dead for readers new to this music.

If a given performance has been issued on an official album, we try to cite that album—for example, *Dick's Picks, Volume 22* (D3:T4). "D3:T4" points to track four on disc three of that album. For these performances, we include a link to an alternate source if possible, usually to Archive.org or sometimes to YouTube.com. For performances that are not part of an official album, we also provide a link to the show as it appears on Archive.org. In many of our reviews, we also refer you to Barry's recordings.

There are three basic types of live recordings available to us. Soundboard recordings are generally the best quality in terms of the music and were usually recorded by the Dead's crew. Audience recordings, by tapers in the audience, do not always rise to the quality level of the soundboards but often more accurately capture the crowd's response and the overall atmosphere. Finally, matrix recordings try to capture both elements by mixing soundboard and audience tapes. Often these are the best to listen to. As mentioned earlier, Barry taped almost 200 shows, and we're pleased to include links to some of those in this book.

Finally, when recommending a performance, we use a standard date format for its first appearance—for example, March 28, 1973. Subsequent references to the date of a show are abbreviated in keeping with Deadhead shorthand: 3/28/73. For example, when asked about your first Dead show, you might answer "3/28/73, Springfield." This combination of date formats provides clarity as well as a little insight for newbies to Deadhead culture.

Readers who are relatively new to the music of the Grateful Dead already may be wondering about these creatures we call "Deadheads." It's actually a loose appellation: if you think you are a Deadhead, you probably are. Deadheads include the thousands of fans who traveled the country following the Grateful Dead at one point or another during the band's thirty-year run from 1965 to 1995 but also include thousands of people who have invested much less time but who love the music. Obviously, Barry and Bob are part of this throng, and for us, the music never stops. We love this music, and it's a major part of our lives.

SOURCES

Before we proceed to the list of the most essential songs, a word about documentation. It has been said that there is more statistical information about the Grateful Dead than anything in the world except baseball. Perhaps. In any case, there is a wealth of archival and statistical information that we gratefully draw on. The most obvious is *DeadBase*, the master compilation of nitty-gritty information about the Dead's live performances. Unless specifically noted, the statistical information and basic performance data about songs in this book are from *DeadBase*, even if we don't provide the specific source in the text. If it's not from *DeadBase*, we provide the source. At the end of this book, we acknowledge other resources we used and recommend.

For lyrics, again, there are multiple sources, but we would be remiss if we did not highlight the great work of David Dodd, whose annotated lyrics website is used in many of the reviews in this book (Intro #4). David's "Greatest Stories" blog on dead.net has also been a great resource on many of the songs in this book (Intro #5).

Dodd's reference-librarian approach makes his work especially useful to people like us. Thank you, David.

There are many other resources available to anyone who wishes to listen to or read about the Grateful Dead. This book would not be possible in its present form without the existence of Archive.org, which we cited earlier. You can gain easy access to specific performances via Deadlists.com or relisten.net, sites that contain links to Archive.org for each performance date. We've also used Deaddiscs.com, also cited earlier, headyversion.com, and other websites for one type of basic information or another. These are usually mentioned in the text. But our gratitude for this fine work must be mentioned here, so thank you! Later in the book, we provide a detailed list of web resources we hope you will find helpful.

With that brief description of some of the backstory, you should be able to begin to enjoy the music of the Grateful Dead, so on with the show. Let's hope that the music never stops. If you'd like to jump right in with our alphabetical listing of essential songs, go for it. If you'd like a peek at the wide variety of music the Dead played, start with the Quick Start Guide that follows next. Either way, we hope this book helps you love this music.

Quick Start Guide

The Grateful Dead were known for the variety of musical genres they incorporated into their musical style. For readers who might like to experience some of this variety before exploring the list of 100 essential songs, this Quick Start Guide is the place to begin. If you are unfamiliar with the Dead's musical eclecticism, first read the lyrics to these songs at dead.net. All of the links in this table are to live performances, and all appear later in the book with additional details.

Genre	Song and Date	Link
Folk	"Peggy-O" (May 7, 1977)	Q.S. #1
Rock and Roll	"One More Saturday Night" (April 8, 1972)	Q.S. #2
Bluegrass	"Cumberland Blues" (March 28, 1973)	Q.S. #3
Country Rock	"Mexicali Blues" (April 2, 1973)	Q.S. #4
Jazz	"Eyes of the World" (March 29, 1990)	Q.S. #5
Classic Dead	"Sugaree" (August 13, 1975)	Q.S. #6
Gospel	"And We Bid You Goodnight" (May 2, 1970)	Q.S. #7
Funk	"Loose Lucy" (March 14, 1990)	Q.S. #8
Blues	"U.S. Blues" (May 7, 1977)	Q.S. #9
Psychedelic	"Dark Star" (April 8, 1972)	Q.S. #10
Love Song	"It Must Have Been the Roses" (April 9, 1989)	Q.S. #11

All song links in this book reference hyperlinks listed under "Features" at https://rowman.com/ISBN/9781538110577. We will do our best to update or replace any links that become outdated.

The 100 Essential Songs

"Alabama Getaway"

Simply put, "Alabama Getaway" (aka Alabama), composed by Jerry Garcia and Robert Hunter, is a rocker. From November 4, 1979, in Providence, Rhode Island, through June 2, 1995, in Mountain View, California, the Grateful Dead played Alabama as a rollicking, fast-paced, get-up-and-dance song. They played it 141 times in all, and eighty-eight of those occurred in its first three years between its first performance in 1979 and the end of 1981. In 1980 alone, the Dead performed Alabama fifty times in their eighty-six shows; only "Drumz" and "Althea" were performed more frequently.

Alabama was often the opening song in the first set: between March 13, 1982, and March 27, 1987, forty-seven consecutive performances of Alabama were show openers. After 1987, Alabama performances tapered off in frequency, and it was not played at all for 416 shows between 1989 and early 1995. In 1995, the Dead played Alabama four times, twice as the show's opening number, including at its final performance on June 2, 1995. In short, "Alabama Getaway" had a relatively short but intense life in the Dead's repertoire.

The lyrics for "Alabama Getaway" (Alabama #1), like those of many Grateful Dead songs, have multiple possible interpretations. Does the song refer to the state of Alabama in some sort of nuanced political fashion? Or is Alabama an individual who is causing trouble for the song's narrator? Biblical references to the "valley of the shadow" only intensify the confrontational theme in the song. It's unclear whether the narrator sees the state of Alabama as a "getaway" or if the song directs the individual called Alabama to "get away." The latter is definitely on the table, the former, perhaps.

On November 4, 1979, at its first performance in a great show Bob attended in Providence, Rhode Island, Alabama was *not* the show's opener, though it did open the second set. Listen to it here: (Alabama #2). The crowd noises before that second set opened were raucous, as usual, but the audience's response to the beginning of Alabama is muted since nobody recognized the song. (Indeed, the audience welcome for the following song, "The Greatest Story Ever Told," (aka Greatest Story) was far more generous.) The fact that the lukewarm reception for the first performance changed dramatically over the years attests to the high esteem in which Deadheads have held Alabama.

Musically, this first version is excellent: solos are extended in the body of the song, and Garcia's voice is strong. Keyboardist Brent Mydland had joined the Dead a few months earlier in 1979, adding both a new and exciting element musically as well as excellent vocals. You can hear both in this version of Alabama. The driving rhythm of the bass line carries the day in this version and is key during the punctuation at the end of each verse and chorus. This version is excellent for a first performance.

On December 28, 1979, in Oakland, a show that was issued in the Dead's *Road Trip* series (vol. 3, no. 1: D1:T8), the musical quality of "Alabama Getaway" is even better than in its first performance a month earlier. The lyrics are clearer, but, typical of an officially released album, the crowd noises are subdued. Listen to an audience recording here: (Alabama #3). As was common with Alabama's dynamics, the song increases in intensity with repeated singing of the final refrain lines, a final guitar solo as an outro, and then a seamless segue into "Greatest Story Ever Told," as was the case in the 11/4/79 show discussed earlier.

The website Dead for a Year (Alabama #4) recommends two versions of "Alabama Getaway" that we also happily recommend: 12/28/79 (Oakland), discussed earlier, and May 15, 1980, at the Nassau Coliseum on Long Island, New York (Alabama #5), when Alabama was the encore. This version was also issued in 2002 on the compilation album *Go to Nassau* (D2:T5), although it is not identified there as the encore. This 5/15/80 version almost seems to be played at double speed—the Dead were not letting the audience go easily and quietly this night. Indeed, as Garcia moves into the outro solo, the audience reaction is immediate and intense, urging him on. He complies. The band ends with a big rock and roll ending.

The final performance of "Alabama Getaway" was on June 2, 1995, when it was the show's opener in Mountain View, California. As you'll see in many of the reviews to follow, the Dead were slowing down in 1995, yet they still could rise to the occasion most of the time. Compared to many earlier versions we recommended, this version of Alabama drags a bit; you can hear the slower tempo in this soundboard recording: (Alabama #6). The quirky musical pause at the end of each chorus and verse is not as prominent as in earlier versions. The outro is less compelling and the segue into Greatest Story (again) is not as seamless as it had been. Yet even in their later years, the Dead played the song quite well, as you can hear on this version.

During the Grateful Dead's thirty-year run, there were major changes in style and concert structure, and many songs evolved in many interesting directions. "Alabama

Getaway," by contrast, was played fairly consistently over the years. It's one of the Dead's essential songs, if only because of its status in the 1980s as *the* opening song. We're happy to include it as our own opening song as well.

"Althea"

Although "Althea" may not be at the top of our 100 essential song list, it is still an enjoyable, laid-back, bouncy tune. Jerry Garcia always seemed to enjoy singing it and did so 272 times from August 4, 1979 (Althea #1), until July 8, 1995 (Althea #2), the penultimate Grateful Dead concert. It was in heavy rotation in 1980, with fifty-nine performances, and in 1981, when it was played forty-four times. After that, performances were less frequent, averaging about ten times a year. It first appeared on the studio album *Go to Heaven* (Althea #3), which was released April 28, 1979. "Althea" has been released officially more than fifteen times over the years. A full list of official releases through 2016 is available here: (Althea #4).

"Althea" is another of the fine collaborations between Garcia and Hunter. Its lyrics demonstrate Hunter's vast knowledge of poetry and classic literature; for example, the lines, "You may be a clown in the burying ground," "You may be the fate of Ophelia sleeping," and "perchance to dream" are all references to Shakespeare's *Hamlet* (Dodd 2005, 296–97).

"Althea" is a love song but not in the usual sense. It starts with the line "I told Althea I was feeling lost," which gives the impression there's a first-person narrator telling his story. Before long, however, Althea herself is offering sage advice on a number of issues facing the narrator regarding his friends' concerns about him being, perhaps, his own worst enemy. For example, she tells him he's "honest to the point of recklessness, self-centered to the extreme." Later, he tells Althea, "I was born to be a bachelor," yet when she replies "Okay, that's fine," he suddenly realizes maybe he really *is* his own worst enemy, leading him to sing, "now I'm trying to catch her." The crux of the love story comes in the last line, where he comments how they are "forgetting the love we bring." You can read the lyrics here: (Althea #5).

Musically, "Althea" is straightforward: a gentle, unhurried, rolling tempo as only the Dead could perform it. The bridge verse illustrates the Dead's ability to change the dynamics of a song by raising or lowering the volume and intensity. In this case it's both. In the versions we recommend, note how the music intensifies during the verse breaks and diminishes when Garcia sings. The strong crowd response after the line "You know this space is getting hot" was always a highlight of performances. Playing the solo as an outro is not unusual for the Dead—many songs have extended outros—but it's done sweetly in "Althea," and the song's coda is short and concise.

As noted earlier, there are many fine versions of "Althea." For Al Franken, long-time Deadhead and former U.S. senator, the choice is clear: Nassau Coliseum on May 16, 1980. In the *Long Strange Trip* documentary, Franken says, "My god, that solo is unbelievable! It was so unbelievably great!" This is a very good version, and

Garcia's solo *is* great; you can judge for yourself here: (Althea #6). Franken even convinces director Amir Bar Lev that it is the best version, though Bar Lev himself had preferred a version from Hampton Coliseum on May 1, 1981 (Althea #7), which is also very good. One interesting thing about the 1980 performance is that "Althea" was performed *both nights* of the two-night run at the Nassau Coliseum, as well as the night before in Uniondale, New York. It's unusual for the Dead to repeat a song three consecutive nights, especially one of Jerry's songs.

In addition to the official recordings, there are *many* versions available at archive. org. Barry saw twenty-four performances of "Althea," the first on May 5, 1980, in Baltimore, and the last in Las Vegas on May 19, 1995. As you listen to our recommendations, remember that "Althea" doesn't lend itself to improvisation, so this limits variation among versions.

First, listen to this performance from Grugahalle, in Essen, then West Germany, on March 28, 1981, accessible here: (Althea #8). This is an FM broadcast recording of "Althea" that is highly recommended at headyversion.com. The Dead played four shows in London before this one in West Germany, and this show had Pete Townsend of the Who sitting in during the second set.

Next, check out this performance from Starlight Theatre in Kansas City from August 3, 1982 (Althea #9), on a nice soundboard recording. This was a hometown show for Barry, and Starlight Theatre was considered one of the best places to see the Dead, even though they played there only three times, in 1982, 1984, and 1985. Now on to Alpine Valley in East Troy, Wisconsin, on July 19, 1989. Barry attended this one, and we both recommend Barry's audience recording (Althea #10). Headyversion.com ranks this as the third best version of Althea! For our final recommendation, we encourage you to listen to this performance from Boston Garden on October 1, 1994 (Althea #11). It's one of the later versions, but everyone including Garcia is in fine form in this very clear matrix recording.

All these are delightful versions of "Althea," and as you peruse our recommendations, others on archive.org, and the official releases, be sure to remember that all of the 1980 and 1981 versions are quite "hair-raising," as Al Franken would say.

"And We Bid You Goodnight"

"And We Bid You Goodnight," (aka Goodnight) is a traditional gospel song attributed to Sarah Doudney and Ira David Sankey. The Grateful Dead adapted and rearranged the song, using Goodnight as the show closer on many occasions. As happens with traditional songs, the title varied over time and from one artist to another, alternately appearing as "We Bid You Goodnight" and "And We Bid You Goodnight." Dead.net, the official web page of the Grateful Dead, uses the latter; Deadbase uses the former. According to Deaddisc.com, the original title of this "traditional 'lowering down' funeral song" was "I Bid You Goodnight."

Under the latter title, the Pindar Family (with Joseph Spence) recorded the version that probably inspired the Dead's arrangement most directly. That version was released on the album *The Music Never Stopped: Roots of the Grateful Dead* (D1:T17). A thirty-second clip of the Pindar Family version is available here: (Goodnight #1). We recommend it both as a predecessor of the Dead's version and also as a contrast to the Dead's arrangement. For the lyrics, see: (Goodnight #2).

The Grateful Dead played Goodnight only sixty-one times: regularly from 1968 to 1970, infrequently from 1971 through 1978, and not at all from 1979 through 1988 and from 1992 through the end of the run in 1995. They revived the song for a few performances in 1989 and performed it eleven times until 1991, when it was dropped from the rotation again. In the early years, Dead shows sometimes did not have separate sets, but when they did, Goodnight was always in the second set and usually the closing song. After 1971, it is almost always listed as the encore. For a song performed only sixty-one times, it's remarkable that there are about two dozen available album releases that include Goodnight. You can see the list here: (Goodnight #3).

Over the years, the Dead played many traditional songs, usually but not always first set songs or early second set songs. They were self-contained and usually played more or less the same way over the years. Goodnight is essential to an understanding of the Dead's music because it was usually an encore sung a cappella or occasionally with a quiet drum backing the singers. The Dead were not always wonderful vocalists, and the fact that they performed an a cappella song is itself notable. That they could carry it off is even more remarkable. Thus, we have a few performances to recommend.

Perhaps the most recognized version of Goodnight is on the *Live Dead* album from 1969, which was issued as a CD in 2003 (D1:T7). This version was recorded on March 2, 1969, at the Fillmore West in San Francisco and is accessible here: (Goodnight #4), a two-minute soundboard recording. (On the CD, Goodnight fades out after only thirty-six seconds.) This is a sweet, mellow performance of the song.

The Dead performed Goodnight on May 2, 1970, at the famous Harpur College show in Binghamton, New York, which was released on *Dick's Picks, Volume 8* (D3:T5). It's also here: (Goodnight #5). On this recording, which times in at 3:20, you can hear the audience clapping rhythmically, and if you listen closely you can hear a guitar. With varying play times, it's not surprising that the lyrics also vary from one performance to another. According to Dead.net, this version from 5/2/70 is the one on which they based their lyrics page, which is linked above. This performance becomes exuberant before ending.

As mentioned earlier, Goodnight was dropped from the rotation after its sole performance in 1978, which was two years to the day (New Year's Eve) of its previous performance in 1976. But after a gap of 756 shows, the Dead broke out the song on July 17, 1989, at Alpine Valley in East Troy, Wisconsin. That performance is available here (Goodnight #6), on a matrix recording in which the crowd's responses are audible. This version comes in at about three minutes.

You can see Goodnight performed as the encore in Hampton, Virginia, in a video from October 8, 1989 (Goodnight #7), a performance that was issued on the album *Formerly the Warlocks* (D3:T6). Garcia can be seen strumming his guitar but there is little guitar sound in the mix.

Whatever the title, seeing "And We Bid You Goodnight" was always a special treat for Deadheads. A so-called acid rock jam band presumably would not tread into the space of gospel music, particularly to perform a cappella. The Dead's success with this song is a good example of why it is difficult to apply quick and easy labels to the band.

"Attics of My Life"

"Attics of My Life," (aka Attics), composed by Hunter and Garcia, may be one of the best-loved songs by the Grateful Dead—at least for Deadheads. Casual listeners might not even know about Attics, since it was performed live only forty-eight times. The first sixteen of these performances were in 1970; from 1972 until 1989, the Dead didn't play the song live at all. Attics's late period breakout performance happened on October 9, 1989, after a gap of nearly 1,100 shows, as the encore. During its performance life after that 1989 show, Attics was almost always played in the second set, usually near the end if it wasn't the encore.

Some listeners might have heard only the version on the studio album *American Beauty*, released in 1970. That remains the standard against which all performances are measured. What the live versions may lack in terms of the vocal quality, however, is made up for by the intensity with which the Dead played the song, not to mention the audience response. Garcia was once quoted saying: "some of these songs, man, when we sang them, they could stand your hair on end, like 'Attics of My Life.'" (McNally 2015a, 202).

Attics is a love song, perhaps the best love song ever written because it's about behavior rather than emotions. See the lyrics here: (Attics #1), and the reader comment that includes a quote from Robert Hunter explaining the song as "about the soul." David Dodd's *Greatest Stories* series has a particularly interesting essay on Attics, including more commentary on the Hunter quote mentioned (Attics #2). In keeping with the idea of both love and soul, Bob has heard these lyrics at a wedding and a funeral, both occasions evoking tears.

Musically, Attics is a slow ballad with little, if any, instrumentation to interfere with the focus on the lyrics. There is no improvisation, no extended outro, just Hunter's poem set to a lovely tune by Garcia. Trust Robert Hunter to get it right: love isn't an emotion or an attitude, it's commitment, it's an action (or many actions), it's behavior that enhances the life of the one you love. In Attics, there is no line that declares: "I love you," and yet Attics is a wonderful love song because "when there was no ear to hear, you sang to me"; "when there were no strings to play, you played to me"; and "when I had no wings to fly, you flew to me." All of this happens over a long period of time; it's a long-term commitment "where all the pages are my days, and all my lights grow old." Moreover, it all occurs under uncertain circumstances, in which "my life is full of cloudy dreams unreal" and "tastes no tongue can know." People of a certain age, including the authors of this book, recognize the value of long-term kindness, both giving it and receiving it, thus we understand love much the way Hunter expresses it in this song. The wonder is that he was able to write this at the young age of twenty-nine!

For listening, you should start with the studio version mentioned above, then move on to live versions. In the studio version (Attics #3), there's instrumentation, but the song feels as if it is a cappella. While listening to the vocals, keep in mind that this is a rock and roll band, not a church choir.

Then, move on to the May 14, 1970, live performance debut at Meramec Community College in Kirkwood, Missouri, available here: (Attics #4). This version precedes the studio version on *American Beauty* by several months. Even allowing for first-time jitters—if the Dead ever actually felt them—you can hear that the vocals cannot compare with the studio version. At this point, Phil Lesh was still singing the high register, which didn't help. There is no real guitar solo in this version, as in the studio version.

The September 27, 1972, performance at the Stanley Theater in Jersey City, New Jersey, was released on *Dick's Picks, Volume 11* (D3:T3) and is available here: (Attics #5). This is one of only two performances of Attics in 1972—a week later the Dead would play Attics for the last time until 1989. Here they played Attics between "Cumberland Blues" and "The Promised Land"—two rockers—so Attics provided quite a change of pace. The vocals still do not meet the studio standard, but they are an improvement over the 5/14/70 performance referenced earlier.

As a bonus for those who wish to hear a version from shortly after the Dead's 1975 return from a hiatus, try May 28, 1976, listed in Scott et al. (1995, 60) as a rehearsal session (Attics #6). Note that there are two versions on this recording. The first one is cut before the end, but the band then resumes from the beginning. The longer of the two versions includes a guitar solo, unlike the studio version on *American Beauty*. It's worth mentioning that although the Dead rehearsed the song, they did not play Attics live for several years after this.

The October 9, 1989, version is the breakout: the Dead played Attics for the first time in almost 1,100 shows, a gap of seventeen years. This show, from Hampton, Virginia, is available as an official release, *Formerly the Warlocks* (D6:T7), and as an audience recording (Attics #7). You can hear the crowd's reaction when the Dead sing the first lines and sense the audience's dilemma: do we cheer this major event or listen reverentially, as the song suggests? It's the latter—you can hear the crowd's reaction in the last minute or so. In this version, vocals at the high end from keyboardist Brent Mydland were a real plus for the overall sound. The instrumentation on this version is even more subdued than on earlier live versions.

On September 26, 1991, at Boston Garden, the Dead played Attics in the Jerry Ballad slot, just before the final song of the second set. This version is available here:

(Attics #8), also an audience recording. The crowd's response to Attics is fun to listen to, with alternating periods of near-silent listening during the verses and loud cheers applauding the vocal lines. Nobody wanted to miss a word, yet everybody wanted to express their joy. The crowd response is especially interesting during the line, "When I had no wings to fly, you flew to me." The crowd response is loud and intense but then cuts off almost completely, as if a choirmaster was directing the audience from the stage. Finally, we recommend listening to Barry's recording of Attics from Phoenix, Arizona, on April 3, 1994 (Attics #9).

We hope these selections convince you that "Attics of My Life" is a superb song, unique among those written by rock and roll bands. To understand the overall range of the music of the Grateful Dead, Attics is essential.

"Beat It on Down the Line"

"Beat It on Down the Line" (aka BIODTL) was composed and first recorded by Jesse Fuller in 1961, so this is not an "old-timey" piece of music per se. However, the Dead's cover arrangement of BIODTL is reminiscent of other songs in that category like "Cold Rain and Snow," "Viola Lee Blues," or even the Dead's cover of Johnny Cash's "Big River." The Dead first performed BIODTL live on March 12, 1966, which makes it one of the oldest songs in the rotation. Its last performance was on October 3, 1994, after 325 performances.

BIODTL illustrates some of the whimsy that occurred at Grateful Dead shows, and we deem it essential for that reason, if for nothing else. Specifically, the number of beats in the intro varied from show to show. This phenomenon became widely known to Deadheads, and *DeadBase* (Scott et al., 1995, 426) documents this listing of the maximum number of opening beats the band played. (Incidentally, the highest was forty-five beats on September 11, 1985; the link to that show is below.)

Musically, BIODTL, a rocker, is part folk song, part blues, part rock and roll but always fun to listen to, always easy to dance to. The tempo varied over the years, but the song remained more or less consistent structurally. The lyrics (BIODTL #1) evoke a typical Grateful Dead narrator struggling with life and persisting in the face of great odds. He works in a coal mine and yearns to get back to the shack where he belongs and where his love is waiting for him. BIODTL was a standard in the first set from 1967 on.

BIODTL's first performance on March 12, 1966, from the Danish Center in Los Angeles (BIODTL #2), is a good place to start listening. First of all, it's remarkable that such a good-quality recording exists from so early in the Dead's touring. The Dead play the song at more or less the tempo that evolved over the years, but there is no evidence of the whimsical counting of the opening beats on that night. The playing style suggests electric folk music, and the vocal harmonies invoke bluegrass. Readers interested in humor should consider listening to the "Heads Up" instrumental and "Ice Cream Break" on the same recording.

On May 19, 1966, at the Avalon in San Francisco (BIODTL #3), BIODTL opened the show, but the available recordings begin after the song has played into the first verse, so again the opening beats are missing. Otherwise, this is an excellent early version of the song. Only a few months later, on November 19, 1966 (BIODTL #4), at the Fillmore in San Francisco, the Dead opened BIODTL with eleven beats, playing a much cleaner, maturer, speedier version. In particular, Lesh's bass line is outstanding, and the band is tight. Garcia's solo certainly keeps up with the accelerated tempo. This is a good sample of the early Grateful Dead. On August 8, 1982, at the University of Iowa (BIODTL #5), BIODTL opens with five beats. Garcia's solo is now more central to the performance, and he extends it an extra verse. This is a good version. By now, the tempo is slower in comparison to 5/19/66 and especially to 11/19/66, which are referenced earlier.

For those who want to hear what forty-five beats sounds like, listen to the start of BIODTL on September 11, 1985, in Oakland (BIODTL #6). This is otherwise a typical version of BIODTL, but because the recording is a high-quality audience taping, it's fun to hear the audience response, both to the song itself and to the number of opening beats. Garcia's solo is delightful.

Finally, we point you to October 3, 1994, at the Boston Garden, BIODTL's final performance (BIODTL #7). This final version starts on a high note, but it's difficult to count the opening beats, since one instrument seems to play five and another instrument four or five, though not at the same time. The tempo is slower. Garcia's solo soars, albeit briefly, as he cedes to Vince Welnick on keyboards for the second part of the solo. The audience response is loud and clear at the onset of the song, and on this audience tape we can hear that this is a sing-along for the Deadheads.

Some might argue that varying the number of opening beats in a song is a gimmick that has nothing to do with the quality of the music. But we take "Beat It on Down the Line" as an essential song because its opening "gimmick" tells us a lot about the Grateful Dead's attitude toward live performances: lighthearted and yet serious about the quality of their music on the one hand while committed to improvisation and taking risks on the other.

"Bertha"

It was early November 1971. Bob's friend Tex walked into the house, put a record on the stereo, and said, "I think you're gonna like this." There are events in all our lives of such significance that we remember exactly where we were. This was one of them for Bob. Tex lowered the needle onto the record and out came "Bertha," the first Grateful Dead song on the *Skull & Roses* album released in late October 1971. The rest, as they say, is history.

"Bertha" was performed live for the first time on February 18, 1971, at the Capitol Theater in Port Chester, New York. From then until its final performance on June 27, 1995, at the Palace in Auburn Hills, Michigan, the Dead performed

"Bertha" 394 times. They performed it every year except 1975, the year the group took a hiatus from touring. The song was always in the rotation, and whenever it opened a show or a second set, Deadheads knew to expect a rousing performance.

In the early years, "Bertha" was usually played in the first set. In 1971, for example, the Dead performed "Bertha" forty-nine times, opening the show with it twenty-five times. In 1977 and 1978, "Bertha" could appear in either the first or second set, and in 1979 it was usually in the second set. Starting in 1981, "Bertha" was usually in the first set: from 1982 through 1995, "Bertha" was the show opener more than fifty times.

In other words, "Bertha" was a punctuation song for the Dead, an attention-getter and a crowd-pleaser. To hear "Bertha" at its rousing best is to understand that immediately. The two-chord intro catches your ear at once; you can't ignore the fast tempo. The crowd roars at the first line: "I had a hard run." Garcia's solo is soaring. The outro with its repetition of "any more" varied from show to show, keeping the audience in suspense, waiting for the tight coda to end the song. "Bertha" *always* received a great response from the audience.

The lyrics (Bertha #1) tell the story of that familiar Grateful Dead downbeat character struggling to make it and having a difficult time, to say the least. He runs into a tree, asks to be arrested, and has to keep moving. Is he simply doing a not-so-great job of running away from someone or something? Is it deeper than that? David Dodd speculates that the phrase "bar door" might be "bardo," "a concept from Tibetan Buddhism that there is an intermediate state between two existences, a space between incarnations. Between lives." See here (Bertha #2) for this and more. If you consider the idea that "Bertha" may be a pun on "birth," these lyrics rise to a different level, and we're dealing with the circle of life. And then there's the probably apocryphal story that "Bertha" was the name given to an electric fan that moved around the Dead's office, threatening fingers and kneecaps.

"Bertha" is a relatively short, self-contained, stable song. Over the years, the principal change was moving Garcia's solo from late in the song, right before the final chorus, to earlier, after the second verse. There's no shortage of officially released versions of "Bertha," as you can see by searching Deaddisc.com. All of these versions are worth your time.

The version of "Bertha" on the *Skull & Roses* album was performed on April 27, 1971, at the Fillmore East in New York City, an evening shared with the Beach Boys. You can hear this performance here: (Bertha #3). This early version has the solo near the end of the song.

The performance on May 9, 1977, in Buffalo, New York, was released in 2017 in the box set *Get Shown the Light* (D2:T1). Here, "Bertha" opened the second set. The solo is performed after the second verse. This version is available as a good-quality audience recording here: (Bertha #4). The band sings "any more" ten times in the coda and immediately segues into "Good Lovin'," a frequent pairing in the 1970s.

For a later version, try March 30, 1989, at Greensboro, North Carolina. "Bertha" appeared frequently in the Dead's rotation, and the longest gap between performances was twenty-three. This is the breakout show, and you can hear an audience recording (Bertha #5). This may be the most enthusiastic recording you'll ever hear, especially during the "Phil bombs," loud punctuation notes from the bass, guaranteed to get the audience to respond. during the solo. If you'd like less audience and more music in the mix, listen to the soundboard recording of the same performance: (Bertha #6). We prefer getting caught up in the spirit of the show with the audience version.

"Bertha" is perhaps one of the Dead's quintessential dance songs, a great way to start a show, and always a welcome presence in the set list. We suggest listening to "Bertha" to start your day, especially on Monday mornings. It'll help.

"Bird Song"

Composed by Jerry Garcia and Robert Hunter, "Bird Song" was written in memory of Janis Joplin, according to Hunter's book of lyrics *A Box of Rain* (1990, 16). The Dead had a long history with Janis, coming of age together in the San Francisco music scene during the late 1960s. She was with them on the famed Festival Express concert train trip across Canada in 1970, and she also performed a duet of "Turn on Your Lovelight" with Pigpen on July 16, 1970, in San Rafael, California, only two months before she died.

The first studio recording of "Bird Song" was on Garcia's first solo album, *Garcia*, released in 1972, but it didn't appear on a Grateful Dead album until the *Reckoning* album of 1980s acoustic performances, released in 1981. "Bird Song" had its first live performance by the Grateful Dead on February 19, 1971, and was last performed on June 30, 1995, with a total of 296 performances. After its debut, it was part of the repertoire until September 15, 1973, and not played again until September 25, 1980, when it was played in an opening acoustic set during of a run of twenty-four shows in San Francisco, New Orleans, and New York. After that run, it stayed in the regular live electric rotation until its last performance in 1995.

In the booklet for the 2004 Garcia box set *All Good Things: Jerry Garcia Studio Sessions*, Hunter says the bird image came from a collage he'd seen years before with a picture of a bird and a quote, which remained with him: "All I know is something in me sang that in me sings no more" (Hunter 2004, 44). This led to the opening line that Deadheads love: "All I know is something like a bird within her sang." One line that typically got the audience singing along is "I'll show you snow and rain." You can find all the lyrics at this link: (Bird #1).

Garcia set the lyrics to a lovely melody and sang it almost like a bird himself. What was a sweet and simple song on the *Garcia* solo album later became a first set powerhouse for the Dead in which the band stretched out with extended jams that offered a taste of things to come in the second set. For such a beautiful and powerful song, surprisingly few official live versions have been released over the years: Deaddisc.com lists fewer than thirty. Fortunately, we have Archive.org to help fill our ears with many performances.

It's a good idea to start with the debut rendition of "Bird Song" on February 19, 1971, in order to see how the song evolved over time. This is an up-tempo performance with the entire band contributing and no indication that it was the first time the band played the song in front of an audience. The soundboard version cuts as the song is wrapping up at about 6:03 (Bird #2), but you can also listen to the entire song on an audience recording that sounds remarkably good for 1971 (Bird #3).

Our next recommendation is one from the "comeback" acoustic performances in 1980 played at Radio City Music Hall in New York on October 27. This is a clear, clean audience recording; no soundboard is available. Even as an acoustic performance, the band stretches out for a full eleven minutes. Stream it at this link (Bird #4), where you can clearly hear the boys in all their acoustic glory.

Continuing in chronological order, check out this delicious version from the UC Berkeley Greek Theatre on July 15, 1984. We recommend this matrix recording in which you can hear the drummers' brushes playing on the cymbals, Mydland's trills on the electronic keyboard behind Garcia's solo, Lesh's bass going where no other bass goes, and Weir's unique rhythm guitar. Stream it at this link: (Bird #5); you'll be glad you did.

After its return to the live lineup in 1980, 1989 was one of three years with the most performances of "Bird Song" with twenty-one. Barry was lucky enough to see seven, one of which was December 9 at the Great Western Forum in Los Angeles. We definitely recommend this thirteen-minute performance. You can stream Barry's fine audience recording at this link: (Bird #6). This was a good year for the Dead, with everyone healthy and Brent Mydland still on keyboards. Garcia shows off his MIDI effects when he solos as a "flute." Best of all, the band gives this performance their signature improvisational jamming that's so special with the Dead's live performance; you'll understand the earlier comment about the band stretching out in the first set.

Another show Barry was lucky enough to see was on March 20, 1992, in Ontario, Canada. By this time, Mydland had passed away and Vince Welnick was doing a nice job on keyboards. This is an audience recording by the famed Oade brothers, and you can stream it at this link: (Bird #7). This version runs more than twelve minutes, and though 1992 sometimes is considered the downward slope of the Dead's career, you'll still enjoy it.

To wrap up our recommendations, we end with one of the last performances of "Bird Song" at the Coliseum in Charlotte, North Carolina, on March 24, 1995. Although this version may not pack quite the punch of the others, it's still a crowd-pleaser, as you'll hear in this soundboard version you can stream (Bird #8). Garcia's voice isn't as strong as it once was, but he's right there, and so is everyone else in the band. Having seen the Dead several times in 1995, Barry remembers the band behind Garcia as a locomotive urging him on, and you'll hear that here.

"Bird Song" is another wonderful Grateful Dead song with a long and storied history, and we've shared as much as we can in our limited space here. It is a classic example of the evolution of the Grateful Dead in later years, when they played extended jams within the song. Enjoy it!

"Black Muddy River"

"Black Muddy River," by Jerry Garcia and Robert Hunter, is a languid and thought-ful ballad that entered the Dead's live rotation relatively late in the game in 1986. It was originally released on the studio album *In the Dark*, recorded and released in 1987. Many of the Dead's songs were played extensively prior to being released on a studio album, but the Dead played "Black Muddy River" only three times live before recording it. Overall, they played the song sixty-six times, mainly in the late 1980s, though they brought it back in 1995 after a gap of almost four years. Except for a handful of early performances in which the Dead played it in the second set, "Black Muddy River" was usually played as an encore.

The lyrics (BlackMR #1) to "Black Muddy River" are interesting and perhaps opaque: like many Grateful Dead songs, this one is given to multiple interpreta-tions. Hunter wrote the poem for this song after Garcia suffered a diabetic coma in 1986. He envisioned images of and had nightmares about death when he wrote it, according to Steve Silberman's interview with Hunter here: (BlackMR #2). It's a sad, mournful song, whether it be about death, old age, or the difficulties in facing life. Yet, as is often the case with Hunter's poetry, there's a sort of dialectic between seemingly overwhelming problems and the ability to withstand, fight back, and perhaps overcome. In "Black Muddy River," Garcia may be singing about what it's like carrying the weight of the Grateful Dead on his shoulders or the bleak realities of life in America during the Reagan years, but the song enjoins us to "dream me a dream of my own" and to "sing me a song of my own." It does *not* allow us to leave the shore of the river, however; whatever the problem is, we can't escape the dialectic.

The Dead played "Black Muddy River" as a slow lament, perhaps to highlight Hunter's lyrics. Garcia's voice was always intense and emotional in his performances of this song, and that reverential tone—perhaps counterintuitive to readers unfamil-iar with the Grateful Dead—carried over into the audience on most occasions. You don't hear shouts and screams during this song.

The first performance of "Black Muddy River" was on December 15, 1986, at Oakland Coliseum, only a few weeks before the band recorded the *In the Dark* album. Given that timing, listeners might expect a fairly polished performance, albeit with some imperfections, as it is the first live performance of the song. We recommend this soundboard recording (BlackMR #3) so you can more clearly hear the quality of the performance. Keep in mind that this is the Dead's first show after Garcia's near-fatal coma five months earlier, so his voice sounds rough. For the song's first live performance, this one is extraordinary.

"Black Muddy River" was not officially released on many albums; Deaddisc.com cites only eight releases as of 2016 (BlackMR #4), but there are some good performances out there. For example, the second of the two box sets from spring 1990, *Spring 1990 (The Other One)* (D2:T11) includes an excellent performance of "Black Muddy River," this time from March 14, 1990, in Landover, Maryland. You can hear it here: (BlackMR #5), which is a matrix recording that combines the soundboard with an audience recording. This may well be the strongest performance of those recommended here. The single loud crowd response is ironic: when Garcia sings "When it seems like this night will last forever," he sings it as a lament, but the audience understandably wants the night to last forever.

There's another excellent performance from the same period, April 2, 1990, at the Omni in Atlanta, which was issued on the *Spring 1990* (D3:T6) box set. Again, "Black Muddy River" is the encore. By now, four years into the performance life of the song, the audience recognizes it immediately, as you can hear on this audience recording: (BlackMR #6). At the same time, the overall sound is more subdued than one might expect at the end of a show. And again there's only one strong crowd response, when Garcia sings the "night will last forever" line. Incidentally, this is the user review website headyversion.com's second favorite performance of this song. We also offer you the "Black Muddy River" from July 29, 1988, at Laguna Seca Raceway near Monterey, California, when it was the encore. This is an audience recording that Barry taped (BlackMR #7), and it captures the appreciative attitude of the crowd after a great show.

For headyversion.com's favorite performance, we have to turn to the very last Grateful Dead show, July 9, 1995, at Soldier Field in Chicago. "Black Muddy River," the first of the two-song encore that night, has the unfortunate distinction of being the last song on which Jerry Garcia was the primary vocalist. On this audience recording, the audience welcomes the band back to the stage for the encore for the first two-plus minutes. This sounds like a typical Dead show audience. Once the song begins, the crowd quiets. On this audience recording (BlackMR #8), Garcia's voice is somewhat strained, but the harmonies from the backup vocals are strong. Keeping the band's level of exhaustion in mind, the music quality of this performance is remarkable.

In spite of all of the problems in the world, "Black Muddy River" is ultimately an optimistic song. Let the world do its worst and yet still "sing me a song of my own." Garcia did it, and so can we.

"Black Peter"

"Black Peter" is a beautiful ballad that occupies a special place in the hearts of Deadheads. The song is recognized as one of the "Jerry ballads," songs performed at a relatively slow tempo toward the end of the second set at Grateful Dead shows. Dead shows usually ended with upbeat, high-energy songs, so songs like "Black Peter" feel like the calm before the storm. Other songs in this category include "Stella Blue," "Comes a Time," "Standing on the Moon," and perhaps "Wharf Rat," all of which are discussed later in this book.

"Black Peter," composed by Jerry Garcia with lyrics by Robert Hunter, appeared on the studio album *Workingman's Dead* released in 1970 as track 8. It was part of the harvest of wonderful songs that emerged during this period. In concert, "Black Peter" was performed 343 times from December 4, 1969, well before its studio release, to June 22, 1995, just two weeks before the Grateful Dead's final show. It was a regular part of the rotation every calendar year except during the 1975 touring hiatus. The Dead performed "Black Peter" forty times in 1970, and more than twenty times per year from 1978 through 1982. In other years, the frequency diminished to a handful of performances each year as the band's repertoire expanded.

Musically, as mentioned, "Black Peter" is a ballad played at a slow tempo with relatively little by way of improvisation or jams. There's usually only a single solo in the song, although it varies in length from one performance to another. Occasionally there's a louder solo in the coda after the last refrain of the line "run and see." This is one of the Grateful Dead's relatively few songs that didn't change much from performance to performance, although the tempo slowed over the years. There were many acoustic performances of "Black Peter," especially early on.

The lyrics (Black Peter #1) for "Black Peter" make the case for why this song is one of the Grateful Dead's essential songs. "Black Peter" is the story of a person on his deathbed. While this significant—to the narrator—event takes place, the conversations and the activities around him are utterly mundane: the talk is of the weather, the wind blowing through the window, the sun rising and setting. The song hits pay dirt with the bridge verse. "See here how everything, lead up to this day," the narrator sings, and yet it's just a normal day, like all the others.

The idea that "everything lead[s] up to this day" is reminiscent of chaos theory or the butterfly effect. We are merely a collection of atoms responding to all the other atoms in the universe: there are no deities governing life; it's just atoms. This materialist view of life, an atomist view of reality, recalls "On the Nature of Things," by the Roman philosopher Lucretius. If we are dead and "cold beneath the ground" tomorrow, as the song intones, so be it. Accepting this view of life is not at all sad, it's liberating; it's perhaps the true meaning of "go with the flow."

These lyrics have prompted interesting essays focusing on their meaning and significance. Oliver Trager has noted that it's uncommon for a rock song to feature a man singing from his deathbed. Peter Wendel, another music historian, said, "It doesn't get any darker or deeper than 'Black Peter,' neither musically nor lyrically." There's more: (Black Peter #2). David Dodd provides an excellent exegesis of this song (Black Peter #3), adding the idea that the dying man, who in the song lives another day, is scolding his visitors for their callous conversations in his presence. He expresses wonderment that a relatively young man like Robert Hunter could have such insight into the ideas that an older person facing death might have. Listen to "Black Peter" to hear how these lyrics are delivered with such deep emotion.

On May 2, 1970, at the famous Harpur College show, the Dead played an acoustic version of "Black Peter" that appears on the album *Dick's Picks, Vol. 8* (D1:T6), also accessible here: (Black Peter #4). This early performance came around the time the Dead were releasing the *Workingman's Dead* album. This is a strong performance with excellent guitar work and vocals.

On October 29, 1977, in Dekalb, Ilinois, "Black Peter" appears in the Jerry ballad slot, just before the final song of the second set. This electric version (Black

Peter #5) is another great version of the song. The tempo is quite slow, even compared to the measured acoustic performance in the 5/2/70 show mentioned earlier. The dynamics are fine throughout the song: fairly soft volume during the verses punctuated by strong musical fills between the verses. The bridge verse in this version is outstanding in its emotional intensity, provoking an appropriate audience response. The coda, including the extended singing of "run and see" and the jam that follows, is also noteworthy. This is as powerful a performance of "Black Peter" as you'll find.

For contrast, listen to "Black Peter" from April 24, 1978, a sweet and mellow performance, available here: (Black Peter #6). For a later performance, listen to July 8, 1990 (Black Peter #7), at Pittsburgh's Three Rivers Stadium. Here "Black Peter" is in its customary Jerry ballad slot. The tempo is slightly faster than the 10/29/77 version, clocking in at about 9:40, compared to that show's twelve-minute-plus version. After the second verse, when Garcia sings, "just wanna have a friend or two at hand," the crowd roars as if they are the friends in question.

Our personal favorite is the December 1, 1979, performance (Black Peter #8) at the Stanley Theater in Pittsburgh. If the 10/29/77 show is a powerful version, this performance is softer, almost sweet, with rolling rhythms in a slow tempo. The solo after the second verse repeats the verse structure twice and shows Garcia's ability to play around the melody. The vocal harmonies in the bridge are about as good as anything performed live by the Dead.

"Black Peter" was a crowd favorite during more than two decades of live performances with its dynamic changes and emotional strength. We hope the lyrics help you meditate on life.

"Black Throated Wind"

"Black Throated Wind" (aka BTW), written by Bob Weir and his longtime lyricist, John Perry Barlow, made its live debut on March 5, 1972 (BTW #1), at Winterland in San Francisco at a benefit concert for Native Americans on Alcatraz. A studio version of the song appears on Weir's solo album *Ace* (BTW #2), with the Dead (minus Pigpen) acting as his backup band. Over the years BTW was performed 158 times, with the last performance on June 28, 1995. Its performance history is unusual, even for the Dead. It was played seventy times in 1972, fewer than twenty times in 1973 and 1974, and then it wasn't played again until 1990. The song, both live and studio versions, times out at less than six minutes, relatively short for Dead songs. BTW is usually found in the first set, where the songs aren't really open enough for jamming. After about 1970, when the Dead transitioned to a standard two-set format, the first set usually consisted of self-contained songs that did not feature extended jams, although there were usually at least one or two songs that did feature jams, perhaps to set the stage for the second set, which usually consisted of extended songs with lots of improvisation.

Barry saw ten versions of BTW, including at his first show on June 16, 1974 (BTW #3), thoroughly enjoying all of them. The song is one of Barry's favorites, although it's not clear why: Melody? Lyrics? Weir's delivery? It's probably the combination of all of them. Barlow's lyrics tell a story, with some interesting lines that are perhaps more literal than those found in most of Robert Hunter's lyrics. "Black Throated Wind" is the story of a hitchhiker reflecting on a relationship that didn't turn out well. He's standing by the interstate carrying emotional baggage and second thoughts: "the woman I thought I once met" ended up doing "better by me than I done by you." Does this indicate that the hitchhiker got the short end of the stick in the relationship? David Dodd, however, points out that the hitchhiker was treated better than he'd treated his partner (BTW #4), which makes complete sense since he's "going back home, that's what I'm gonna do."

The most interesting performance for Barry—and perhaps for everyone in attendance that night—was in Landover, Maryland, on March 16, 1990 (BTW #5), when Weir returned it to the repertoire for the first time since October 19, 1974, a sixteen-year gap! For the Landover version, Weir and Barlow reworked the lyrics significantly. Apparently one or both were unhappy with the lyrics, thus the years-long break between performances. But the lyric changes didn't last. They reverted to the original lyrics after only a couple of performances; by the fifth time they played the revised version on October 27, 1990 (BTW #6), at the Zenith in Paris, France, only a handful of the new lyrics remained.

Surprisingly, we hear fewer changes than those reported by David Dodd (2005, 187). He indicates changes to the second chorus from "keeps on pouring in and speaks of a life that passes like dew" to "whispers like sin and speaking of life that passes like dew." However, the one change that did remain from the short-lived "new" lyrics is in the third verse. The line "So I give you my eyes and all of their lies" became "So I give you my eyes, they were just a disguise." Regardless of how long the new lyrics remained, this is another example of the Dead's evolution during their thirty-year career. "Black Throated Wind" has been officially released on more than fifteen albums, and most of the recordings are from the early years of the Dead. The complete list of official releases is available here: (BTW #7).

In addition to the five versions of "Black Throated Wind" already suggested, here are a few more. Start with a soundboard recording that's quite good from the Europe '72 tour at Wembley Pool in London on April 8, 1972 (BTW #8). Next, go to an audience recording of a much later performance at Deer Creek, near Indianapolis, on June 6, 1990: (BTW #9). Barry attended that show and remembers well Jerry's guitar sounding especially clear. Finally, there is another fine soundboard recording of one of the last performances from the Dead's final year from February 21, 1995, in Salt Lake City (BTW #10).

After checking out all these versions, you'll notice what we commented on earlier: BTW is a first set song that doesn't change much from version to version. You may or may not enjoy "Black Throated Wind" as much as we do but be sure to give it a fair listen.

"Box of Rain"

"Box of Rain" is one of the Grateful Dead's most significant songs as well as an unlikely standout of their shows. Its significance is evident: among other reasons, Robert Hunter, who wrote the song with Phil Lesh, entitled his published collection of lyrics *A Box of Rain*. Moreover, "Box of Rain" is the last song the Dead performed live, as the second encore on July 9, 1995, their final show. Although disguised by the upbeat tempo, "Box of Rain" might rank as one of the Dead's best love songs. But in terms of performance, "Box of Rain" was an unlikely hit because Lesh, though considered by many a musical genius, is not an accomplished singer.

The pattern of the Dead's performances of "Box of Rain" reflects the strength of Lesh's voice. The Dead performed the song 161 times. Of these, almost fifty performances occurred in 1972, when they introduced the song, and 1973. Until then, Phil had been singing backup vocals at the high end of the register, though not always successfully. Around 1973, his voice gave out, and he did not sing for several years after 1973, except for backup vocals in "Truckin'." "Box of Rain"—and Phil's voice—came out of retirement in 1986 and was played at least eight times every year after that through the end of the Dead's run.

During the first third of its performance life, "Box of Rain" was mostly a first set song; in the middle third, from about 1986 to 1990, the Dead played it in either set; and in the final five years, it became a second set song, with several performances as the encore. The song became increasingly important to the Dead—and to Hunter—since "big songs" tended to be played regularly later in their shows. Unlike many second set songs, "Box of Rain" never included significant improvisation or jams. It was played consistently from its first to its last performance.

The lyrics for "Box of Rain" can be found here, along with other insights into the song (Box of Rain #1). Hunter says: "Phil Lesh wanted a song to sing to his dying father and had composed a piece complete with every vocal nuance but the words. If ever a lyric 'wrote itself,' this did—as fast as the pen would pull" (Hunter 1990, 26). On one hand, the lyrics describe the end of life: "you're tired and broken, your tongue is twisted . . . thoughts unclear." But on the other hand, the repeated line— "What do you want me to do, to do for you"—stresses the love of the caretaker for the dying person, love as commitment, kindness, and the communication of both.

Hunter closes the song with one of the finest stanzas of poetry of his career. It begins, "It's just a box of rain, I don't know who put it there, believe it if you need it, or leave it if you dare." To what does the opening "it" refer: Life? The universe? Love? A "box of rain" is a literal impossibility, but figuratively Hunter imagines it as "the world we live on," which makes sense if thinking of the planet as a box. The stanza closes with "Such a long, long time to be gone and a short time to be there." That could be said of anyone's life, but Deadheads take it further, in hindsight, of course, as commentary relating to the Dead's performing life, not to mention Garcia's life, which ended only a month after the final performance of "Box of Rain."

"Box of Rain" first appeared on the studio album *American Beauty* in 1970; this is one of the Dead's songs that was *not* played live before it was recorded in the studio. The song appears on about twenty other official recordings. The first live performance of "Box of Rain" took place on September 17, 1970, but we recommend starting with the October 9, 1972, performance at Winterland in San Francisco, when the Dead played it in the first set. You can hear a soundboard recording here: (Box of Rain #2). The Dead deliver a very good performance in this version.

On March 20, 1986, in Hampton, Virginia, the Dead brought "Box of Rain" out of retirement after a gap of seventy-seven shows. They closed the first set with the song, much to the delight of the audience. You can hear a good version of the song in this matrix recording: (Box of Rain #3). Garcia's solo in this version is particularly beautiful and mellow.

As mentioned earlier, the Dead's final performance of "Box of Rain" was also their final song ever, in Chicago on July 9, 1995. You can hear this version here: (Box of Rain #4). This matrix recording captures both the soundboard music and the audience responses. Although the band may have been exhausted after a long tour, they rise to the occasion for this version. Garcia plays his usual folk-inspired short solo.

The Grateful Dead may have intended "Box of Rain" to be the coda for the tour on 7/9/95, but of course it became the coda to an era. For Deadheads, it's never been the same since that performance. In 2015 at Soldier Field in Chicago, the surviving members of the Dead along with other musicians played three shows commemorating the fiftieth anniversary of the Grateful Dead, the *Fare Thee Well* shows. There, at the same venue as their final performance in 1995, they opened the first of the three shows on July 3, 2015, with "Box of Rain," bringing it full circle.

"Brokedown Palace"

"Brokedown Palace" (aka Brokedown) is another sweet ballad from Garcia and Hunter, one that fits into the river and water theme of several of their other songs, such as "Black Muddy River," "Big River," and "Lazy River Road." It was first performed live at the Fillmore West in San Francisco, August 18, 1970 (Brokedown #1), and it was nearly always part of the Dead's active repertoire except for 1976 and 1978. Overall, the Dead played Brokedown a total of 215 times live, with the last performance on June 25, 1995 (Brokedown #2), at RFK Stadium in Washington, D.C. The lovely studio version of it appeared on the outstanding 1970 album *American Beauty*, which is highly recommended: (Brokedown #3).

Hunter wrote the lovely lyrics while living in London. The storyteller bids "fare you well my honey" as he leaves "this brokedown palace." If a man's home is his castle, as the old saying has it, then these lyrics easily could be reflections on one's own death, the breaking down of one's own "palace" or body. The narrator is "going home" and "resting [his] bones," yet will leave something behind as he plants "a weeping willow on the bank's green edge." It ends with "fare you well, fare you well, I love you more than words can tell," a perfect song for an encore. And after 1977, that's when Brokedown was performed most often. Bob never fails to come to tears at this point in the show—and not because it meant the show was nearly over.

As is usual with Hunter lyrics, all is open to interpretation. Is the storyteller leaving, dying, or simply reflecting on life? You decide. David Dodd offers some enlightening comments about the lyrics and their meaning on his "Greatest Story Ever Told" blog (Brokedown #4), including a wonderful vignette by Ken Kesey after his son's death. These comments help put Grateful Dead biographer Dennis McNally's comments in perspective when he calls Brokedown "a death song, but a death that is part of the peace that passeth all understanding. It is the death of the old and accomplished, an ending of dignity and serenity" (2002, 376).

In keeping with its role as an encore, Brokedown was a contained song with a stable structure—no Deadhead expected significant improvisation or extensions. It's a 4/4 song with plenty of minor chords to set the emotional, reflective tone. Brokedown reflects Garcia's musical genius: when a song is about the lyrics, as is the case with Brokedown, he doesn't let the music become the star of the show. Instead, Garcia allows the music simply to be the stage upon which the poem is recited. Be sure to read the beautiful lyrics, which you can find here: (Brokedown #5).

In addition to Brokedown's long history of live performances and the studio version mentioned earlier, the Dead officially released more than twenty albums that include Brokedown, including four box sets. A full list through 2016 is available here: (Brokedown #6). Nearly every version of "Brokedown Palace" is online at archive.org. Here are a few we recommend, all of which are ranked highly at headyversion.com.

First, check out October 3, 1980, at the Warfield Theater in San Francisco (Brokedown #7), which is ranked at the top of the headyversion.com list. When you listen to this clear audience recording, you'll hear the crowd's excitement as the song begins to play. Then notice how truly quiet they become to the point of reverential silence. This is a sign of the respect Deadheads have for the Dead and their music. For Deadheads, it's all about the music. You'll find this in nearly every Dead performance of ballads.

Next give a listen to June 8, 1977, at Winterland Arena in San Francisco (Brokedown #8). This matrix recording is ranked the third best performance of Brokedown by headyversion.com users. It runs two minutes longer than 10/3/80, and it has Keith Godchaux on keyboards with Donna Godchaux singing backup vocals, whereas 10/3/80 had Brent Mydland on keyboards and backup vocals.

Barry recorded this Brokedown, the fourth he saw, which was the encore from June 21, 1986, at the Greek Theater in Berkeley (Brokedown #9). This was a sweet, mellow performance after a great show; however, the most memorable performance he saw was in Colorado at the Town Park in Telluride on August 16, 1987 (Brokedown #10). This version was again the show's encore, but it didn't go as planned. Not long after they started playing, it was clear there were problems musically, and the band began to hesitate, some members actually stopping. Even Jerry was having trouble singing and playing on key. Finally he stopped and said, "Wait a minute! This is all fucked up! We're in the wrong key. You people are used to this—the altitude and all. Forget all that happened!" This elicited a roar of approval from the audience, and the band started over again, this time without incident. This is another example of the unpredictability of Grateful Dead performances, as well as the understanding and appreciation of Deadheads—no one expected perfection, only a good time. Yet when the band righted itself after starting again, the beauty and depth of feeling was fully there.

You won't go wrong with any of our recommended versions. And you'll benefit even more if you listen to several to hear Garcia's underrated voice deliver Hunter's sweet lyrics.

"Brown Eyed Women"

The Grateful Dead introduced "Brown Eyed Women" (aka BEW), a mid-tempo ballad and folk song, in 1971. Robert Hunter is the lyricist and Jerry Garcia composed the music. The Dead performed BEW 347 times, playing it consistently every year after its introduction on August 23, 1971, through its final performance on July 6, 1995, just days before the Dead's final concert. From 1971 through 1979, the Dead played BEW about two dozen times a year, gradually tapering down the frequency, so that in 1994, for example, the last full year of touring, they played it only eight times in eighty-four shows.

Statistics like that give weight to the uniqueness of the Grateful Dead: most rock bands tour with a relatively limited repertoire, playing basically the same show every time out, whether it be their greatest hits or latest album. In 1994, the Grateful Dead played 145 different songs in those eighty-four shows, and no song except "Drumz," the drummers' solo, was played more than twenty-eight times. The Dead played "Touch of Grey," their biggest hit, only twelve times in 1994. The fact that "Brown Eyed Women" was played "only" eight times speaks to the strength of the band, not to the popularity—or lack thereof—of BEW or any other song from the "old days."

BEW is one of the Dead's songs that never appeared on a studio album. It first appeared on the classic *Europe '72* album (D1:T8). Almost fifty live versions of BEW have been released, according to deaddisc.com. BEW started out as a song that the Dead played in either the first or second set, but it gradually became a first set song—after 1978, it was never played in the second set.

The title is puzzling: is it "Woman," which makes more sense in terms of the lyrics? Or "Women," as Dead.net and this review have it? It was woman, singular, on the original album release and at least until the 2001 CD release of *Europe '72*, but it's women, plural, everywhere else, including all recent issues. Obviously, this is not an earth-shattering question, but it may say more about Deadheads and their quest for details than anything else.

The lyrics (BEW #1) follow the lives of typical Dead characters, in this case a poor farmer, Jack Jones, a moonshiner living in the hills during the Depression, and his wife, Delilah. The song is narrated by one of their eight sons, the only one who turned bad, allegedly because he "didn't get the lickin's that the other ones had." Jones the moonshiner is more of a mystery: he works hard, he persists, his liquor is strong, yet the roof falls in one winter because of the snow, causing Delilah's death. As a result, the "old man never was the same again."

In the end, we lose everything: It's a message we hear in many Grateful Dead songs, including "Stella Blue," "Row Jimmy," and perhaps even "Box of Rain." Yet there's another message also frequently heard in the Dead's canon, namely that love, commitment, and persistence in the face of obstacles are the things that make life worth living. This Hunter poem may be interpreted as the great cosmic questions about life or simply about the minutiae of moonshining: whether the bottles were clean, who chopped the hickory for the still, the ox that took up the yoke so the fields could be plowed, and so forth.

"Brown Eyed Women" is a mid-tempo ballad that began its musical life at a faster tempo, as you can hear in one of our recommendations. Later they slowed it down, and it became more of a folk song about the Depression era in the United States. The song has an excellent musical and vocal bridge, narrating when the "roof caved in."

For an early version, listen to the Dead's performance on October 19, 1971, at the University of Minnesota, available here: (BEW #2). This is a show at which the Dead introduced no fewer than six new songs, and Keith Godchaux's first show as keyboardist. This version has a speedier tempo than later versions, in contrast with the version on the *Europe '72* album, for example.

Next we jump ahead to May 8, 1977, the fabled Barton Hall Cornell University concert, released in 2017 in the *Get Shown the Light* box set (D1:T9). This is the Holy Grail of Grateful Dead shows—most Deadheads have heard a circulating tape of this show. It's also accessible here: (BEW #3). (This is an audience recording by famed early taper, Jerry Moore.) Here the tempo has settled into the groove that fans are more accustomed to hearing on this song. Garcia's solo is melodic, and the support from the rest of the band equally so. Given the fame of this particular show, it's no surprise that this version is voted number one at the headyversion .com website.

Eight years later, on June 30, 1985, in Columbia, Maryland, the Dead played another characteristic version of BEW, in what by now had become the song's typical style. A good matrix recording is available here: (BEW #4). Garcia's voice is not at its strongest, but background vocals, now with Brent Mydland in the band on keyboards, are better than some versions from the 1970s. Garcia's guitar, however, is at its strongest on this version. We especially enjoy the "Phil bombs," as Lesh punctuates the chorus a couple of times.

"Brown Eyed Women" was a consistent part of the rotation for the Grateful Dead for twenty-five years and earned a cherished place in the canon. It's not a signature song, but it certainly isn't a one-off composition, either. It's an essential part of the "meat and potatoes" of the Dead's musical diet. BEW is good listening for its lyrics, for placing the Dead in the mainstream of Americana roots music, and for the enthusiastic reactions captured on audience recordings.

"Candyman"

"Candyman," by Garcia and Hunter, appeared on the Grateful Dead's *American Beauty* album in 1970, one of their most accessible and popular albums. One of the cornucopia of songs that emerged from around 1969 to 1971, "Candyman" was performed live 277 times and was played every year except for the group's hiatus in 1975. The first live performance was on April 3, 1970, in Cincinnati, during an acoustic set, where it was followed by the Everly Brothers hit "Wake Up Little Susie." In fact, twenty-one of the song's forty-nine performances in 1970 were in acoustic sets—we recommend one below. Its final live performance was on June 30, 1995, in Pittsburgh. "Candyman" appears a handful of times in the second set; it was primarily a first set song.

The lyrics to "Candyman" (Candyman #1) speak to a familiar theme—the downtrodden hero attempting to make a go of life. Our hero gambles, seduces, plays his guitar, and even threatens to blow Mr. Benson—Hunter's personification of the overclass—"straight to hell." That line always starts a hearty roar from the assembled Deadheads, more because it's anti-authority than because it's pro violence. Finally, the narrator (or perhaps it's Garcia) works the circuit, appearing here, appearing there, eventually returning: "the Candyman comes 'round again." The Candyman character may be an outlaw, but he has something for everybody, whether it's music, drugs, sex appeal, or vengeance.

David Dodd offers interesting insights into these lyrics (Candyman #2), in which he stresses the anti-authoritarian tendencies of Deadheads, not to mention the sense of being outcast from a society that often dismissed the Grateful Dead as little more than nostalgic relics of the 1960s.

Musically, as with many first set songs, "Candyman" is not a song with a lot of improvisation or extended jams. It's stable in structure, with a slow to medium tempo. What is notable is the vocals. On the *American Beauty* studio album, the harmonies are true, and Garcia's work on pedal steel guitar is accomplished. The Dead are often less successful in live performances when it comes to vocals, but "Candyman" was usually the exception. For example, listen to May 28, 1977, in Hartford, released on the album *To Terrapin* (D2: T2) and accessible here: (Candyman #3). On this audience recording, listen to the sing-along. This solo is gentle and soaring, and the band provides perfect backing, a rolling sound the Dead perfected. The harmony test comes with the vocal bridge after the solo: exquisite. The intensity increases after the final chorus, for an instant, until the coda. This version may be the standard against which other live versions are measured. (We still think the studio album is the definitive version.)

In an earlier acoustic performance, May 7, 1970, at MIT in Cambridge, Massachusetts, for example (Candyman #4), the song starts slowly and the tempo seems slow, almost ponderous. The acoustic playing is fine, and Garcia sings this as a solo until the harmony bridge. This "Candyman" shows the band's ambitious approach to live music, changing aspects of the music to see what worked best. Comparing this show to the Hartford 1977 performance, it's evident that the structure is consistent but the quality differs. It was apparently a polite audience at MIT, but we're not sure that's a good thing.

Spring 1990 was a good touring season for the Grateful Dead. They performed "Candyman" on May 6, 1990, in Carson, California, available here: (Candyman #5). This electric version starts at the same mellow level as most electric versions, with that rolling backing sound from the band. The intensity picks up in the third verse and then backs off for the final chorus and coda. This is a good late version.

In addition to the three performances mentioned earlier, we recommend "Candyman" from *Dick's Picks, Volume 8* (D1:T7), the Harpur College show in Binghamton, New York, on May 2, 1970, and available here: (Candyman #6). This is an acoustic version and "Candyman" is cut after the first verse, so it's a short performance, with the Dead quickly moving into "Cumberland Blues." It's an early version—maybe the Dead were still working on it.

We also like the version of "Candyman" on *Dick's Picks, Volume 20* (D3: T6), from Syracuse, New York, on September 28, 1976 (Candyman #7). The tempo is a bit slower. This is a good recording for audience responses, especially to the Mr. Benson line, at about 2:40. The vocal harmonies are tighter than on many other versions. We also recommend the "Candyman" on *Dick's Picks, Volume 34* (D1:T7), from Rochester, New York, on November 5, 1977 (Candyman #8). This audience recording is an excellent version for both the tempo and the vocal harmonies. Finally, you should listen to Barry's great audience recording of "Candyman" from July 29, 1988, at the Laguna Seca Raceway near Monterey, California (Candyman #9).

Critics of the Grateful Dead's vocal skills should treat themselves to a mid-1977 version of "Candyman." This is good music. Listen to it, dance, and sing along, especially if you need to vent because of something your own "Mr. Benson" has done—and we all have one, don't we?

"Casey Jones"

The Grateful Dead played many "traditional" and "old-timey" songs adapted from oral history or early recordings from the 1920s. Among these are their "story songs" based on actual events or individuals. We include three of these in this book: "Dupree's Diamond Blues," "Stagger Lee," and "Casey Jones." Although based on some of the events in the life of Casey Jones, an engineer during the early twentieth century from Cayce, Kentucky, this is an original song composed by Jerry Garcia and Robert Hunter.

Musically, "Casey Jones" has a steady beat that suggests the rhythmic sound of a train, and the song builds toward a crescendo that might be the demise of the train and the engineer in a deadly accident. There's not a lot of improvisation in the song, which builds to an energetic coda that usually repeats the last chorus several times. In the early years, it sounded like a folk song in tone, but that changed, and it became a rocker with a powerful, pulsating rhythm driving the song.

The Dead performed "Casey Jones" 312 times beginning in mid-1969, though irregularly. In its first three full years in the rotation, from 1970 to 1972, the Dead played "Casey Jones" 199 times, more than any other song during those years. Performances dropped to thirty-five shows in 1973 and to only ten shows in 1974. After the 1975 touring hiatus, the Dead never played it more than seven times a year and didn't play it at all from 1985 to mid-1992. The song's glory days were definitely its early years. Until around 1977, "Casey Jones" might be played at any point during the show, including many times as an opener. After the 1975 hiatus, its placement was usually as the encore.

The lyrics in "Casey Jones" tell the story of a locomotive engineer who is "driving that train, high on cocaine" and who dies in a collision with another train. The lyrics are here: (Casey #1). Those who don't know the lyrics might focus on the "high on cocaine" line, but this is in fact an anti-cocaine song and worth appreciating for that reason alone, not to mention the fun of the performance. Most of the lyrics are straightforward, but as usual, Hunter's lyrics run deeper. In this case, a favorite aphorism for Deadheads is: "Got two good eyes but we still don't see."

"Casey Jones" first appeared on the album *Workingman's Dead* in 1970, but it was performed live fifty or more times before that. It has appeared on at least seventy other albums issued by the Dead; the full list is here: (Casey #2). Deadbase lists the first performance of "Casey Jones" as June 20, 1969, but the earliest performance of the song available at Archive.org is two days later, June 22, 1969, in Central Park in New York City. That performance (Casey #3) is not great quality. The first two minutes of this recording is a jam before the song starts. This version has a much faster, only slightly funky tempo and style. Most of the characteristic riffs are not yet included, but the repeated lines of the outro are indeed there from the beginning. As mentioned earlier, readers are encouraged to listen to early versions of these songs as a basis for comparison with later, more evolved performances.

Only a few months later, at the famous February 14, 1970, show at the Fillmore East in New York City, the Dead played "Casey Jones," a performance released on *Dick's Picks, Volume 4* (D1:T2) and accessible as a soundboard recording here: (Casey #4). This version is the funky, pulsating song we now recognize as the "standard" "Casey Jones." Compared with the 6/22/69 show mentioned earlier, it almost sounds like a different song.

Prior to its closure, the Fillmore West in San Francisco staged a series of shows during the summer of 1971. The Grateful Dead's show, July 2, 1971, included Bob's favorite version of "Casey Jones." That version is on the compilation album *Fillmore:*

The Last Days and here: (Casey #5). (This show was broadcast on FM radio, and the recording includes a radio voice in the first minute.) The outro here is particularly fun and pulsating.

We also recommend three additional shows that span the years during which "Casey Jones" was played less frequently. The first is from August 4, 1974, in Philadelphia, a show issued as *Dick's Picks, Volume 31* (D2:T8), when the Dead played "Casey Jones" as the encore. It's accessible here: (Casey #6). By this time, the very funky outro with drum flourish had been added to the song. Second, we suggest June 20, 1992, in RFK Stadium in Washington, D.C., when the Dead broke out "Casey Jones" after a gap of 549 shows. This version features an actual diesel train horn in the intro and an enthusiastic crowd response, not to mention the sing-along. Hear it at this link: (Casey #7). The outro isn't as intensive as in earlier versions, but the funky coda is still cool.

Finally, on December 16, 1992, in Oakland, California, the Dead played "Casey Jones" as the encore. This version is on *Dick's Picks Volume 27* (D3:T4) and accessible here as a matrix recording: (Casey #8). This version captures the audience's reaction: part of the great fun of this song is the increasing audience enthusiasm with each repetition of the song's chorus in the outro. The song's increasing intensity transfers to the audience and maybe vice versa.

The musical tone of "Casey Jones" brings to mind the motif of the song: full-speed-ahead recklessness. The pulsating rhythm evokes the hard-driving pistons of the steam locomotive featured in the song. Yet at another level, it's just a hard dancing, fun song. So keep on dancing.

"Cassidy"

"Cassidy" is an upbeat tune written and composed by the Grateful Dead's "other" songwriting team: Bob Weir (music) and John Perry Barlow (lyrics). It was first recorded on Weir's solo studio album *Ace*, which was released in 1972 as the eighth and final track on the album. Weir performed the vocals and the Grateful Dead were his backing band.

"Cassidy" was first performed live on March 23, 1974, at the Cow Palace, near San Francisco, at the first "complete" "Wall of Sound" show. The Dead performed "Cassidy" 334 times during the next twenty-one years. They performed the song at least a dozen times each year until 1991, except for 1986, when the Dead played only forty-six concerts. After 1991, the number of performances dropped. "Cassidy" was also played acoustically several times in 1980. Its final performance was on July 6, 1995, in Maryland Heights, Missouri, where "Cassidy" closed the first set.

"Cassidy" was named for the daughter of Rex Jackson and Eileen Law, both part of the Grateful Dead's support team/family. The lyrics (Cassidy #1), however, refer in part to the legendary Neal Cassady, an early participant in Kesey's Acid Tests and the protagonist in Jack Kerouac's *On the Road*, as well as a huge influence on the Grateful Dead. For more on Neal Cassady and the song "Cassidy," look here: (Cassidy #2).

Like many Grateful Dead compositions, the lyrics in "Cassidy" have multiple levels of interpretation as well as adages that speak to life in general. In this case, for example, note "Fare thee well now, let your life proceed by its own design" and "let the words be yours, I'm done with mine." Lyrics such as these can be taken as advice to baby Cassidy, what Neal Cassady said before his sudden death in Mexico in 1968, or simply the lyrics wrapping up the song. In teaching introductory courses on the Grateful Dead, Bob has used these lines as his sign-off at the end of the course.

The first performance of "Cassidy" was on March 23, 1974, and was released on *Dick's Picks, Volume 24* (D1:T8) and is also here: (Cassidy #3.) This version timed in at 3:37, which is much shorter than later versions. Bob Weir and Donna Jean Godchaux both performed the vocals throughout the song. This first performance is solid musically, as are the vocals, but it's "folkier." It's not the rocker that "Cassidy" would become. After the final verse is sung twice, the song ends abruptly. There's only one short solo within the body of the song.

The song's next performance was more than a year later because of the Grateful Dead's 1975 hiatus. The June 3, 1976, performance in Portland, Oregon (Cassidy #4), timed in at 5:20. There's a more elaborate solo within the body of the song, showing the Dead's characteristic multiple use of "lead" instruments. The bridge after the last verse has emerged by this time, although it's relatively terse and quickly leads back to the final verse. The character of the song has shifted toward the rocker end of the spectrum, compared to the first performance on 3/23/74.

By December 3, 1981, five years after the 6/3/76 Portland show, "Cassidy" showed more signs of evolving. Listen to it here: (Cassidy #5). The timing is 5:23, but the tempo is considerably faster. Keith and Donna Godchaux had left the Grateful Dead by this time, so Weir sings the vocals by himself. The solo within the song is more refined, with Weir playing the main lead for this song. The difference from earlier versions lies in the bridge after the last verse: "let the words be yours, I'm done with mine." This bridge, virtually nonexistent in the two previous shows discussed earlier, is now extended for about two minutes with Garcia, Weir, and Phil Lesh all playing lead.

Ten years later, on February 24, 1992, at the Oakland Coliseum—available here (Cassidy #6)—the tempo is still fast and the vocals are shared with Vince Welnick, now on keyboards. The bridge after the last verse is again longer (about three minutes) and now also more ethereal and unstructured. This is an excellent performance.

Over the years, "Cassidy" evolved from a short, sweet, straightforward song in the folk genre into an upbeat rocking song that included a longer, spacey musical interlude. Because of this sort of evolution in performance over the years, "Cassidy" is an essential Grateful Dead song. It's also worth noting that when the surviving members of the Grateful Dead scheduled their fiftieth anniversary shows for Chicago on July 3, 4, and 5, 2015, they called the event the Fare Thee Well shows.

"Caution (Do Not Stop on Tracks)"

By the late 1960s, the Grateful Dead had established their credentials as a primo jam band. "Caution (Do Not Stop on Tracks)" (aka Caution) is one of the early great jam pieces in their repertoire.

On the *Anthem of the Sun* album, the studio version of Caution is attributed to Ron McKernan ("Pigpen"). Other sources list the Grateful Dead as a unit as composers. What seems clear is that McKernan wrote the lyrics—more about this later. Crediting the music to the Grateful Dead as a group recognizes the essentially improvisational nature of the song and of the band's musical style back in the day: there's not much by way of a single coherent set of music to this song beyond the basic rhythmic pattern.

The lyrics for Caution are straightforward (Caution #1) but fluid in performance. You'll hear more or less the same lyrical themes on different versions of Caution: the gypsy woman, the touch of mojo, and repetitions of "all I/you need." But you'll also hear a great variety of different lyrics in different versions, because McKernan improvised some of the lyrics for many, if not most, performances. For more on this, see David Dodd's piece about Caution here: (Caution #2).

Anthem of the Sun was issued in 1968, but the Dead played Caution live on at least nine occasions before 1968. The first known live performance was on January 8, 1966, at the Fillmore Acid Test in San Francisco, but there's a studio version of Caution in the Grateful Dead's box set *So Many Roads* (D1:T2) from November 1965. Caution's final live performance was on May 11, 1972, at Rotterdam, in the Netherlands, during the Dead's Europe '72 tour. Overall, the Dead played Caution fifty-six times. Pigpen died in early 1973, and the Grateful Dead never played Caution after 1972.

Caution was always a fluid piece, usually part of a longer, continuous piece of music. Since there was often no discrete intro nor coda to Caution at those early shows, you often couldn't tell when Caution began or ended. You can best recognize Caution when Phil Lesh starts to play a characteristic bass line, which varied but usually stood out with its fast tempo.

Pigpen comes in with vocals at some point, although when that happens varied from performance to performance. Apart from the musical improvisation that is characteristic of Caution, even the vocals—and the timing of the vocals—reflect the open-ended approach to jamming that the Dead were known for in the late 1960s. Caution might seem to be over, but the following song may be simply an interruption. Soon enough, you hear the bass line again and realize that Caution is back for another round of improvisation.

A very early version of Caution from November 3, 1965, is accessible (Caution #3), when the Dead played the song in a studio setting. This version suggests why the song would be attributed to Pigpen: it's just over three minutes long and the first two minutes feature a harmonica solo by Pigpen, followed by the lyrics. Unfortunately, this version cuts off after 3:15 or so. On later versions, Garcia's lead guitar does most of the song's introductory section, so this 11/3/65 version with the harmonica dominating is an interesting early version to hear. It's also a good version for identifying Phil's characteristic bass riff.

The Dead played a particularly accessible version of Caution on November 8, 1969, at the Fillmore in San Francisco. That show was issued in 1995 as *Dick's Picks, Volume 16* (D3:T1&T3), and you can listen to it here: (Caution #4). In this version, Caution is part of a continuous long jam that had begun not quite an hour earlier with "Dark Star." In this version, Caution begins slowly: in fact, there's only a hint of Lesh's characteristic bass line initially, with a clearer riff at about 3:05. The tempo is still slower than what we expect in Caution, but at about 10:05, the pace picks up and the bass line is clearer. Shortly thereafter, Pigpen's vocals kick in. At what appears to be the end of the song, the Dead segue into "The Main Ten."

When the Dead finish that interlude, there's a teasing riff from "Death Don't Have No Mercy" before they return to Caution. We mention this tease because it exemplifies the Grateful Dead's approach to preparing a set (song) list for their shows. In short, there usually was *no* fixed set list; determining which song to play next was often based upon who introduced the notes to a song as a suggestion that might or might not be taken up by the whole band. In this case, the suggestion is not taken up, and the band resumes Caution for another nine minutes of improvisation, including another round of vocals by Pigpen. This was one of the great improvisational jams by the Grateful Dead; there may be no better example of their full-speed-ahead style of music, at least in 1969.

To truly appreciate the Grateful Dead's full trajectory, "Caution (Do Not Stop on Tracks)" is one of the most essential songs in the early history of the band. Early Deadheads fully bought into the Dead's jamming style—or they didn't remain Deadheads for long. There are many anecdotes about fervent Deadheads abandoning the Dead when they started to shift their emphasis away from this kind of music after 1969 and toward the country rock style heard on the albums *American Beauty* and *Workingman's Dead*, both of which date from this time period.

"China Cat Sunflower" > "I Know You Rider"

We have focused on individual songs so far, but Deadheads generally believe that the flow of one song into another paints a better overall picture of the music of the Grateful Dead. The medley of "China Cat Sunflower" (aka China), composed by Jerry Garcia and Robert Hunter, and "I Know You Rider" (aka Rider), a traditional song, is our first pairing.

The China > Rider medley was a fixture in the Grateful Dead repertoire, full stop. The Dead performed China 554 times and Rider 550 times. Between 1970 and their last show in July 1995, the Grateful Dead played China > Rider some 530 times. Given these statistics, you can see why the sequence of these two songs is essential for an appreciation of the Grateful Dead.

From 1970 through 1995, Deadheads had a good chance of hearing this signature two-song medley. Rarely were there more than ten concerts between performances of China > Rider. The exception to this is a gap of 198 shows from 1974 to 1979, which included the band's 1975 hiatus. During that gap, there was only one performance of China > Rider, on December 29, 1977.

The lyrics for "China Cat Sunflower" (China #1) have befuddled many. Suffice it to say that though these lyrics appear non-intuitive, there are anecdotes in Deadhead lore to the effect that the lyrics made perfect sense as an accompaniment to psychedelics. We'll leave it at that. In an unaltered state of mind, we can simply accept the lyrics as part of the song, as opposed to forcing a precise interpretation of the story. On the other hand, lyricist Robert Hunter has said, perhaps tongue-in-cheek, as quoted by David Dodd (China #2), "Nobody ever asked me the meaning of this song. People seem to know exactly what I'm talking about. It's good that a few things in this world are clear to all of us."

By comparison, the lyrics for "I Know You Rider," a traditional piece of music arranged by the Grateful Dead, are perfectly clear. The song talks about one of the recurring characters in Grateful Dead lyrics: the wanderer, perhaps a down-at-the-heels loner, looking for better luck in life: "The sun's gonna shine in my back door some day." The song has a rich musical history that goes back to early blues, and variations were performed as folk songs in the mid-twentieth century.

We recommend listening to some early, separate performances before turning to performances of the medley. The first live performance of China took place on January 17, 1968 (China #3), at the Carousel in San Francisco, where it timed in at less than three minutes. This version is played at a lightning tempo, but most of the elements are in place, including Weir's characteristic lead riff introducing the song. The solos here do not include the tonal key shift that appears in later versions. On March 12, 1966, at the Danish Center in Los Angeles, the Dead performed Rider (China #4). Musically, this version is played at a faster tempo than in later years, but as with China's first performance, the elements are all there. You can call this early version an electrified folk song.

Three and a half years later, on October 24, 1969, the Dead played an early version of China > Rider as a medley at Winterland in San Francisco, available here: (China #5). (Even at this relatively early date, someone in the audience taped the set, for which we are grateful indeed.) The musical elements of later versions are in place: the tempo of each song is slower than in the early performances of the separate songs. The jam between the two songs, though short, raises the level of intensity, consistent with the jamming the Dead were known for in 1969. The standard dynamics in "I Know You Rider" are there already.

As noted above, there are hundreds of versions of China > Rider, and most, if not all, are accessible to anyone who wants to spend weeks on just this medley, either via the Archive.org website or albums issued by the Grateful Dead. Find a full listing of these albums—there are almost ninety—at deaddisc.com (China #6). The version from May 3, 1972, in Paris, France, that appears on the Dead's album *Europe '72* is a standard version with which all Deadheads are familiar (China #7).

China > Rider was often performed as the closing number of the first set and occasionally for closing the second set. It was more often used to open the second set, but placement varied: it could be played anywhere in the show. A relatively rare sequence from June 26, 1974, in Providence, Rhode Island, a show Bob saw, has the medley in the second set after a two-and-a-half-minute spacey jam. Moreover, ever the improvisers, the Dead then began China itself with an extended jam before singing the first verse. This is an interesting version to listen to, if only for those two dimensions, and you can hear it here at a link that begins with the jam: (China #8).

Up until this point, China > Rider has been described as back-to-back songs with a jam in between. But occasionally the Grateful Dead slipped a specific sequence of notes called the "Mind Left Body Jam" (aka MLBJ) into the typical China > Rider jam. Although this happened on many occasions, MLBJ is generally not listed as a separate song in the metadata of China > Rider itself: it doesn't usually appear in the set lists. MLBJ consists of a simple four-note sequence that listeners recognize when they hear it. In the same 6/26/74 Providence show, the Dead included the MLBJ at the end of the jam after "China Cat Sunflower." This version of China > Rider is one of the great ones, in our estimation.

There is no evidence that we are aware of that the Dead planned (or didn't plan) to use "Mind Left Body Jam" in specific performances of China > Rider. But, in magical moments, use it they did. For a second great example, check out November 11, 1973, at UCLA's Pauley Pavilion, a show released by the Grateful Dead as *Dave's Picks, Volume 5* (D1:T8&T9) and here: (China #9). This is an excellent show overall with a very good version of China > Rider. MLBJ is an interesting piece of the Dead's puzzle—they played it many times over the years but rarely with attribution as a song. See a detailed description of the jam here: (China #10).

We would be remiss if we didn't highlight one of the great crowd response moments in Grateful Dead music. In Rider, Garcia sings: "I wish I were a headlight on a north-bound train," and continues: "I'd shine my light through the cool Colorado rain." Over the years, the audience began to respond with a rousing cheer to this line: it's obvious to most Deadheads that Garcia was in fact the headlight, no need for wishing. Soon, the Dead themselves were pumping up the volume at this specific moment in the song, making the cheers resonate ever more loudly.

The same 6/26/74 Providence show illustrates these dynamics well. And for another example, listen to December 29, 1977, at Winterland in San Francisco. This show was issued as *Dick's Picks, Volume 10* (D2:T4&T5) and is accessible here: (China #11). This is an audience recording, so you can hear the crowd responses more clearly. At these moments in Rider, the interactions between the band and the audience were palpable and wonderful to experience. For a soundboard recording of the same show, which allows the music to come through more clearly, look here: (China #12). That 12/29/77 show has an amazing second set, with China > Rider embedded in a long set of music that starts with "Playing in the Band" (aka Playing), continuing through China, Rider, "China Doll," "Drumz," and "Space," flowing to "Not Fade Away" before the reprise of Playing to end the set.

Now that we've convinced you that China > Rider was an unbreakable pair, it's time to remind you that the Grateful Dead were anything but predictable. Here's a performance of the two songs with "Crazy Fingers" sandwiched between them from July 29, 1988, in Monterey, California, at the Laguna Seca Raceway. Listen to Barry's recording of the three songs (China #13). Don't forget you are listening to three consecutive items at this link. This is an enjoyable, fast-paced version of both China Cat and Rider, with particularly strong crowd responses for both Bob Weir and Jerry Garcia at key moments. "Crazy Fingers" between the two songs is a special treat.

The China > Rider medley is perhaps *the* quintessential musical piece performed by the band, at least in the minds of many Deadheads. We hope you enjoy its many versions, and don't forget to sing along.

"China Doll"

"China Doll" easily may be the darkest song in the Grateful Dead's repertoire. To illustrate this point, the original title was "The Suicide Song," as lyricist Robert Hunter told Blair Jackson in a 1988 interview in the Deadhead magazine *The Golden Road* (Jackson 1988, 36). This song was written by Garcia and Hunter and made its live debut on February 2, 1973, in Los Angeles. The studio version appeared on *From the Mars Hotel*, released in 1974. One live acoustic version was also released on the two-LP *Reckoning* album in 1981, from the 1980 run of shows that included an acoustic set. In total, the Dead played "China Doll" 114 times; its last performance was October 11, 1994. "China Doll" was not always a regular part of the active rotation; it appeared sporadically. There were no performances in 1975, 1976, 1978, 1982, or 1995, and in the years it was played, it may have been played only once.

In the Jackson interview mentioned earlier, Hunter explains that the lyrics are a sort of a dialogue between someone who has shot himself and someone "sort of like a guardian angel." This offers listeners background for understanding the story, though the opening line, "A pistol shot at five o'clock," and then "before I hit the ground" should leave little doubt regarding the song's content. Hunter calls "China Doll" "a terrifying song," albeit one with "some affirmation of how it can be mended." Despite the darkness, Garcia's reading of the lines offers hope for the mending that Hunter mentions. Hunter seems to concur: "the song is eerie and very, very beautiful the way Jerry handles it." You can find all the lyrics here: (China Doll #1).

Musically the song is written in 4/4 time and played very slowly. It can't be called a ballad; it's really a dirge or requiem. Perhaps because it is such a quiet song, "China Doll" was included in several acoustic performances in the fall 1980 run of shows, with seven versions at the Winterland Theater in San Francisco and two at Radio

City Music Hall in New York City. Deaddisc.com provides a list of performances that has been released on official albums.

Barry didn't see "China Doll" performed until June 14, 1985, and then saw it only twelve times total. Although shorter than many, running less than six minutes, one of the performances that we recommend (and is also recommended at headyversion. com) is from Alpine Valley in East Troy, Wisconsin, on July 18, 1989. In the matrix recording of this performance, you can hear the crowd's excitement when they recognize what's coming. Garcia uses an unusual effect on his guitar while Mydland backs him with a nice harpsichord sound: (China Doll #2). A version that we like even more, which Barry also saw live, is from three days earlier at Deer Creek Amphitheatre, near Indianapolis, on July 15, 1989, which is nearly eight minutes long. Garcia's guitar is clearer, and he plays a mellow horn sound. You can hear Barry's excellent audience recording here: (China Doll #3). There are some weird electronic noises in a couple of spots.

The debut of "China Doll" at Stanford University on February 9, 1973, was the first Wall of Sound show. An excellent soundboard can be found here: (China Doll #4). For a first performance, this is quite polished, with good backup vocals overall. Headyversion.com's top pick for "China Doll" is from June 20, 1974, in Atlanta: (China Doll #5). This is an excellent soundboard recording, and you can clearly hear Weir's backup guitar, along with Lesh on bass, Godchaux on keyboards, and Kreutzmann on drums. The backup vocals are not as strong as those from the 1970s *Working Man's Dead/American Beauty* era, however. A later version from June 16, 1990, at Shoreline Amphitheatre in Mountain View, California, is a high-quality audience recording: (China Doll #6).

In addition to the one acoustic official release of "China Doll" on *Reckoning*, there are a couple of other acoustic versions we recommend, both of which are matrix recordings that combine an audience recording with a soundboard recording. The first is from Winterland in San Francisco on October 9, 1980 (China Doll #7), and the second is from Radio City Music Hall in New York City on October 26, 1980 (China Doll #8). In both you can hear the audience reaction while also appreciating Garcia's exquisite guitar playing. The backup vocals are also well done.

Listening to "China Doll" is a remarkably emotional experience. Though the song is about a suicide, it is so touchingly played and sung that it becomes captivating and enchanting rather than depressing or dark. At least that's how it affects us, and we hope it does the same for you as well.

"Cold Rain and Snow"

"Cold Rain and Snow" (aka Cold Rain) is a traditional song arranged by the Grateful Dead with updated lyrics. It's one of the Dead's "old-time" songs, this one based on an old folk song and "murder ballad," in which the protagonist is nagged to the point that he murders his wife. The Dead's version of the song includes the nagging but not the murder. Traditional old-time music was old-style country music based primarily on English folk songs. This genre developed as oral tradition music into the twentieth century, when it started to be recorded. For an insightful essay on old-time music, look here: (Cold Rain #1).

The Grateful Dead played Cold Rain 241 times, performing it every year from 1966 to 1995. They probably also played it in 1965, the year the band formed, but recordings from this early period are scarce. Since Cold Rain appeared on the Dead's first studio album, *The Grateful Dead*, it's probably safe to say that Cold Rain is the song in its repertoire that was played over the longest period of time—essentially for the band's entire thirty-year run.

The first documented live performance was on February 25, 1966, in Los Angeles, at the Sunset Acid Test, less than three months after their first performance as the Grateful Dead (rather than as the Warlocks, as the band previously had been known). Cold Rain's final performance was on June 19, 1995, at Giants Stadium in East Rutherford, New Jersey. Cold Rain was almost always a first set song and frequently the opener for the show. When it appeared in the second set, it was often the second set's opener.

The Dead played "Cold Rain and Snow" as a quick tempo song, with vocal harmonies that always received a response from the crowd. The precursor version of the song by Obray Ramsey is on the album *The Music Never Stopped: Roots of the Grateful Dead* (T1), where the song is called "Rain and Snow." Ramsey plays it as a dirge-like lament and the only instrument is a banjo. The Dead's version was far more upbeat, but the roots are clear.

As mentioned earlier, the Dead adapted the oral tradition lyrics from the oldest versions of the song. For the Dead's version of the lyrics, look here: (Cold Rain #2). There's no murder ballad here, but the idea of a nagging partner remains, perhaps to be followed by a quick departure from the scene if our protagonist's patience runs out: "I ain't gonna be treated this-a-way" and "going where those chilly winds don't blow." It's worth noting in passing that Barry proposed to his wife during the set break on August 14, 1991, immediately before the Dead opened the second set with "Cold Rain and Snow." We view this as a coincidence, not an omen.

The February 25, 1966, performance (Cold Rain #3) at the Sunset Acid Test at the Ivar Theater in Los Angeles is the Grateful Dead's first documented live performance of the song. Considering the date, this is a good soundboard recording. Though not a folk song, Cold Rain clearly has a bluegrass overtone.

On May 11, 1978, in Springfield, Massachusetts—a killer show that Bob attended, by the way—the Dead opened with "Cold Rain and Snow." This version appears on *Dick's Picks, Volume 25* (D3:T1) and is also available here: (Cold Rain #4). This is a standard performance, perhaps a little less upbeat than other versions. Garcia plays a pleasant, mellow solo. The band eventually raises the energy level of the song, as well as the crowd's response, with repeated singing of the title line ("run me out in the cold rain and snow") in the outro. When compared to the first performance discussed earlier, listeners can hear the development of the song from its earliest roots into a polished opening song.

For a show from the 1980s, try September 5, 1985, at Red Rocks in Colorado, always a good venue for the Dead: two shows later at this venue, they would render the "Star Spangled Banner" on the kazoo, not to mention "Frozen Logger." This show (Cold Rain #5), however, opens with a solid "Cold Rain and Snow." Incidentally, this matrix recording, which mixes a soundboard recording with an audience tape, is attributed to the Oade brothers, well known tapers. And finally, from the 1990s, listen to the Orlando, Florida, show from April 9, 1991: (Cold Rain #6). This is a solid performance—in later years the Dead added a flourish during the final verse, which can be heard on this version at about 4:50.

"Cold Rain and Snow" is not necessarily one of the Dead's greatest songs, but it's essential to a good overall understanding of the band's roots. It's the song they played over the longest period of time during their run, adapting it from early American oral and folk traditions. It's not simply a song, it's Americana and *roots*.

"Comes a Time"

October 19, 1971, in Minneapolis was quite a night for the Grateful Dead and Deadheads alike: six new songs premiered, including "Comes a Time," (Comes #1), and Keith Godchaux joined the band on keyboard, supplementing Ron "Pigpen" McKernan, who was struggling with health issues. "Comes a Time" is a lovely Jerry Garcia and Robert Hunter composition that had only sixty-six performances between its premiere and final performance on October 9, 1994, in Landover, Maryland. Further limiting access, the song wasn't recorded in a studio until it appeared on Garcia's "solo" *Reflections* LP in 1976. It didn't appear on a live recording until 1995, when one of the Europe '72 performances was released on CD as *Hundred Year Hall*. Who knows why the Dead would do this? It's unlikely there's a simple answer, although Dead biographer Dennis McNally reports that they were too busy absorbing Keith into the band to do any recording (2002, 413). In any case, "Comes a Time" is an essential Grateful Dead song.

This is an emotional song with touching lyrics from Hunter, although they may be interpreted as about hiding or holding emotions in. For example, "you've got an empty cup only love can fill"; "you get so far away from how it feels inside"; and "till the day may come when you can't feel at all" show us the emotional void facing the singer/narrator. The opening line is most familiar to Deadheads, "Comes a time when the blind man takes your hand and says: Don't you see." The lines combine to show us the danger of unexpressed feelings: eventually feeling nothing at all. Hunter's poetry always focused on communicating, and this song expresses that in spades.

If you listen to the debut performance mentioned earlier, you'll find a special treat—a verse not included in Hunter's book of lyrics nor in David Dodd's. In it the narrator expressed his feelings in a negative way and now must live with them. You'll hear this verse at about 4:24. It tells of expressed emotions better left unexpressed, and it seems odd that it wasn't retained in the song since it sheds light on why the singer/narrator holds in his emotions. Here's the little-documented verse:

The words come out like an angry stream,
You hear yourself say things you could never mean.
The heat cools down and you find your mind
You've got a lot of words you've got to stand behind.

Along with the "official" lyrics, Dodd includes this verse in his artsite.com blog (Comes #2), but no mention of it appears anywhere else that we've found. This otherwise undocumented verse appears before the last chorus, and it was part of the song for the first eight performances. There were also a few other minor lyrical variations in these first performances, such as "blind man takes your arm" instead of "hand." It was not until December 1, 1971 (Comes #3), in Boston, when the song as we know it was first performed.

Musically, "Comes a Time" is a slow ballad with strong Garcia vocals that drive the emotional points home. In the early versions, he uses falsetto during the line in the final chorus, "got an empty cup." Along with his beautiful but heart-wrenching guitar solo, this is a powerful Grateful Dead song.

There are several live official releases of "Comes a Time." In addition to the *Hundred Year Hall* CD mentioned earlier, it can be found on more than a dozen releases, one on the more recently released *May 1977: Get Shown the Light* box set from May 9, 1977. All of the releases are at deaddisc.com (Comes #4). We recommend starting with the version from May 9, 1977, in Buffalo, New York: (Comes #5). This is a very long (eleven minutes), very slow version that sounds especially good with Donna Godchaux backing Garcia's vocals on the chorus. Garcia's long solo to close the song is particularly strong and emotional, and the entire performance demonstrates again how powerful the spring 1977 tour was for the Dead.

Of the sixty-six performances of "Comes a Time," Barry was extremely lucky to have seen nine live. The first version Barry heard, and one that we recommend, was in Kansas City on February 9, 1979 (Comes #6). This audience recording captures the near-silence of the audience; its respect for this soft, emotional song isn't typically found among rock and roll enthusiasts. We also recommend a performance Barry saw at the Greek Theatre in Berkeley, California, on June 14, 1985 (Comes #7). This show was the first of a three-show run celebrating the Dead's twentieth anniversary. It's a memorable performance for Barry, since it was this show that convinced him to "get on the bus" and see multiple shows each year. It is an excellent soundboard recording.

Finally, we suggest the final performance of "Comes a Time" on October 9, 1994 (Comes #8), in Landover, Maryland. This audience recording again shows the audience's appreciation when the song begins, as well as their respect for the need for silence as the song progresses. The Grateful Dead created a unique listening experience, which created a unique Deadhead culture. At a Dead concert, the purpose was simple: listen to the music. So give a listen to one or more of the performances we've shared.

"Crazy Fingers"

If there's a single essential Grateful Dead song that gets short shrift, it's "Crazy Fingers." Yet this is a great piece of music, as well as one of Robert Hunter's greatest poems.

Imagine listeners who have heard only Grateful Dead songs like "Casey Jones," "Sugar Magnolia," or "Caution (Do Not Stop on Tracks)." Play "Crazy Fingers" for them and they will be amazed that it is a Grateful Dead song: the music is lilting and playful with a hint of reggae. This song shows how difficult it is to pigeonhole the Grateful Dead. It's a song that illustrates the eclecticism of styles the Dead played in each show. "Crazy Fingers" is a beautiful song deserving of more recognition.

"Crazy Fingers," composed by Jerry Garcia and Robert Hunter, was first played on June 17, 1975, at Winterland in San Francisco. It was played 144 times and was performed regularly, if infrequently, between 1975 and 1995, save for one long gap between mid-1976 and mid-1982. Its last performance was on July 5, 1995, in Maryland Heights, Missouri, at Riverport Amphitheater, just a few days before the Grateful Dead's final show at Soldier Field in Chicago. "Crazy Fingers" was a staple in the second set of the show, usually as part of an extended uninterrupted sequence of songs.

"Crazy Fingers" sets a lilting tone: it's a beautiful piece of music. It has little by way of extended solos or jams during the body of the song. It's one of the Dead's songs that follows roughly the same pattern each time out, at least until the coda. This is not to say that the solos were canned: Garcia explores and improvises but usually within the stable, consistent structure of the song. Over time, the solos are similar, but certainly not identical. Moreover, Phil Lesh, on bass, plays the song differently each time out. Typically, the coda to "Crazy Fingers" stretches out: Garcia explores the motif while the band prepares to segue seamlessly into another song. These coda sections varied greatly in length and style as the song developed over the years.

The absence of extended solos during the vocal portion of "Crazy Fingers" highlights the lyrics. Indeed, to appreciate why this is an essential Grateful Dead song, you must pay attention to the lyrics (Crazy #1). "Crazy Fingers" tells the story of a long-enduring romance, of life with its perils and pleasures, its surprises and insights, our hope and ultimately our resignation when faced with chaos and fate. Yet love endures. The carousel of life keeps spinning, and before you know it, it's midnight. Finally, in a Zenlike twist, if we reach for the brass ring, we usually fail, but we still keep trying.

During their 1975 hiatus from touring, the Dead worked on new songs, as well as the album *Blues for Allah*. "Crazy Fingers" debuted during this period on June 17,

1975 (Crazy #2), opening the first full Grateful Dead show of 1975. The song never opened a Dead show again, nor did it ever close a set. Unlike many Dead songs (see our review of "Cumberland Blues," for example), "Crazy Fingers" emerged in this first performance nearly as polished as it ever became. Perhaps because of the complexity of the music, it might be said that "Crazy Fingers" reversed the normal developmental process: the last performances were generally not as vibrant and developed as the first ones. But whomever it was who said that Garcia's guitar sounds like the pealing of a bell may well have had this first performance of "Crazy Fingers" in mind.

The Dead's second performance of "Crazy Fingers" was at the band's next show, August 13, 1975, at the famous Great American Music Hall show, which was eventually issued as the album *One from the Vault* (D2:T3). You can hear a soundboard recording here: (Crazy #3). Already the song had migrated to the second set, where it resided for most of the remainder of its run. In what was to become a familiar pattern, the song segued into "Drumz" after an extended coda jam. This excellent performance might be the standard against which other versions of "Crazy Fingers" are compared. Among other things, the keyboards are excellent and more prominent in the mix than on many Dead songs.

"Crazy Fingers" from June 9, 1976, at Boston's Music Hall, as well as most of this show, was issued in the Grateful Dead's series *Road Trips, Vol. 4, No. 5* (D1:T5), also accessible here: (Crazy #4). This is another excellent performance, about one year into the performance life of "Crazy Fingers," again illustrating the Dead's improvisational skill. The body of the song follows the standard pattern, but after the final verse the band extends a solo jam off into spacey realms, this time *without* segueing into another song. On this night, it's a first set song, but the first set at a Dead show was never without at least some improvisational exploration. "Crazy Fingers" delivers for this show.

At the Worcester, Massachusetts, Centrum on April 8, 1988 (Crazy #5), "Crazy Fingers" is sandwiched between "Playing in the Band" and "Uncle John's Band." This musical performance is lively, evocative of the earliest versions of the song from twenty years earlier. Garcia's vocals are a bit flat and his voice sounds strained at times. Examples of this kind of nonstop sets are countless—probably no Dead show exists without at least one example. The flow of music from one song to a second to a third is always a highlight of Dead shows. This 4/8/88 sequence is a good example; if you have time, listen to all three songs in sequence.

We also like March 26, 1995 (Crazy #6), which has strong backup vocals in support of Garcia, as well as an extended coda with hints of "Spanish Jam." On May 5, 1995 (Crazy #7), Garcia's voice is relatively weak in comparison. As with the previous example, the extended coda features a strong bass line and hints of "Spanish Jam." The final performance of "Crazy Fingers" was on July 5, 1995, which Barry recorded: (Crazy #8). At the Dead's previous show at Deer Creek, fans stormed the gates and tore down fences, and on this date, there were death threats against Jerry Garcia. Perhaps those factors affected the quality of this performance of "Crazy Fingers," which sounds flat compared to the bouncy, lively versions of earlier years.

"Crazy Fingers" enjoyed a long, productive run during twenty years of the Grateful Dead's life as a touring band. The band delivered solid, familiar performances throughout the run, with perhaps some decline in the lilting quality of the song toward the end. The lyrics, however, endure with their amazing insights into the patterns of our lives. Perhaps *because* it isn't ear-blasting rock and roll, "Crazy Fingers" is an essential song in the Dead's repertoire.

"Cumberland Blues"

The Grateful Dead always have been known for the wide range of influences in their music. Early on, Garcia collected bluegrass tapes and his ambition was to play with Bill Monroe, the bluegrass legend. At the same time, the Dead always adapted music to their own style, no matter where they found it in musical Americana. "Cumberland Blues" (aka Cumberland) is a good example: it's not technically bluegrass, because they primarily played the song with electric instruments and drums and it doesn't include a banjo. But as the Grateful Dead played it, Cumberland certainly evokes the bluegrass genre: the music and the vocals both have a bluegrass sound.

Most Deadheads have heard the (perhaps apocryphal) story about the old geezer who heard "Cumberland Blues" performed by the Grateful Dead and supposedly commented that it was a great bluegrass song but the original composer would be aghast at what the band did to it. The joke is on the old geezer, of course: "Cumberland Blues" was composed by Robert Hunter and Jerry Garcia, the Dead's great songwriting team, along with Phil Lesh. Cumberland first appeared on the 1970 studio album *Workingman's Dead*, along with so many other great Grateful Dead songs.

Cumberland was performed more than two hundred times over the years and played regularly, except for a long gap of 394 shows between 1974 and 1981. It was a regular part of the first set. Cumberland's final live performance, which was also the Grateful Dead's final show, was on July 9, 1995, at Soldier Field, Chicago. You can hear that version here: (Cumberland #1). At that final show, we hear the song after twenty-five years of performances. The vocals are strong, the music is even stronger and more confident; it's a mature performance.

"Cumberland Blues" is one of the Dead's many songs that focus on working people struggling to eke out a living; see the lyrics here: (Cumberland #2). Cumberland tells a story of someone in the working class and by extension the working class itself: the difficulties of managing both work and a personal life, complications involving love, and monetary gain and loss. For example, should the protagonist stay to work at the mine or move on to greener pastures? Dodd's Greatest Story blog offers more about Cumberland: (Cumberland #3).

"Cumberland Blues" is played in the key of G and seems deceptively simple, since the solo jams are primarily focused around that one chord. But the breaks, especially later in the song, get more complicated, with extra measures inserted. Not to say that bluegrass music is "simple" in its structure, but Cumberland pushes the genre, typical of the Grateful Dead's approach to older traditional songs, folk songs, blues, and so forth. The Dead always added something of their own to whatever they played.

"Cumberland Blues" was introduced in live performance on November 8, 1969, but for an early performance, we turn to the Cumberland from November 15, 1969, a week later and the Dead's next show, available here: (Cumberland #4). This version has a slower tempo than others and the vocals are rough.

Probably the most well-known performance of Cumberland is from April 8, 1972, in London, during the Dead's Europe '72 tour, which was issued on the *Europe '72* album, with a CD version issued in 1990 and reissued in 2001 (D1:T1). You can access it here: (Cumberland #5). This is a polished performance of Cumberland, although this live performance may have been overdubbed in the studio after the tour. You can also hear Cumberland on dozens of albums of live performances: here's the list at deaddisc.com: (Cumberland #6).

"Cumberland Blues" holds a special place in Bob's heart: it was the first song played at his first Grateful Dead show, March 28, 1973, a show that took place shortly after Pigpen's death. This performance was issued on *Dave's Picks, Volume 16* (D1:T1) and is accessible here: (Cumberland #7). Like probably most first-time attendees, Bob was mesmerized by the enthusiasm in the audience, the colorful garb, the dancing, and the fact that no joint touched the same lips twice. In short, the experience was a great success. Cumberland was also a success that night: it has a lilting bouncy intro that included a short solo by Garcia, generally tight vocals (including Lesh's), and longer solos between verses (including a "lead bass guitar" solo by Lesh). Garcia's playing is crisp and confident. The coda is tight, as befits a bouncy bluegrass song.

As you can see—and hear—from its performance history, "Cumberland Blues" is a representative song in terms of evolution of the Dead's music over time. Bluegrass music always has been heavily dependent on tight vocal harmonies, which was never a strength of the Grateful Dead. In other words, Cumberland was always a risk, yet the Dead were never known to shrink from a musical risk. Their success over the years in facing risks makes "Cumberland Blues" an essential Grateful Dead song.

"Dancin' in the Street"

"Dancing in the Street" (aka Dancin') is a cover song by Marvin Gaye, William "Mickey" Stevenson, and Ivy Jo Hunter that was first recorded by Martha and the Vandellas, who had a number two *Billboard* Hot 100 hit single with it in 1964. It has been recorded many times by many performers including the Mamas and the Papas, the Kinks, Van Halen, and the Everly Brothers. The Grateful Dead added Dancin' to their live performances early in their career, on July 3, 1966, at the Fillmore Auditorium in San Francisco. They played it a total of 123 times, with the last performance on April 6, 1987. It has an unusual performance history. It was performed only once in 1971 and then disappeared from the active song list until June 3, 1976, during the Dead's comeback tour after their 1975 hiatus. Then it was regularly performed through 1979, when it disappeared again. It was played once, July 7, 1981, but it wasn't played again until June 24, 1984, when it was played a handful of times until it was gone for good in 1987.

Although there's a soundboard recording of the July 3, 1966, Fillmore performance, that recording unfortunately does not include Dancin', though you can find other songs from that very early show here: (Dancin' #1). Other early recorded versions of Dancin' are hard to find, but you can hear an up-tempo, ten-minute version from March 18, 1967, at the Winterland Arena in San Francisco here: (Dancin' #2), and a slower and much longer rendition on May 6, 1970, on the MIT campus in Cambridge, Massachusetts here: (Dancin' #3). The band really stretches out on this one, as you'd expect in a seventeen-minute song, and Jerry leads with his delightful improvisation, the band following right along.

The first official Grateful Dead recording of Dancin' was their "disco-influenced" version for the *Terrapin Station* LP released in 1977, in which it was titled "Dancin' in the Street." According to Donna Godchaux, this disco arrangement was due to Mickey Hart's love of the *Saturday Night Fever* movie soundtrack from 1977 (Jackson and Gans 2015, 250). To the surprise of many Deadheads who might have expected original songs on a single, the *Terrapin Station* version was released as a seven-inch single with "Terrapin Station" as the B-side, also in 1977. There have been about twenty official recordings of "Dancin' in the Street"; the full list is available here: (Dancin' #4).

Musically, Dancin' is a cover song that most Deadheads love because of the Grateful Dead's ability to take a short song like the original and stretch it out with delicious jams. The long jams started early in the song's performance history, as mentioned earlier, and then evolved into the disco-influenced versions from 1976 through 1979. But in the few late-1980s versions, it was rearranged again as a more "psychedelic pop" version in which the band still could stretch out musically quite effectively with wonderful long jams. For a remarkably detailed discussion about the performance history of Dancin', check out the 1999 essay by Daniel J. Dasaro and Christian Crumlish on the Deadessay blog here: (Dancin' #5).

Unfortunately, we have seen few performances of this song live. Barry saw only four performances of Dancin' in the 1980s. One of them, the version from Municipal Auditorium in Kansas City on July 7, 1981, is not as strong as the other versions he heard later in the 1980s. It isn't as energetic or jamming as other versions, as you can hear for yourself on this eight-minute soundboard recording: (Dancin' #6.) The second version Barry heard was when Dancin' opened the show on June 14, 1985, at the Greek Theatre in Berkeley, California. Although it is more energetic and the band much tighter, the song does not stretch out like those from the 1960s and 1970s: (Dancin' #7).

Here are some other earlier versions we recommend, including some of the "disco" versions, which we particularly enjoy, especially May 11, 1978, in Springfield, Massachusetts, a show that Bob attended. Weir muffs the opening line, but after that he and the rest of the vocalists stretch out a delightful twelve minutes of classic Dead jamming with Jerry's Mu-Tron filter kicking ass on his solo: (Dancin' #8).

The 2017 *May 1977: Get Shown the Light* eleven-CD set and *Cornell 5/8/77* three-CD (D2:T1) release of the classic Barton Hall show from May 8, 1977, is also a true gem, disco or otherwise (Dancin' #9). Barry remembers hearing this for the first time while driving and nearly going off the road after about twelve minutes of heavenly jam!

Here are two early versions of Dancin' that are primal Grateful Dead energy. First is March 18, 1967, from Winterland, with plenty of jamming without the benefit or need for later guitar technology: (Dancin' #10). Next is from January 24, 1970, at the Honolulu Civic Center in Hawaii. It's more laid back than the Winterland version but shows how the early Grateful Dead matures as a band and musicians: (Dancin' #11). Finally, we'll leave you with this one from the Beacon Theatre in New York City on June 14, 1976: (Dancin' #12).

Turn it up and get your dancing shoes on. If you're like us, you'll find "Dancin' in the Street" a Deadhead's dancin' dream.

"Dark Star"

If there's a single song that truly embodies the Grateful Dead's music in the deepest way, it has to be "Dark Star." The lyrics and tune are just the beginning! This is the song that first demonstrated the unique improvisational capabilities that make the Dead unlike any other band. As a result, it's fair to say that "Dark Star" is an acquired taste due to the nearly infinite number of places it can take the listener with its remarkable unstructured playing; it is psychedelia at its peak. It was at this time in the late 1960s in which the Dead learned to "mind meld," anticipating where the rest of band would be going musically. Official Dead biographer Dennis McNally referred to this psychedelic band as an "elite jazz fusion ensemble," and in our opinion they became improvisationally as capable as jazz greats Miles Davis, John Coltrane, and others (2002, 300).

"Dark Star" made its live performance debut on December 13, 1967, in Los Angeles, but no recording is available. The second live performance on January 17, 1968, in San Francisco was recorded and can be heard here: (Dark Star #1). This one is just over four minutes long with a speedy tempo and limited improvisation, but that would soon begin to change. Indeed, change is what "Dark Star" is all about, with the Dead always showing themselves and their audiences something new, fresh, never heard before, and never heard again. By 1968 the improvisation was already blooming, as you can hear on this performance from March 16 that clocks in at more than seven minutes (Dark Star #2).

When the studio version was released as a 45 single in April 1968 (Dark Star #3), it was short and sweet: only about two-and-a-half minutes long with no improvisation. But when the first live version was released in November 1969 on the Dead's two-LP album *Live Dead*, the song was more than twenty-three minutes long and is considered the benchmark for all versions of "Dark Star." Although twenty-three minutes is a long performance, many versions far exceeded that, with some more than forty-five minutes long. These are not for the faint of heart, but if you've acquired the taste for improvisation, you'll love them all.

The lyrics were written by Robert Hunter, and the music was said to be composed by all members of the band while rehearsing for a series of performances in Rio Nido, California, in September 1967. The studio version from the 45 single was later expanded to just over three minutes when it was released on the two-LP *What a Long Strange Trip It's Been* in 1977. In this version, Hunter added an additional verse that appears on only this LP version. Each short verse well describes what that band put into their music, such as, "Dark star crashes, pouring its light into ashes." If you understand that, you'll understand the music. You can read all the lyrics here (Dark Star #4), including the additional ones Hunter added on the LP version.

"Dark Star" was played frequently after its 1967 debut, with twenty-nine performances in 1968 and sixty-five performances in 1969. It was played less frequently through 1974 and then disappeared from the repertoire because the band had developed their improvisational chops by this time in songs such as "Playing in the Band," "Sugaree," "Bird Song," "Uncle John's Band," and others. "Dark Star" reappeared on New Year's Eve 1978 at the closing of the Winterland Arena in San Francisco after an absence of 187 performances and subsequently was played only four times until 1989, when it was performed at the Coliseum in Hampton, Virginia, on October 9 after a gap of 359 shows, with the Dead billed as "formerly the Warlocks." This Hampton show was officially released on *Formerly the Warlocks* in 2010 (D5:T4), or you can listen to this matrix recording that shows the crowd's excitement: (Dark Star #5).

After that performance, "Dark Star" continued to be part of the live catalog, with a handful of performances each year through 1994. In total, the Dead played "Dark Star" 219 times. A multitude of live performances have been released over the years, for which we can be eternally grateful because of the unique character of each; you can see the complete list here: (Dark Star #6). Fortunately, many other versions are available at Archive.org.

We've already provided links to the short studio version, the second and eighth performances, as well as the later 1989 "return" in Hampton, Virginia. For other great versions, we begin with a relatively late performance from the Nassau Coliseum on Long Island, New York, on March 29, 1990: (Dark Star #7). It features Branford Marsalis on saxophone, a guest musician who "gets" Grateful Dead music. So settle in for this tasty eighteen-minute soundboard version. Next we suggest a performance from the Europe '72 tour. Although every "Dark Star" on this tour is worth hearing, listen to this one from April 8 in London: (Dark Star #8). It is an outstanding soundboard recording that runs more than thirty minutes.

Bob saw a thirty-two minute performance in Springfield, Massachusetts, on March 28, 1973 (Dark Star #9), which we recommend. But be warned: it was his first Dead show, and after indulging in much that was offered, he then fell asleep on the floor of the Civic Center during that "Dark Star." We don't think you will, though.

Barry saw a seven-minute version at Deer Creek, near Indianapolis, on June 23, 1993 (Dark Star #10). Though short, it shows what the Dead could do with their MIDI electronics in the later years, and it's one of their last five performances. Finally, we recommend a more primal twenty-one-minute version of "Dark Star" from April 20, 1969 (Dark Star #11), in Worcester, Massachusetts, as a real contrast—and as a reminder of how this essential Grateful Dead song's voyage began.

"Days Between"

"Days Between" (aka Days), was one of the last Garcia/Hunter collaborations; it debuted February 22, 1993 (Days #1), at the Oakland Coliseum Arena. It was performed only forty-one times, the last one on June 24, 1995 (Days #2), at RFK Stadium in Washington, D.C. For Barry, it's one of the most beautiful and poignant songs ever performed by the Dead. In the 2017 *Long Strange Trip* documentary, Dennis McNally, the Dead's publicist and biographer, referred to it as Garcia and Hunter's "last masterpiece." Phil Lesh, in his autobiography *Searching for the Sound* called it "achingly nostalgic."

Days was one of three songs Garcia and Hunter wrote during a flurry of composition in early 1993. It was never issued on a studio album, although it was to be included on the uncompleted album that the band was working on before Garcia died on August 9, 1995. Interestingly enough, David Dodd points out that the term "days between" now means to many Deadheads the period of time between Garcia's birthday, August 1, and the anniversary of his passing on August 9 (Days #3).

Some readers may be unfamiliar with "Days Between" because of its relatively few performances during the last two-and-a-half years of Dead concerts. Others may have dismissed it because it seems totally different from other Dead songs: it could be considered a dirge. It's a slow ballad with an unusual song structure and irregular lines that unfold while the lyrics look back at the past. When it was played, it was another of the "Jerry ballads" appearing toward the end of the second set.

In a 2015 *Rolling Stone* interview by David Browne, Robert Hunter comments that the lyrics represent his feelings about the history of the Dead and his and Jerry's place in it. He also says that with those lyrics Jerry could "leave you in a puddle," which he usually did and continues to do for both of us personally even when listening to recordings. Hunter goes on to say he and Garcia wrote it in an entirely new way for them: he gave Jerry the first verse and began to write the second while Jerry worked out the first verse melody on an electric piano. This process continued with Hunter writing a verse ahead of Jerry. Both were looking forward to using this "strange and irregular construction" again on other compositions, but Garcia's passing ended that possibility.

The lyrics are quite beautiful with lines such as "Summer flies and August dies, the world grows dark and mean." Or "Phantom ships with phantom sails set to sea on phantom tides." And "there were days between polished like a golden bowl, the finest ever seen." The lyrics are worth reading: (Days #4). David Dodd points out at that link that there are fourteen lines in each verse, which is consistent with the form of a sonnet, although the lines are much shorter than those of a sonnet. Each of the four verses in "Days Between" refers to a season of the year, though not chronologically. All this adds to the song's unique structure.

Outstanding versions of "Days Between" are limited due to the small number of performances and also Garcia's declining health and voice. This became obvious in the two-and-a-half-year period when the song was being performed. In fact, only two performances have been officially released. There's a lovely studio rehearsal version that's eleven minutes long on the first album released after Garcia's death, *So Many Roads*, a five-CD box set. That version was recorded February 18, 1993 (Days #5), only four days before its live debut. The *Long Strange Trip* documentary soundtrack album has a very good live version from Madison Square Garden on October 18, 1994: (Days #6). This one is nearly fourteen minutes long.

There are other live versions as well. Barry was lucky enough to see and record nine. His favorite of those is from September 24, 1993, at Boston Garden. You can hear Barry's recording here: (Days #7). Other notable versions include June 22, 1993 (Days #8), at Deer Creek Amphitheater near Indianapolis, the first performance of Days that Barry saw. Both of these are highly rated at headyversion.com. One of the last versions Barry saw was December 19, 1994 (Days #9), at the Oakland Coliseum. This one takes a bit longer to really get started, but then it really soars. This is the second highest rated performance on headyversion.com

In the *Long Strange Trip* documentary, Dennis McNally referred to three members of the Grateful Dead as geniuses: Jerry Garcia, Phil Lesh, and Robert Hunter. Hunter was a poetic genius, and this song's lyrics certainly demonstrate it. Garcia's melody builds and then retreats in each of the four verses, providing a perfect foundation for this poem. It's heartbreakingly beautiful, as Garcia seems to deliver the story of his life so near its end. Listening to so many recordings of Days for this book emphasized the power of this song. Without a doubt, "Days Between" is one of the essentials from the Grateful Dead.

"Deal"

"Deal," by Hunter and Garcia, was a true workhorse song for the Grateful Dead. They played it live 423 times between 1971 and 1995, which ranks it as the fifteenth most played song in the rotation. The Dead performed "Deal" 120 times between 1971 and 1974, and even once during the 1975 hiatus. After 1975, "Deal" was again prominent in the rotation through 1980, when its frequency began to taper off. "Deal" was first recorded on Jerry Garcia's solo album *Garcia*, released in 1972.

Its first live performance was February 19, 1971, and its last was on June 18, 1995, near the end of the Dead's thirty-year run.

On the surface, "Deal" tells the story of a card shark giving advice, a theme somewhat reminiscent of "Loser," another song that focuses on a hapless character who apparently tries to make his living playing cards. But the tone in "Deal" is more positive and much less literal. You can see the lyrics here: (Deal #1). On another level, our narrator is speaking to an individual with whom he has had some kind of long relationship, telling that person to be careful about his or her next step: "Watch each card you're playin', play it slow." Good advice for all of us. Perhaps "Deal" is not only about cards.

Musically, "Deal" evolved during its years in the rotation, maybe as much as any single Grateful Dead song. In the beginning, it was a mid-tempo song with a cowboy/ folk song feeling to it. Later, "Deal" became more of a high-energy rocker: the solos were extended, and the outro became a major event, often used to close the first set on a high note.

In the early 1970s, "Deal" appeared in either the first or the second set. By 1973, it was consistently played in the first set, with only a handful of performances in the second. There are dozens of available live performances of "Deal" issued by the Grateful Dead, with a full list here: (Deal #2). We recommend a few of these later, but you can find hundreds of versions at the Archive.org website if you wish to explore on your own.

Start with the first live performance of "Deal" on February 19, 1971, at the Capitol Theater in Port Chester, New York. Here the Dead played it as the fifth number in the second set. That show was released on the album *Three from the Vault* (D2:T5) and is available here: (Deal #3). This first performance shows no first-time jitters or inconsistency. It's an excellent benchmark performance with which to compare later versions. Besides the solos, pay attention to the slight variations in the way Garcia emphasizes some of the vocal lines.

The October 20, 1974, performance of "Deal" at Winterland in San Francisco was the last before the 1975 hiatus from touring. It's available on a soundboard recording here: (Deal #4). The intro is slightly longer here, and it is a good version if you want to concentrate on the interplay among the musicians in the solo: Lesh, Weir, and Godchaux play complementary lines that make this version sound something like Dixieland jazz. The outro is not yet as extended as it would become later in the run.

On June 25, 1988, in Hebron, Ohio, the Dead closed the first set with "Deal." This version gives you a sense of how the song transformed into a powerhouse. This show is notable because it marks the first time occasional keyboardist Bruce Hornsby sat in with the Dead, in this case playing accordion. This performance is accessible here: (Deal #5). Lesh's bass is prominent in this audience recording; it's a good chance to hear "lead bass." If you prefer a more balanced mix, try this audience recording: (Deal #6). You can hear Bob Weir's rhythm work more clearly. In this performance, the solo after the final verse is extended as the band moves in the direction of serious improvisation. By now, "Deal" has transitioned from about five minutes to more than seven-and-a-half minutes, despite the faster tempo.

By the 1990s, the Grateful Dead often weren't reaching the performance heights they had enjoyed in earlier years, but the spring 1990 tours were excellent. So we turn to March 28, 1990, at Nassau Coliseum on Long Island, New York, for our last pick. This show is available as part of the 1990 box set *Spring 1990 (The Other One)* (D1:T8), and it is available here as well: (Deal #7). "Deal" is the closer for the first set, so you can compare the 6/25/88 first set closer to this one.

This 3/28/90 performance is a great audience recording: there's a good crowd response and a lot of singing along. Garcia's early solo is gentle, almost sweet for such a rocking song. However, there's no mistaking the energy in the second solo after the first round of extended vocalizing of the signature lines. And the crowd went right along with the band, leading it all to a great coda. This is an excellent recording if you want to capture not only the way "Deal" changed over the years, but also for a sense of what it was like to be in the audience at a Grateful Dead show. Nothing like it.

"Deal" is not one of the Grateful Dead's signature songs, but it's a fun, enjoyable song. The lyrics are worth attention, for starters. A Deadhead looking to describe how the Dead evolved can look to this song as a prime example. As a first set closer, "Deal" brought the energy level to a high that would last through the set break and get everyone ready for the second set.

"Dire Wolf"

From fossils, we know that the dire wolf was a common predator in North America until it went extinct about 10,000 years ago. It was larger than a gray wolf, though not the size of the marauding demons seen on the television series *Game of Thrones*. We know that George R. R. Martin, author of the book series, is a fan of the Grateful Dead's music, so it's no surprise that he would use the dire wolf as a predator.

The predator motif emerges in the Grateful Dead's song "Dire Wolf," another of the rich trove of songs that emerged during the 1969 to 1971 period when the Dead were transitioning from psychedelic rock to a somewhat more conventional emphasis on shorter songs that reflected, for example, the cowboy rock genre. "Dire Wolf" was written by the Garcia/Hunter team and appears on the album *Workingman's Dead*, issued in 1970, as track 3.

The lyrics of "Dire Wolf," available here (Dire #1), tell the story of a solitary down-and-out gentleman trying to survive a fierce winter. He is threatened at every turn: by the weather and even by the fact that he cuts the cards to the queen of spades, the "card of death." Disaster is apparently inevitable, but he pleads: "Don't murder me." Another perspective suggests the individual's problems might be self-inflicted: a life of debauchery that is now exacting its toll, as the dire wolf "collects his due." There's duality in many Grateful Dead songs; this one asks: are we victims of external forces or the creators of our own fate? For insights into the lyrics, including commentary by Robert Hunter, see the first link in the previous paragraph. For other insights, see the comments here: (Dire #2).

The Grateful Dead performed "Dire Wolf" 226 times between 1969 and 1995, and they performed it every year except during the hiatus in 1975. You'll have guessed by now that the Dead often played new songs frequently during their first year or two. "Dire Wolf" is no exception. They played "Dire Wolf" sixty-three times in 1969 and 1970. The frequency tapered off after 1971, with only a handful of performances most years. In 1970 and again in 1980, several of the performances were acoustic. The electric version of "Dire Wolf" was a fixture in the first set at Dead shows.

For an early acoustic version, listen to May 5, 1970, the Harpur College show in Binghampton, New York, issued as *Dick's Picks, Volume 8* (D1:T4) and here: (Dire #3). This is an energetic performance with crystal clear vocals and strong guitar playing. The enthusiastic audience response makes this version fun to listen to.

In Eugene, Oregon, on January 22, 1978, the Dead delivered a solid electric performance of "Dire Wolf." Vocals are strong, including the backup vocals by Donna Godchaux. The solo is also strong. This version times in at 4:35 and was released on *Dave's Picks, Volume 23* (D1 T2). It's also accessible here: (Dire #4).

For a late version, listen to May 29, 1995, in Portland Meadows, Oregon, accessible here: (Dire #5). This is an up-tempo version of "Dire Wolf," with Garcia's tired voice still strong enough to carry the song. This recording clocks in at just over four minutes: the first several seconds are "tuning and noodling," as are the final fifteen or twenty seconds. So this is a short, quick version of the song. As with many songs in the repertoire, this "Dire Wolf" shows little decline by the 1990s.

And check out headyversion.com's fan favorite "Dire Wolf" from April 16, 1978, in Huntington, West Virginia. You can hear it here: (Dire #6). The music here is sweet from the outset, with that rolling sound the Dead perfected. By the end of the solo, however, Garcia has raised the intensity—the dynamics in this version are worth listening to: in the course of a single song, the Dead take it from a comfortable folk tune to a soaring rocker and then back to the folk tune by the end of the song.

Finally, listen to this upbeat early "Dire Wolf" from Santa Rosa, California, on June 27, 1969 (Dire #7). Surprise! This early version has Bob Weir on vocals and Jerry Garcia on pedal steel guitar.

"Dire Wolf" was born fairly complete in 1969 and did not change much through the years, at least in terms of structure, tempo, or timing. It's an essential song partly for the lyrics, but also because it's an excellent example of the type of songs the Dead played after 1970, especially in the first set.

"Dupree's Diamond Blues"

Reaching back into the roots of American music, the Dead performed a few songs like "Dupree's Diamond Blues" (aka Dupree's), traditional songs based on true stories or events. We include other similar songs in this compendium, including "Casey Jones," earlier, and "Stagger Lee," coming later. Though it's a traditional song, the Dead's version is original, composed by Jerry Garcia with lyrics by Robert Hunter. See the lyrics and read additional background about the history of the song and its alternate titles here: (Dupree's #1).

The lyrics are about crime and sex. One crime is Dupree's murder of a sales clerk in the jewelry store: the clerk simply wants Dupree to pay for the diamond he wants. A second crime occurs when the judge at Dupree's trial turns out to be intimately familiar with Dupree's girlfriend, who apparently gets around. Both Dupree and the judge seem to be having a relationship with the same woman. The song is based on true events that occurred in South Carolina. See the earlier link for details.

The Dead performed Dupree's eighty times over the years, albeit irregularly. After its first performance on January 24, 1969, they played it sixteen times that year and then not again until 1977. They did not play it from 1979 to 1981, performing it occasionally from 1982 until 1990, and then dropping it from the rotation except for a single performance in 1994. From 1982 on, Dupree's was always a first set song, except for its breakout performance on August 28, 1982, when it was the encore.

Musically, Dupree's is a slow to mid-tempo song played in a ragtime style with more than a hint of comic, funky irony. There are rather abrupt—for the Dead—intro and coda sections to this short song, which usually timed in at about four minutes. There is relatively little improvisation or instrumental solos here, especially in the early performances.

The first performance, on January 24, 1969, in San Francisco, is available here: (Dupree's #2). It's always illustrative to listen to the first performance of a song in order to compare it with later performances. For example, listen to April 26, 1969, in Chicago, just three months later. That performance is on *Dick's Picks, Volume 26* (D1:T1) and here: (Dupree's #3). This version, the show's opener, has as slow a tempo as you'll ever hear on this song.

As mentioned earlier, Dupree's has three separate breakout performances due to the long gaps in its performance life. The first of these was on October 2, 1977, in Portland, Oregon, after a gap of eight years and 561 shows. Listen to it here: (Dupree's #4). This is a "Betty Board" recording, with what is likely the best sound quality of any of these recorded performances. This version has a notable Garcia solo. The second breakout performance is from August 28, 1982, after a gap of 338 shows, in Veneta, Oregon, when Dupree's was the encore. Listen to it here: (Dupree's #5). The tempo is a little faster, but the song still times in at about six minutes. This is a good quality audience recording, so some crowd response carries into the mix. As the song developed over the years, the Dead emphasized solos a bit more, as you can hear in this version, including a little fun in the coda. This breakout show was also ten years after the famous "Sunshine Daydream" Veneta show from August 27, 1972.

The third breakout performance took place on August 13, 1994, in Madison Square Garden in New York City after a gap of four years and 342 shows. This was also Dupree's final performance. There is an excellent audience recording here: (Dupree's #6). The Grateful Dead had a huge repertoire of songs: in 1994 alone, the last full year of touring, they played 145 different songs, many of them, like Dupree's, only once. Either this song was pulled from distant memory, which is remarkable, or they rehearsed it and updated it, only to play it one time, which is equally remarkable. At any rate, you can hear imaginative solos in this version, a good final stop on our tour of Dupree's.

Dupree's is a fun ragtime tune that appeared from time to time in the Dead's repertoire and then disappeared for years on end. Can we identify with this story/song? Well, many of us have purchased a diamond for someone special, but few of us have shot the sales clerk, we presume, so you decide. Whatever your pleasure, Dupree's was always fun to listen to, always a bit funky, and a great song to dance to. We hope you enjoy listening to it as much as we do.

"El Paso"

"El Paso" is a cover song written by Marty Robbins, who had a number one *Billboard* Hot 100 hit with it in 1959, when it was on his *Gunfighter Ballads and Trail Songs* LP. The Grateful Dead performed "El Paso" 388 times in concert beginning on July 14, 1970 (El Paso #1), in San Rafael, California, until July 5, 1995 (El Paso #2), in St. Louis, almost twenty-five years to the day. It's another cowboy song for Bob Weir, who must be a fan of Robbins's work since he also covered Robbins's "Big Iron" on the 1976 album *Kingfish*, when Weir was also part of that band. Unlike other cowboy songs, "El Paso" could take off with beautiful, soaring guitar lines by Garcia. This is a cover song that many Deadheads love.

Despite being played 388 times, El Paso's performance history was spotty. It was absent from their repertoire in 1983, played only three times in 1984, absent again for two years from March 1987 until March 1989, when it was played once that year, once in 1990, once in 1991, twice in 1992, and once in 1993. Then it returned actively to the song lineup in 1994 and 1995.

The lyrics tell a similar story as several of the Dead's other cowboy songs like "Mexicali Blues" and "Me and My Uncle." The narrator/storyteller is in a West Texas cantina and has fallen in love with a "Mexican maiden" named Felina, who has cast a spell on him with her "wicked and evil" eyes. Before he knows it, another cowboy comes to the cantina and shares a drink with Felina, which leads the storyteller to challenge "his right for the love of this maiden" by shooting him. He races away to hide out in the badlands of New Mexico but ultimately isn't able to stand being away from "the wicked Felina." When he returns to El Paso, he's nearly surrounded by cowboys who are "shouting and shooting" as he races to the cantina. Of course, he's shot and as he lies dying, Felina finds him, kisses him, and cradles him in her arms "that I'll die for." You can find all the lyrics here: (El Paso #3).

Musically, "El Paso" is in 3/4 time, which makes it nearly a polka, but the fast tempo brings a racing excitement to the music and gives Garcia the opportunity to shine with his quick backing licks as Weir sings; it's a delightful duet between Weir and Garcia. Ultimately, Garcia's playing behind Weir *makes* this song. Of course, the rest of the band also shines. Like most of their cowboy songs, it's short, generally clocking in at no more than four minutes, but the tempo and energy always got the crowd up and shaking their bones.

"El Paso" first appeared as an official Grateful Dead release on the 1976 *Steal Your Face* LP, which was live recordings from the Grateful Dead's October 1974, run at Winterland in San Francisco. This album received a lot of negative feedback from fans and even band members due to problems with the master tapes as well as the pressure of a deadline to deliver a live album to United Artists to fulfill the Dead's contract with them. In fact, when all the Grateful Dead albums from 1973 through 1989 were remastered and included in the *Beyond Description* box set, *Steal Your Face* was the only one omitted. "El Paso" has since appeared on numerous official recordings, and you can see a complete list through 2016 here: (El Paso #4).

Barry saw "El Paso" seventeen times, starting with his first Dead concert on June 16, 1974, and ending with his next to last on July 5, 1995, which was the song's last performance. The June 16, 1974, version is quite good, with Weir introducing it as "a tune of death and destruction" (El Paso #5). Seeing the Dead play at the Greek Theatre in Berkeley, California, was always a treat, and Barry certainly enjoyed the version he heard there on June 20, 1986: (El Paso #6). Jerry's playing is different on this version with fewer rapid guitar fills and Weir's voice is a bit rough. Barry especially liked the version from June 28, 1992 (El Paso #7), at Deer Creek in Noblesville, Indiana, since the song had been played only ten times since he had last heard it almost six years earlier in December 1986. Phil's bass is strong in the soundboard mix, which clearly shows his contribution.

We also recommend the last version played on July 5, 1995, at Riverport Amphitheatre near St. Louis; the link for it is provided earlier in this section. This one features Weir on acoustic guitar with a few missed notes by Garcia at the end. Finally, we recommend the "El Paso" played at the University of Alabama's Coliseum in Tuscaloosa on May 17, 1977, in this nice soundboard/audience matrix recording: (El Paso #8). Jerry is hot on this version.

Regardless of the version, we know you'll agree with our positive sentiments about "El Paso." Be sure to practice your polka steps when you dance.

"Estimated Prophet"

"Estimated Prophet" (aka Estimated) is one of those songs most Deadheads look forward to hearing since it's one that opens up for some wonderful jazzy jamming that truly makes it one of the essentials from the Dead's catalog. Estimated is a Bob Weir and John Perry Barlow composition. It joined the performance repertoire on February 26, 1977, at the Swing Auditorium in San Bernardino, California: (Estimated #1). This was a memorable show because it also introduced the "Terrapin Station" suite. For its debut, Estimated was played in the first set, as it was the following night as well as six other times in early 1977. After that, Estimated was always a second set song.

"Estimated Prophet" was played 390 times from 1977 until its last performance on June 28, 1995, near Detroit, Michigan (Estimated #2). It was clearly a mainstay for the Dead in concert. The studio version is the first track of the *Terrapin Station* album first released on July 27, 1977, which you can hear it at this link: (Estimated #3). It was later released on CD in 1987 and again in 2004, with an expanded and remastered version as part of the *Beyond Description* box set. "Estimated Prophet" frequently segued into "Eyes of the World" (aka Eyes); in fact, that pairing was played 178 times. On fourteen other occasions the pairing was Eyes > Estimated, which occurred most often in 1990. Generally, Estimated followed "Scarlet Begonias > Fire on the Mountain" in the second set, which provided some awesome dancing time.

By this time in the Dead's career, having taken a hiatus in 1975 and early 1976, they had a dedicated and passionate following of Deadheads, a small number of whom considered Jerry Garcia a messiah. Barlow talks about this in a number of places including the *Long Strange Trip* documentary released in 2017. Barlow, in addition to being a childhood friend of Weir as well as his songwriting colleague, was also a member of the Dead's "inner circle," having even served as tour manager for a period. This led Weir and Barlow to write Estimated, which was about a crazed fan who has a vision of a "prophet on the burning shore" with "voices telling me" "might and glory gonna be my name." The lyrics also include several references to biblical passages such as "like an angel, standing in a shaft of light"; "the sea will part before me"; and "fire wheel turning in the air." There are several direct and indirect references to California as well, such as "knocking on the golden door" (or Golden Gate) and "standing on the beach." The lyrics can be interpreted as describing a crazed fan—or not. You can find the full lyrics to Estimated here: (Estimated #4); other perspectives about the lyrics are in David Dodd's *The Complete Annotated Grateful Dead Lyrics* (2005, 270–72) and his Dead.net blog here: (Estimated #5).

Musically, Estimated has a unique opening that lets listeners know immediately what song is coming. It's written in a 7/4 time signature, although it isn't the only Dead song with an unusual rhythm—check out "Lazy Lightning > Supplication" or "Playing in the Band," all reviewed later in this book. What makes this song special to some listeners is the long, extended jamming that is some of the best jazz the Dead ever played. In fact, in a 2014 *Rolling Stone* article, David Fricke reminds folks of

"Lesh's original model for the Dead's improvising aesthetic: John Coltrane's classic modal-liberation quartet of the early 1960s." After Weir had finished his vocal raves, Garcia put his wah-wah pedal to great advantage in Estimated, and they took the audience to wonderful jazzy spaces.

"Estimated Prophet" has appeared on many official recordings; you can find more than forty versions on multiple *Dick's Picks* volumes, *Dave's Picks* volumes, and numerous box sets. You can see a full list of releases through 2016 here: (Estimated #6).

Barry saw and recorded Estimated twenty-nine times between February 10, 1979, in Kansas City, and April 2, 1995, at the Pyramid in Memphis. Estimated is definitely one of his favorites. You can find the 2/10/79 version of it here: (Estimated #7). Be sure to check out the rest of the show—it had such a rousing crowd response that there was a second encore. Other notable versions of Estimated include April 19, 1982, at the Baltimore Civic Center in Baltimore, Maryland (Estimated #8); October 26, 1989, at the Miami Arena in Miami (Estimated #9); and May 15, 1977, in St. Louis, Missouri (Estimated #10).

One special version of Estimated that we highly recommend happened on March 29, 1990, at the Nassau Coliseum in Uniondale, New York. This performance featured guest saxophonist Branford Marsalis and was officially released on the three-CD *Wake up to Find Out: Nassau Coliseum, 3/29/90* (D2:T2), in 2014. Weir commented in the Fricke article mentioned earlier that the spring 1990 tour "was the high point for that era," and this version of Estimated supports that statement. Marsalis's familiarity with the Dead, according to the Fricke article, "was from the "Truckin' era," but you wouldn't know it from this performance. Marsalis's saxophone fits the song like a comfortable glove in this fifteen-minute version of "Eyes of the World." As Marsalis said of this night, "I didn't grow up just playing jazz. This was like going home." Listen for yourself here: (Estimated #11).

The recommendations we've offered provide a good cross-section of performances of "Estimated Prophet" through the years. Don't limit yourself to only one or two of these—check them all out for a taste of one of the jazzier improvisational songs in the Dead's catalog.

"Eyes of the World"

Jerry Garcia and Robert Hunter wrote "Eyes of the World" (aka Eyes) in 1973, and it debuted along with five other new songs on February 9, 1973 (Eyes #1), at the Roscoe Maples Pavilion on the Stanford University campus in Palo Alto, California. Eyes became a regular part of the live performance catalog, averaging about fifteen shows a year, and it was played 381 times in total until its last performance on July 6, 1995. Except for seven performances, Eyes always was played in the second set. In 1977 when "Estimated Prophet" was first introduced, it quickly became the most common predecessor to Eyes, and the combination of the two was common as a lead-in to "Drumz" and "Space" at the halfway point of the second set.

"Eyes of the World" is another lyrical gem from Robert Hunter, although it's not easy to interpret it literally, as is often the case with his lyrics. Who wouldn't be surprised to "wake up to find out that you are the eyes of the world"? What does that mean? Does a nuthatch really have "wings a mile long"? And can one go wherever "the heart has its beaches, its homeland, and thoughts of its own"? Ultimately, listeners can interpret these lines for themselves alone—as the eyes of the world.

You can find the complete lyrics at AZLyrics.com (Eyes #2) or at David Dodd's Annotated Grateful Dead Lyrics site: (Eyes #3). Dodd, of course, offers some background for some of the more esoteric lines such as "the heart has its seasons," which was probably influenced by seventeenth-century mathematician and theologian Blaise Pascal. Another interesting connection for a possibly deeper understanding is a book on Buddhist practice titled *You Are the Eyes of the World*, which is "helpful to anyone trying to integrate their spirituality into daily life" according to one Amazon .com reviewer: (Eyes #4). Perhaps that's what Hunter was trying to tell us—or not.

Musically "Eyes of the World" shows, again, how well the Dead worked together. This is a song that often showcased Phil Lesh on bass, or "lead bass," as is often said. Written in 4/4 time, Eyes is not necessarily a rocker, but it is up-tempo and quite a good dance song.

Eyes is often used as one of the best examples of the Grateful Dead as a jazz ensemble, especially when paired with "Estimated Prophet." Eyes is a fluid song with jams between each of the vocal verses and, on many occasions, an extended jam in the intro before the first verse. In later years, the band usually segued out of Eyes after the last verse, perhaps with a short jam. In the early years, Eyes often included a tremendous outro jam that could last ten minutes or longer, taking the song through a variety of chord changes before ending in tight syncopation.

"Eyes of the World" had its studio release on the album *Wake of the Flood*, released in 1973: (Eyes #5). This was also the first record issued by the Dead's own Grateful Dead Records, which is a story in itself. There are nearly fifty official releases of Eyes, and you can see the full list through 2016 here: (Eyes #6). It was also released on the more recent *May 1977: Get Shown the Light* box set.

On March 28, 1973, in Springfield, Massachusetts, Bob's first Dead show, the band played Eyes right after "Dark Star," which provided the return to "normalcy," a transition from unstructured improvisation, as in "Dark Star," to relatively more structured songs, late in the second set. That show is available on *Dave's Picks, Volume 16* (D3:T3) and is accessible here from a matrix audience/soundboard recording: (Eyes #7). You can hear Weir's amazing work on rhythm guitar, and at about 6:20 in this version, the band finishes singing the verses and launches the outro. Listen for the syncopation at about 10:40; it seems to come out of nowhere. The band then segues seamlessly into "Playing in the Band." Bob danced away in Springfield that night and still dances to it whenever he hears it. To us, the outro to "Eyes of the World" captures the essence of the Grateful Dead.

Barry saw Eyes at his first show in 1974, as well as his last show in 1995. He saw thirty-seven versions in total. We recommend the first one he saw, from June 16,

1974, in Des Moines, Iowa: (Eyes #8). The jamming in this long version is amazing as they change styles many times. You'll wonder how they could morph from Eyes to the next song so smoothly and seamlessly until you finally realize what you're hearing is now "Big River," of all things!

Here are some other fine versions of Eyes worthy of attention. What many consider the best version of "Eyes of the World" is from March 29, 1990 (Eyes #9), at the Nassau Coliseum on Long Island, with guest Branford Marsalis. This fifteen-minute performance is truly outstanding due to the marvelous interplay between Marsalis and the Dead. Marsalis was remarkably able to fit right in with the Dead whether they were improvising or not, and he returned to play with them several more times in the 1990s. You can read comments from Marsalis himself in the "Estimated Prophet" review earlier. This version of Eyes was on the official two-CD release *Without a Net*, a collection of live performances between October 1989 and April 1990. The full concert, including Estimated, was released on the three-CD *Wake up to Find Out: Nassau Coliseum, 3/29/90* (D2:T2).

Eyes was played as an encore on a few occasions. One of those was on *Dick's Picks, Volume 12* (D2:T1) from June 26, 1974, at the Providence Civic Center, a show Bob attended. It is also available on a matrix recording here: (Eyes #10). Another stunning later version is filler on *Dick's Picks, Volume 17* (D3:T8) from March 31, 1991, at the Greensboro Coliseum in Greensboro, North Carolina. This is one of the longest versions, running twenty-three minutes, and you can find a lovely audience recording here: (Eyes #11). Plus, it's not often that you can hear Garcia play "flute" on his MIDI, as he does in this stretched-out version.

The last performance of Eyes was on July 6, 1995, at Riverport Amphitheatre near St. Louis: (Eyes #12). It was Barry's last show and certainly not the Dead's best version, but it's surprisingly strong given Garcia's health at this time. It opens the second set and runs about nineteen minutes. Garcia's voice is strong throughout. Though his playing has its ups and downs, the band wails away to be sure the song has the energy it deserves.

Whatever versions you choose to hear, you're not likely to be disappointed with "Eyes of the World."

"Feel Like a Stranger"

"Feel Like a Stranger" (aka Stranger), composed by Bob Weir and John Perry Barlow, was first performed on March 31, 1980, halfway through the Grateful Dead's thirty-year run. That year, the Dead played eighty-six shows, and Stranger was performed in forty-one of them, quite a high percentage. Its frequency tapered off after 1981, but the Dead continued to perform Stranger at least five to ten times every year until 1995. In 1980, its first year in the rotation, Stranger was played in both the first and second sets. By November 1980, Stranger established itself as a first set song, and after 1981, it rarely turned up in the second set. Stranger's final performance was on July 5, 1995, at Riverport Amphitheater in Missouri. Barry saw this show and remembers it well, since he and his wife found Bob Weir and Vince Welnick (the Dead's keyboardist) in their hotel bar the night before and got pictures. The crowd at the show was not as lighthearted as at most shows, since the July 3, 1995, show at Deer Creek had been cancelled due to crowd control issues and a death threat for Garcia.

Stranger was the opening song at dozens of shows over the years, right up until the end of the Dead's touring in 1995. Using it as an opening song makes perfect sense musically, since it establishes the parameters for a good Grateful Dead show: It's generally played as an upbeat song, one that is hard *not* to dance to. It has changes from one section of the song to another. It allows for improvisational solos in the body of the song. It has an extended outro section, which is "structured" only in the sense that the same chords are used from one performance to another. At the same time, the outro is improvisational because of the way Garcia expands beyond a close reading of a particular riff to playing a more free-form version. And it closes with a tight, high-energy riff that's difficult to ignore. If you heard Stranger as the show's opener, you knew it was going to be a good show!

The lyrics in Stranger seem to speak directly to the experience of the singer, Bob Weir, namely singing a song onstage, with someone shooting him glances and him wondering "just what you've got." Could this be simply a "groupie" song? Notwithstanding that perspective, many lines evoked strong crowd responses, particularly "it's gonna get stranger, so let's get on with the show." Bob's favorite line might be "just like running a red light . . . no point in looking behind us, no." (Not that he has.) Find the lyrics here: (Stranger #1).

On May 4, 1980, in Baltimore, two months and a handful of performances into the touring life of Stranger, the Dead played it as their third song of the show, ending a three-song nonstop performance that began with "Mississippi Half-Step Uptown Toodleloo," followed by a powerful, rocking "Franklin's Tower," and then Stranger. The audience that night was treated to a prime example of the Dead's flexibility and unpredictability, since the band rarely began a show with three longer songs, each with extended improvisation. This version of Stranger is a good one, worth listening to for the funky tempo and interesting keyboard fills, not to mention Garcia's outro solo and the band's counterpoint approach to supporting that solo (Stranger #2). At the end of the song, Weir gives a short speech, endorsing drummer Bill Kreutzmann for president in the 1980 election. Barry attended this show and remembers being mildly annoyed by someone yelling "Dark Star" throughout the show. He also remembers being thrilled to successfully smuggle recording equipment on the second try after being turned away by the first security guard.

The April 2, 1990, show at the Omni in Atlanta has a powerful version of Stranger. This show was issued in the box set *Spring, 1990* (D1:T1) and is also accessible as a good audience recording here: (Stranger #3). The Dead opened the show with Stranger. (Be advised that there are about three and a half minutes of noodling and tuning before Stranger begins in this version.) There is the usual robust crowd response when Weir sings: "let's get on with the show." Weir's scat vocals begin at about six minutes into the recording, followed by an excellent Garcia outro solo. Brent Mydland's backup vocal adds greatly to the song's intensity and provokes crowd responses as well.

The final performance of "Feel Like a Stranger" was at Riverport, in Maryland Heights, Missouri, on July 5, 1995, only days before the Dead's final show. You can hear it here: (Stranger #4). As with the 4/2/90 show discussed above, Stranger this night was the opener for the first set. Weir's vocals are as good as ever, as are the backup vocals, although Brent Mydland is no longer with the band at this point and Vince Welnick is the new keyboard player/vocalist. The tempo of this version is slower, with less counterpoint in the funk. Weir's scat vocal section is well done. By 1995, Garcia's voice may have been unsteady, but his guitar work usually rose to the occasion, and the outro solo in this version is no exception. The coda riffs perhaps aren't as well played as in earlier versions, yet this is still a good version to listen to for purposes of comparison with earlier shows, which crackled with energy.

"Feel Like a Stranger" is a high-powered song that illustrates a lot of what the Grateful Dead could accomplish in a live performance. Even though the norm in the first set for most shows was shorter, self-contained songs, Stranger was a frequent choice as the opener for shows. Stranger usually may have been "self-contained" in the sense that it often did not segue into a subsequent song without a break. But there the similarity ends, for Stranger also had copious doses of improvised vocalizing, not to mention Garcia's outstanding and extended solo in the outro. Add to that a punchy ending, and you have an essential Grateful Dead song.

"Foolish Heart"

This Garcia/Hunter collaboration was one of their later additions to the Grateful Dead songbook. It made its performance debut on June 19, 1988, at Alpine Valley in Wisconsin, available here: (Foolish #1). The studio version of "Foolish Heart" was released on the Dead's last studio album, *Built to Last*, on Halloween 1989. This song was also in one of the Dead's few music videos, which you can see here, done with the studio version of the song: (Foolish #2). In total, "Foolish Heart" was performed eighty-seven times, with the last on June 27, 1995, at the Palace in Auburn Hills, Michigan, available here: (Foolish #3).

"Foolish Heart" might be called an "anti-love song," since Hunter's lyrics are a cautionary tale about giving your love to someone with a foolish heart. Garcia does a fine job of singing this up-tempo, semi-rocker with the repeated warning to "never give your love, my friend, unto a foolish heart." We are told there are many things you *can* do: "carve your name in ice and wind," "speak with wisdom like a child," "sign the *Mona Lisa* with a spray can," or even "bite the hand that bakes your bread," but *never* give your love to a foolish heart. The consequences can cause problems, such as going astray, losing sleep, and cursing! All the lyrics can be found here: (Foolish #4).

Some of the other late arrivals by Garcia and Hunter did not remain long in the playbook, including "Believe It or Not," "Built to Last," and "When Push Comes to Shove," but "Foolish Heart" must have resonated with Garcia, since it stayed in the repertoire every year after its debut. It also has plenty of room for the band to stretch out and jam, which those other songs do not. "Foolish Heart" was typically played in the second set, as it was in its debut, though it did appear in the first set eleven times and once as the encore. The debut performance ran about six minutes, but that changed quickly; by the fifth performance it was already running more than nine minutes. Most performances run ten or eleven minutes or more, which made it a crowd-pleaser that got everyone on their feet. It usually features a couple of long jams, with the second reaching a musical peak.

Since "Foolish Heart" was a late arrival to the repertoire and performed relatively few times by Grateful Dead standards, it has been released on only a handful of official recordings: only about ten different performances. Here's a list of all the albums and box sets where you can find "Foolish Heart": (Foolish #5). Barry saw twenty-six performances of "Foolish Heart," and they were all enjoyable. We won't recommend all of them, of course, but here are some of the versions he saw, along with several others that are all worth checking out.

Start with a performance from Alpine Valley in Wisconsin on July 19, 1989, accessible here: (Foolish #6). This jamming version runs nearly twelve minutes, and Barry remembers being in the "tapers" section behind the pavilion for it. This version is ranked number two at headyversion.com. Next we suggest March 19, 1990, at the Hartford Civic Center: (Foolish #7). This is a good quality audience recording; Phil's bass is a standout. This version runs more than eleven minutes and is ranked number one at headyversion.com: (Foolish #8). We don't necessarily agree, since we prefer the July 19, 1989, version, but it's definitely a very good version.

East Coast crowds always brought lots of energy to Dead shows, and that's apparent in this performance of "Foolish Heart" at Madison Square Garden on October 13, 1994: (Foolish #9). As mentioned earlier, this version has a long ending jam, followed by Garcia wailing repeatedly on "unto a foolish heart."

Finally, we'll close with a version from 1995, on February 21 in Salt Lake City: (Foolish #10). This is a clear soundboard recording from a year that has earned a bad rep for less than stellar performances. That isn't the case with this performance, however. Garcia and the band are fully engaged and spot-on in this ten-minute version. Enjoy!

Though added late to the rotation, "Foolish Heart" was illustrative of the Dead's style in later years.

"Friend of the Devil"

Written and composed by John ("Marmaduke") Dawson, Robert Hunter, and Jerry Garcia, "Friend of the Devil" (aka FOTD) originally may have been intended for

Dawson's New Riders of the Purple Sage band, but Garcia added the bridge section ("got two reasons") and claimed the song for the Grateful Dead, according to musicologist Oliver Trager (1997, 125). The Dead first performed FOTD on March 20, 1970. The Dead played a whopping 142 shows in 1970, performing "Friend of the Devil" in thirty-six of them. FOTD was a regular in the rotation, especially after the 1975 hiatus: beginning in 1976, they played FOTD more than a dozen times every year into the 1980s, although the frequency tapered off beginning in 1984. FOTD's final performance was on June 24, 1995, at RFK Stadium in Washington, D.C.

For most of the three dozen performances of "Friend of the Devil" in 1970, the song appeared in an acoustic set. After 1970, all performances were with electric instruments. Occasionally, the Dead played FOTD in the second set, but it was definitely a first set song: after 1979, there's only one appearance for FOTD in the second set. The lyrics for FOTD, which you can see at (Friend #1), tell the story of a by now familiar Grateful Dead character, the cowboy on the run who may or may not have committed crimes here and there along the way. He must in fact make deals with the devil to survive: the song's title, after all, makes that clear.

Musically, many Grateful Dead songs evolved over time, but perhaps no song evolved as drastically as FOTD. It began life as a catchy folk tune and eventually transformed into a slow ballad that ultimately might have qualified as a "Jerry ballad,"—the penultimate song of the second set—although FOTD never made it that far into the set list, however.

April 24, 1970, available here (Friend #2), is a good example of "Friend of the Devil" as an acoustic performance. Although the audio quality of this audience recording is lacking, it nevertheless captures the folk tone of FOTD. For a better quality acoustic version of the song, see *Dick's Picks, Volume 8* (D1:T3). This performance, from May 2, 1970, the famous Binghamton, New York, Harpur College show, is also available here: (Friend #3). This version has a lengthy intro section. You can tell that the Dead are changing their musical approach: this FOTD is a long way from the full-speed-ahead psychedelic jams of the late 1960s.

October 19, 1974, accessible here (Friend #4), from Winterland in San Francisco, is an early electric performance of "Friend of the Devil." This is the song's last performance before the Dead's 1975 touring hiatus. The tempo here is a little slower than in the acoustic shows mentioned earlier, and the drums are more prominent, as is the bass line. But overall, it is still played as a folksy song: you won't hear a lot of the dynamic changes typical of most Grateful Dead songs, nor the extended improvisations, until the second solo starts to sound more rocking than folk. By the end of the song, the band has reverted to a more folk-like sound.

June 4, 1976, in Portland, Oregon (Friend #5), is the first performance of FOTD *after* the hiatus. You can hear significant differences between this version and the previous one from a year and a half earlier. First, the tempo is much slower; there are background vocals; and the instrumentation is closer to the staccato style of several other Grateful Dead songs. FOTD has now become a ballad and is no longer a folk song, at least in the style of playing: Garcia's solo now reflects the improvisational playing around the melody that we have become used to hearing. You can also hear this slower style on a recording Barry made at the Greek Theater in Berkeley, California, on June 21, 1986: (Friend #6).

Finally, we recommend a still later version from July 2, 1989, in Foxboro, Massachusetts, some thirteen years after the 6/4/76 performance discussed earlier. Here the Dead opened the second set with FOTD (Friend #7). In this performance, the tempo is faster, the keyboards are more prominent in the solo, and Garcia is all over the guitar in the best sense possible. Most of this song is played staccato style. But after the solo and the vocal line "she's my heart's delight," when the volume has dropped, the Dead incorporated a power riff that brings the song (and the audience) back to the high levels of energy throughout the song. In these later performances, this riff always provoked a strong audience response.

Some songs in the Grateful Dead's repertoire remained more or less unchanged over the years, but others evolved, sometimes significantly. "Friend of the Devil" is one of the latter. It's an essential Grateful Dead song not simply because it replays a familiar theme in Dead music—the outlaw on the run—but also because of its evolution over the years. The last performance discussed here from 7/2/89 is a good recording for hearing this song's evolution: FOTD progresses from a three-minute folk song to an eleven-minute Grateful Dead song. FOTD evolved from a catchy folk tune played on acoustic instruments, to a full-out rocking ballad much closer in spirit to, for example, "Sugaree" or "He's Gone," than to folk music.

"Goin' Down the Road Feelin' Bad"

"Goin' Down the Road Feelin' Bad" (aka GDTRFB) is a Grateful Dead arrangement of a traditional song. It's not an original composition, yet it feels so much like one of the Dead's own songs. The song has a history as a working-class folk song, and versions are attributed to Woody Guthrie and the blues singers Sonny Terry and Brownie McGhee. You can listen to and watch a more contemporary bluegrass version from 2007 by the Carolina Chocolate Drops (GDTRFB #1).

The Grateful Dead played GDTRFB 293 times beginning in 1970, performing it at least once a year thereafter through the end of their run. In the early years, GDTRFB was played frequently—for example, forty-nine times in 1971, when the band played eighty-two shows. There's a similar pattern in 1972. After that, GDTRFB appeared far fewer times per year, but the song was always in the rotation, even during the hiatus in 1975, when the Dead played it twice during their four performances that year.

The lyrics for GDTRFB are straightforward: once again we hear the story of an itinerant working stiff struggling to make it in life in the face of obstacles, who is tired of "being treated this-a-way." Verses varied on different occasions, as might be expected from a traditional song with its own history; you can see these lyrics and the variants here: (GDTRFB #2). Reading these lyrics as a series of verses leaves one feeling that this is a very sad song, and the reality it portrays may indeed be sad. But listen to the way the Grateful Dead play it—it will lift your spirits.

GDTRFB was nearly always a second set song, usually played close to the end of the set. From its first appearance in 1970 through about the middle of 1973, GDTRFB was almost always paired with "Not Fade Away" (aka NFA). Sometimes that was just the two songs, one after the other, but quite often the Dead bracketed GDTRFB with NFA, a sequence that came to be familiar to Deadheads at the end of the second set during those years. After 1973, GDTRFB preceded NFA occasionally, but Weir chose to sing other songs after GDTRFB, including "One More Saturday Night," "Good Lovin'," and, later on, "Throwing Stones," among others. On nearly every occasion, no matter what song followed GDTRFB, the sequence was fast paced and rocking, as befits the end of the second set.

Probably the most famous iteration of the paired sequence of these two songs is the version that appears on the two-LP album *Grateful Dead* (aka *Skull & Roses*), in which NFA preceded GDTRFB on the album. That version was recorded on April 5, 1971, in New York City (GDTRFB #3), a soundboard recording. Like the *Europe '72* album, *Skull & Roses* is a collection of several different live performances, so it doesn't include the jam or "Lovelight," which actually followed GDTRFB on 4/5/71.

The June 8, 1977, performance of GDTRFB in San Francisco is especially good for listening to a sequence of songs: NFA > GDTRFB > "Johnny B. Goode." This version was released on the boxed set *Winterland June 1977: The Complete Recordings* (D6:T4) and is also available here: (GDTRFB #4). The Dead start the song as a moderately rocking folk song with a rolling beat, but the intensity builds as the verses are completed, especially after the final chorus. Four minutes into the song, you can tell the volume is increasing, and by the end of this solo, we're no longer in "folk song" territory. This is the Grateful Dead at their best: playing as a Dixieland ensemble with each instrument complementing the others—it almost seems as if everyone is playing lead. If you listen to this version a second time, you'll be able to appreciate the work of Weir, Lesh, and Keith Godchaux all the more. And of course this version is from the spring of 1977, arguably among the Dead's best touring seasons.

For those interested in watching a video of a live version of GDTRFB, we recommend the Dead's performance at Alpine Valley, Wisconsin, on July 17, 1989, which is available here: (GDTRFB #5). It's a treat to watch the interaction between Garcia and keyboardist Brent Mydland. Bob Weir's rhythm is clear on this version, and he does his usual great playing. The dynamics here are excellent: Garcia brings it down and then back up near the end of the song.

Finally, we mentioned earlier that the Dead played GDTRFB less frequently as the years passed and as they separated it from "Not Fade Away." On June 22, 1992, in Burgettstown, Pennsylvania, the Dead broke out GDTRFB after a gap of fifty-seven shows. It's available here as an audience recording: (GDTRFB #6). This version may not match the intensity of the 1977 version mentioned earlier, but it shows the Dead at their best in the 1990s, not always their best decade.

GDTRFB is a special song for Bob. On October 2, 1972, while the Dead were playing a show in Springfield, Massachusetts, Bob found himself at a conference in Dubrovnik, Yugoslavia, unable to attend the show. Two days later, at the airport in Dubrovnik, he spotted a young man with a Dead decal on his guitar case. They chatted and soon were both singing GDTRFB to the delight of many locals and to the consternation of Bob's colleagues. It's a wonderful memory—and should that (no longer young) man read this, he should please contact Bob.

We hope you enjoyed our little excursion into the world of "Goin' Down the Road Feelin' Bad," in which the lyrics are sad but the music is happy. This is definitely one of the essential songs for Deadheads.

"Good Lovin'"

"Good Lovin'," a cover song the Grateful Dead performed 428 times, was written by Arthur Resnick and Rudy Clark. There were several recorded versions in the early and mid-1960s, the most famous of which was by the Young Rascals. The Dead first performed it live in 1966, the only documented performance of the song that year, but they probably played it more times in those early years. Of the 428 performances, the Dead played "Good Lovin'" ninety-one times in 1969 and 1970, including sixty-seven performances in the 142 shows during 1970 alone. These figures support the notion that the Dead played the song at least a few times before 1969.

In those early years, the lead vocalist on Good Lovin' was Ron (Pigpen) McKernan, the Dead's original keyboardist. We often overlook the fact that Pigpen was as much a front man for the Dead as Garcia or anyone else in those years, with several showstoppers including "Midnight Hour" and "Lovelight." Those two songs shared Pigpen's improvisational talking performances, sort of a vocal solo during which time the band settled into quiet backup mode while Pigpen riffed on whatever lines he came across. In contrast, "Good Lovin'" was a jam tune, with the musicians taking over the middle segment of the song. The lyrics are not at all subtle, and you can see them here: (Good Lovin #1).

Of some interest is the fact that the Dead released "Good Lovin'" on their studio album *Shakedown Street* in 1978, in which it had the honor of being the first song on the album. The Dead did not record many cover songs on studio albums, although Jerry Garcia did so on his solo projects. "Good Lovin'" may hold the record for the most live performances prior to studio release than any other song—more than twelve years. There were of course many performances released on live albums—Deaddisc.com lists dozens of releases here: (Good Lovin #2).

The first performance on May 9, 1966, can be heard here: (Good Lovin #3). That this soundboard recording exists at all is amazing, and we must thank our friend David Gans for the remixing on this very early recording. This version has a lightning fast tempo, which changes over the years. Lesh provides an intense, throbbing bass line. The middle portion of the song is a jam rather than vocal improvisation. This version times in at about four minutes, a short version compared to what would come later.

On December 12, 1969, in Los Angeles, the Dead played "Good Lovin'" in the second set. This version has been issued on *Dave's Picks, Volume 10* (D2:T7) and can be heard here as well: (Good Lovin #4). This version is bracketed around a drum solo, and the total time including the drum solo is just over six minutes. Pigpen's vocals are clear and strong on this soundboard recording.

On May 2, 1970, at Harpur College in Binghamton, New York, the Dead played a much more mature version of "Good Lovin'," which was issued on *Dick's Picks, Volume 8* (D2:T8) and is accessible here: (Good Lovin' #5). This version has the intro that we are more familiar with, starting with drums, then each instrument in turn joining the fray. This version brackets a drum solo and picks up again after the drums. The total timing of the two "Good Lovin'" segments is more than twelve minutes compared to the four minutes in the 5/9/66 show mentioned earlier. The jam here is a high energy improvisation of the style the Dead delivered in the late 1960s. At about 7:30 of the second segment, the band slows the tempo, anticipating the final set of vocals from Pigpen. This is a classic Pigpen-era version of the song.

September 3, 1977, is the famous Englishtown, New Jersey, show that was released on *Dick's Picks, Volume 15* (D2:T2). "Good Lovin'" times in at six minutes and is accessible here: (Good Lovin #6). Pigpen had left the band in 1972, and Bob Weir became the primary vocalist on the song about a year and a half after Pigpen left. The tempo is a bit slower in this 1977 show, the music more polished but less improvisational. This version times in at about six minutes, which may reflect the fact that it was the second song of the second set rather than a blockbuster at the end of the set. Between the vocals from Weir and the absence of a high energy jam, this version is more refined and polished, less raw and raucous. This is a standard version for "Good Lovin'" during the middle years of the Dead's run.

For a later version, we turn to April 2, 1990, at the Omni in Atlanta, a show that was released in the *Spring 1990* box set (D3:T5). There's a good matrix recording here: (Good Lovin #7). At this point, the Dead were sharing the vocals: Weir sang the first verse and Brent Mydland the second. This version times in at around seven minutes. The jam after the second verse is straight ahead, and the jam after the third verse includes the vocal improvisation by both Weir and Mydland, which became characteristic of the song in later years. The song builds in intensity toward the end and ends the second set for this show.

With different vocalists over the years and with varied timings, "Good Lovin'" shows the evolution of a single song over a thirty-year period, illustrating the ways the Dead could make a cover song their own.

"Greatest Story Ever Told"

"Greatest Story Ever Told" (aka Greatest Story) is a Bob Weir and Robert Hunter composition that debuted live at the Capitol Theater in Port Chester, New York, on February 18, 1971 (GSET #1). Its final live performance was June 27, 1995 (GSET #2). Greatest Story was performed a total of 280 times. The studio version was included on Weir's 1972 "solo" LP *Ace* (GSET #3), which featured the Grateful Dead as his backup band. During its early years, Greatest Story was played in either the first or second set; in 1981 it shifted almost exclusively to the first set. It was a regular part of the repertoire but was dropped after the band's 1975 hiatus, reappearing in 1979 and then remaining in the lineup for the rest of the band's career.

The lyrics to "Greatest Story Ever Told" are a lot of fun, with many biblical references including the opening line, "Moses came riding up on a guitar" and "Abraham and Isaac sitting on a fence." It also has several ironic twists, such as "I asked him for mercy, he gave me a gun," and "I asked him for water, he poured me some wine." You can find the complete lyrics at this link: (GSET #4).

According to Dennis McNally (2002, 393, 438), the rhythm for Greatest Story was inspired by a tape Mickey Hart had made of the sound of a pump on his ranch. Weir picked up on it and added chord changes, then Hunter also got involved, drawing on "Froggy Went a-Courtin'" for the tempo and the lyrics. When Weir asked to replace "guitar" with "quasar" in the opening line, "Moses came riding up on a guitar," Hunter's growing frustration ultimately led him to discontinue acting as Weir's lyricist. However, if you listen to the debut performance from February 18, 1971 (GSET #5), you'll hear "guitar" rather than "quasar." Weir continued to wrestle with the last word of the line for the next two performances, singing "Moses come ridin' up in a bar car" on February 19, 1971 (GSET #6), and February 20, 1971 (GSET #7), before finally settling on "quasar" on February 21, 1971 (GSET #8). As a side note, Hart also made a song inspired by the pump tape, calling it "The Pump Song" (GSET #9), which he included on his first solo album, *Rolling Thunder*, released in 1972. When the Dead's *Reckoning* album was released in 1981, Hart was added to the songwriting credits.

Musically, "Greatest Story Ever Told" is another up-tempo rocker that always got the audience on their feet dancing. It always began with a fast, staccato bass beat from Lesh to let everyone know what was coming. In later versions in the mid-1980s, it opened with a two-note chord from Weir. This is "just a song," as Mickey Hart would say, meaning it was more about the lyrics than the music—"songs" limited the band's ability to improvise. Although most versions of Greatest Story might sound similar, the Dead always added wonderful variations in each performance, particularly noticeable in Garcia's solos.

Greatest Story has been officially released more than thirty times, and you can see a full list through 2016 here: (GSET #10). To appreciate the fun and danceability of Greatest Story, try some of our recommendations in addition to the performances we've already mentioned. The August 27, 1972, performance (GSET #11) in Veneta,

Oregon, is often mentioned as the best; you can judge for yourself. Garcia goes for it with his solo, and, so does everyone else! The day was hot, and so is this version, which can also be seen in the official video release, *Sunshine Daydream*.

After being absent from the live lineup for 207 performances, Greatest Story returned on February 17, 1979 (GSET #12), in Oakland, which also happened to be the last show with Keith and Donna Godchaux. This is another fine example of how simple differences from one performance to another kept the audience coming back for more.

Beginning with his first Dead show on June 16, 1974, Barry saw sixteen versions of Greatest Story. Of these, the June 16, 1974 (GSET #13), version is worth checking out. Garcia does great wah-wah work while Weir sings lead with Donna Godchaux and Lesh backing him on vocals. Barry also saw two later shows, which we both recommend, that demonstrate how the band and song matured while keeping the audience engaged. First, give a listen to this performance on April 9, 1987 (GSET #14), in Chicago. It's memorable for Barry because he was stopped by security as he tried to sneak his recorder in without a taper's ticket. He managed to get it in but missed the Greatest Story opener. Finally, listen to this crystal clear soundboard from September 18, 1994 (GSET #15), at Shoreline Amphitheatre in Mountain View, California. It's the next-to-last performance Barry saw and one of the last seven from the Dead—and it shows the band still in fine form.

"Hard to Handle"

"Hard to Handle" was composed in San Francisco in the 1960s by the great Otis Redding. The Grateful Dead were familiar with Redding, having opened shows and performed with him. The Dead first played "Hard to Handle" in February 1969, with vocals by Ron McKernan (aka Pigpen), and performed it often and regularly until August 1971, around the time McKernan became too ill to perform. The Dead played "Hard to Handle" more than one hundred times between 1969 and 1971, when it was dropped from the rotation.

The Dead reprised the song for two shows on December 30, 1982, and on the following night, New Year's Eve 1982. The latter version featured Etta James and the Tower of Power horn section and is available on video here: (Handle #1). This performance was arranged by the guests, not the Grateful Dead, so this is not the "Hard to Handle" as played by the Dead, as you'll hear later. From this performance it might also be noted that the Dead were not always a great backup band: on this occasion, with the possible exception of Bob Weir, they seemed to coast. In their defense, this was the third set of a long evening.

We chose to include this cover song for two main reasons. First, it highlights Pigpen, one of his songs long remembered and *not* adapted by the surviving members of the Dead after his death in March 1973. Second, the Dead played "Hard to Handle" as a funky hip-hop song with an upbeat tempo and not as a mournful blues song.

To hear what the Grateful Dead sounded like in late 1969 through 1971, with full-speed-ahead jamming, listen to "Hard to Handle." The lyrics for "Hard to Handle" are available here: (Handle #2).

The Grateful Dead Guide here (Handle #3) makes picking recommended versions of "Hard to Handle" much easier. For a detailed analysis of dozens of performances of "Hard to Handle" by the Dead, visit the website. Due to space constraints, we cannot match this in-depth analysis. That page also contains many direct links to the Archive.org website, so you can choose from raucous early versions to more polished and funky later versions. We recommend two specific shows, however.

On April 29, 1971, at the Fillmore East in New York City, the Dead played a funky nine-minute version of "Hard to Handle" (Handle #4). This version starts slowly and picks up when McKernan starts his vocal improvisations after the second verse and chorus. When he stops singing/talking, the band picks up the intensity level even more as they extend the improvisation. They segue into a four-note jam toward the end of the song, which finally gets organized and brings the jam to its conclusion, when Pigpen reprises the final verse and chorus.

August 6, 1971, at the Hollywood Palladium is what we consider the best performance of "Hard to Handle," an opinion shared by both the headyversion.com website and the Grateful Dead Guide. This version is available on the album *From the Phil Zone* (D1:T6). One might think that albums issued by the Grateful Dead would be soundboard recordings made by their own crew. This performance is the exception, an audience tape. The liner notes describe the performance as the "hyperdrive version," which seems accurate. An audience recording is accessible here: (Handle #5). The Grateful Dead Guide provides a different link, which is also an excellent recording, perhaps from the same source: (Handle #6). Listening to the audience respond to this song is a lot of fun, especially as the song progresses and Garcia picks up the lead, supported by an expressive bass line from Lesh. Pigpen reprises the singing at about 7:00, leading the band to a tight ending.

We intentionally downplay cover songs in this book, but some had to be included. Younger Deadheads may not be as familiar with the Dead's early work, when the *Live Dead* album, with its extended jams and raucous energy, represented the state of the art. "Hard to Handle," as the versions we recommend attest, is an important part of that early legacy. Our sincere thanks to whoever taped these shows in 1971.

"Hell in a Bucket"

"Hell in a Bucket," (aka Bucket), by Bob Weir and John Perry Barlow, is a rocking teaser, a song that takes us toward the darker side of life, at least a little. Bucket's lyrics (Bucket #1) take us on an urban tour: this is neither country rock nor cowboy music. And though many Grateful Dead songs include struggles and obstacles, Bucket is about love turned bad with a heavy dose of revenge—or at least getting the last laugh. In the Dead's official video of this song, our narrator, drinking in the

Bucket, a bar, shows a biker a picture of his lover, urging him to pursue her so that she'll see that the narrator is a bargain compared to the biker.

That's the main theme of the song: she'll carry on in her wanton ways, but ultimately she'll pay the price and our hero will have survived and "won," if winning is an option at all. In Bucket, the saints don't come marching in: it's the "snakes come marching in." But apparently, survival, too, has its price, since our hero appears to be drinking his life away, as the title's word play suggests. But at least he's "enjoying the ride," which isn't such a bad way to go through life—maybe Bucket has a more positive message than we first imagine. David Dodd's Greatest Story blog on Bucket (Bucket #2) is worth reading in this context.

The Grateful Dead introduced "Hell in a Bucket" on May 13, 1983, at the Greek Theater in Berkeley, California. Only a handful of original songs were introduced by the Dead later than 1983, and most were ballads such as "Days Between," "Foolish Heart," "Lazy River Road," and so forth. Bucket may have been the last rocker introduced by the Dead. The Dead performed Bucket 216 times, an average of more than sixteen times a year. Bucket's final performance was on June 30, 1995, in Pittsburgh at Three Rivers Stadium.

Bucket was almost always a first set song, and often the opening song of the show. When Bucket was in the second set, it usually opened that set. The Dead used Bucket to get the show rolling, to get the crowd on its feet and dancing. "Hell in a Bucket" is also one of only six songs for which the Dead made a music video for MTV, a very big deal in the late 1980s. You can see it here: (Bucket #3).

"Hell in a Bucket" is a song that illustrates the Dead's tendency to extend the codas of their songs with repeated iterations of a final line, in this case "enjoying the ride," with Bob Weir improvising on the phrase while increasing the intensity level. Even on May 13, 1983, at its first performance (Bucket #4), Bucket included this kind of extended outro, although it's more subdued than it would become in later performances. At that show, Bucket was not the opener, and naturally enough, the crowd responses are somewhat muted, since the audience couldn't anticipate the hook lines. But you can hear that Bucket's structure was already in place—the song did not change much over the years.

For two other excellent performances, we recommend these shows released in the *Dick's Picks* series. The first is October 14, 1983, in Hartford, Connecticut, only a few months after Bucket's first performance. This performance is on *Dick's Picks, Volume 6* (D1:T9), and you can hear it here: (Bucket #5). The tempo has picked up a bit, and the bass line is more compelling—this is one of those performances in which Lesh plays both lead bass and bottom line bass, which means he's working hard. Bob was at this show and clearly remembers Bucket, especially its extended ending. It felt like the end of the first set, but it was not, as the Dead did a quick segue into "Day Job." At this show, the combination of those two songs made a great closing for the first set.

The second is from September 16, 1990, at Madison Square Garden, where Bucket was the show's opener. This performance is on *Dick's Picks, Volume 9* (D1:T1) and here: (Bucket #6). On this audience recording, you can almost feel the electricity as the band gets ready to open the show. This is a solid, mature performance with a lot of audience participation. If you're a Deadhead, you know what this means. If you're a newbie, this is a good recording to hear what that was like. The audience even helps Weir when he forgets a verse and applauds the punctuation at the end of the first solo. This version has a tremendous coda.

By June 30, 1995, the final performance of Bucket, in Pittsburgh (Bucket #7), the Dead were close to the end of what would turn out to be their last tour. Bucket was the show's opener: Weir's vocals are fine, Garcia's leads are solid, and Lesh's bass line carries a good beat. This performance has a typically extended coda. This audience recording conveys a sense of the atmosphere at the show, including a big cheer during the line "at least I'm enjoying the ride."

Unfortunately for all of us, however, the ride was almost over, as it would turn out, in terms of the Grateful Dead's touring life. But we still have "Hell in a Bucket" to help us enjoy the ride. Keep dancing!

"Help on the Way" > "Slipknot" > "Franklin's Tower"

These three songs, "Help on the Way" > "Slipknot" > "Franklin's Tower" (aka Help > Slip > Franklin), give you two essential songs in one review, with a bonus, "Slipknot," thrown into the mix. These three songs were not always played together, although they did appear together when they were first performed live on June 17, 1975 (HSF #1) (HSF #2), at Winterland in San Francisco during the Grateful Dead's touring hiatus. (Surprisingly, this performance of "Help on the Way" has no lyrics.) This trio was played again when they made their recording debut on the *Blues for Allah* LP later in 1975, (HSF #3). This trio is the way most Deadheads think of each of these songs, as one awesome combination, so in this review, we'll discuss all three songs.

Help is another delightful Garcia and Hunter collaboration. Musically it seems to have some of the same flavor as "Blues for Allah," given its rhythm and melody. The lyrics have a number of lines that grabbed Deadheads' attention and became part of the cultural language. For example, the opening line, "paradise waits," always seemed to tell the crowd what was coming when it opened the show, as it often did. Hunter, as usual, lets his thoughts fly with "poised for flight, wings spread bright" or "don't stop to run, she can fly like a lie." You can find the full lyrics for Help here: (HSF #4).

Slip is an instrumental "composed" by Garcia, Keith Godchaux, Phil Lesh, and Bob Weir. Slip as a jam appeared on its own twice in 1974, before Help or Franklin were played. First it was sandwiched between a nineteen-minute "Eyes of the World" and "China Doll" in Atlanta on June 20, 1974 (HSF #5), and then it was played between a twenty-one minute "Dark Star" and "Stella Blue" on July 25, 1974, in Chicago (HSF #6). In total, Slip was played a total of 112 times in concert including 110 times following Help. The pairing of Help > Slip was absent from the active repertoire from October 11, 1977, until March 25, 1983, and again from September

12, 1985, until October 8, 1989, and there were only two performances in 1985. Help > Slip was played only three times without Franklin.

"Franklin's Tower," on the other hand, was continuously in the live repertoire after its debut in 1975 and was performed 221 times in total. Franklin is another Garcia and Hunter collaboration. It's a bubbly, buoyant tune that immediately got the crowd on their feet to dance. The lyrics invite everyone to join in, which the crowd would do, especially on the chorus, "roll away . . . the dew." Other lines in which the crowd sang along include "if you get confused listen to the music play" before Garcia would take off with a guitar solo. The crowd would join in again with "may the four winds blow you safely home again" and "if you plant ice you're gonna harvest wind." You can read the full lyrics for Franklin here: (HSF #7).

David Dodd's Annotated Grateful Dead Lyrics site reproduces a wonderful essay from Robert Hunter in response to a critic's comments about the Dead's lyrics being "meaningless." Hunter is notoriously quiet about his lyrics, so nothing we can say here better explains "Franklin's Tower" or the meaning of *any* of his lyrics. Be sure to read "Fractures of Unfamiliarity and Circumvention in Pursuit of a Nice Time" here: (HSF #8). Dodd's site also has a link to a delightful tongue-in-cheek essay by Andrew Shalit that suggests the song is about Ben Franklin and his special technique for making a bell sound better. It's a hoot! Dodd's Dead.net blog touches a bit on both these essays (HSF #9), or you can find the full version for Shalit in Dodd's Annotated Grateful Dead Lyrics entry (HSF #10).

In addition to the studio release of Help > Slip > Franklin on the *Blues for Allah* album, there are surprisingly few official releases, given the stature of this trio of songs and the number of times they were played together. The excellent live version on August 13, 1975, from the Great American Musical Hall in San Francisco was later broadcast on FM radio and is available on *One from the Vault* (D1:T2–4) and here: (HSF #11).

The *30 Trips around the Sun* eighty-CD box set has three versions, one of which is especially interesting from September 28, 1975. It was during the Dead's "hiatus" and only one of four live performances in 1975. This one is from Lindley Meadows in Golden Gate Park in San Francisco and has the following song lineup to open the show: Help > Slip > "The Music Never Stopped," "They Love Each Other," "Franklin" and then on to the rest of the one-set performance, which was the last Grateful Dead concert until June 1976. You can also listen to the September 28, 1975, performance here: (HSF #12).

The *May 1977: Get Shown the Light* box set also has a fine version, from May 9, 1977, in Buffalo, New York, which opens the show. Headyversion.com lists it as one of the best versions, and you'll understand why when you hear this more-than-thirty-minute performance of these three songs. You can also hear it here: (HSF #13). If you're a newbie to Grateful Dead music, you may be skeptical about a thirty-minute performance of anything. But trust the Deadheads: thirty minutes of nonstop Dead is wonderful and it didn't happen often enough. You can see all the official releases of the wonderful trio of songs here: (HSF #14).

When Help > Slip was absent from live performances, Franklin continued being played regularly, as mentioned earlier. Franklin was included on the live *Dead Set* two-LP album and the later CD in the *Beyond Description* box set. There are a few other official releases with nice versions of it, which you can see here: (HSF #15).

Barry saw "Franklin's Tower" performed alone only fourteen times without Help > Slip. The first Franklin he saw in Baltimore on May 4, 1980, was eleven minutes long, and you can listen here to a very nice audience recording (HSF #16). The second version he saw was August 3, 1982, in Kansas City at Starlight Theatre, and we highly recommend it. This is a jumpin' eleven-minute performance you can hear in this great matrix recording: (HSF #17).

On September 6, 1983, at Red Rocks Amphitheatre overlooking Denver, Barry saw his first of twelve Help > Slip > Franklin performances, another version we highly recommend. This performance is twenty-five minutes long and begins with a wonderful example of Lesh doing lead bass. Although Help is short at little more than three minutes, Slipknot makes up for it at nine minutes, and then it goes into a thirteen-minute Franklin. Sweet! Take a listen to a very good matrix recording here: (HSF #18). We also recommend another fine performance at Deer Creek near Indianapolis on June 28, 1992, when the trio opened the show. It's not the longest version, but it's a respectable eighteen minutes and very well played. You can hear the crowd's appreciation on this matrix recording here: (HSF #19).

One last version we recommend that is certainly worth hearing is from October 9, 1976, in Oakland, California, which featured the Who on the bill as well. The Dead's second set lineup is the reason we recommend this particular performance: "Saint Stephen" > "Not Fade Away" > "Saint Stephen" reprised > Help > Slip > Drumz > "Samson and Delilah" > "Slipknot" reprised > Franklin > "One More Saturday Night." The Encore: "U.S. Blues." You can find all of it on Archive.org (HSF #20). Give yourself time to enjoy this whole second set and turn up the volume!

Enjoy all the versions we've recommended in this review. If you get confused, just let the music play!

"Here Comes Sunshine"

"Here Comes Sunshine" (aka Sunshine) is an intriguing Garcia and Hunter song. Oliver Trager describes it as "the Grateful Dead at their sublime Beatlesque pinnacle" (1997, 175). And yet there's mystery around this song as well.

Sunshine first appeared on the *Wake of the Flood* studio album, released in 1973: the name of the album is the first line of the lyrics of this song. The Dead had played the song twenty times before they went into the studio, not an unusual pattern for the band, working out the details onstage before recording. That said, the Grateful Dead played Sunshine live only sixty-five times; almost half of these performances were in 1973, one in 1974, and then none until 1992. Therein lies the mystery: why so few performances of such a beautiful song? Why such a long break of eighteen years (a gap of 1,213 shows)? This last is more easily answered in the breach: for all practical purposes, Sunshine had been dropped from the rotation, but according to Trager, apparently Sunshine was reprised because of a suggestion by keyboardist Vince Welnick, which led to the 1992 breakout (1997, 1,750).

The lyrics in Sunshine, available here (Sunshine #1), speak to a familiar trope in Hunter's poetry, the struggling character mired in poverty who nevertheless persists in the face of adversity, from the flood referenced in the song to more general life circumstances: "good to know you got shoes to wear," and "been down before." At the same time, there is optimism in the chorus, which repeats the line "here comes sunshine!" And there's simplicity in the lyrics: short lines sung sweetly.

Musically, Sunshine is a gem. The music is mid-tempo with recognizable phrases, especially between verses. After the second verse and chorus, the band opens the song to an extended improvisational jam. Compared to similar jams in the late 1960s, the Sunshine jam seems gentle but the artistry comes through. Toward the end of this jam, the band comes together for a series of tight, elegant phrases before launching back into the jam. In other words, you hear a kind of structured improvisation, as counterintuitive as that might sound. Later in the song, the Dead sing the third verse and chorus, following that with a syncopated musical bridge, and then relaunching the jam. This extended jam ends with a similar tightening of the phrasing and a coda that consists of the band singing the chorus one last time.

One of Bob's favorite performances is from March 28, 1973, in Springfield, Massachusetts, his first Grateful Dead show. That night, the band opened with "Cumberland Blues," familiar because it had already been released on the *Europe '72* album. Sunshine was second, and Bob remembers being totally entranced by this "new" song: it had so much jamming but at the same time the band was tight. That show was later released as *Dave's Picks, Volume 16* (D1:T2), but not before a young friend sent Bob a tape of that show as a Father's Day gift. Very cool! You can also access a good matrix recording of this show here: (Sunshine #2). This was only the tenth live performance of the song, and it times in at about 8:45, considerably shorter than the Tampa show described later. This live version took place before the Dead recorded their *Wake of the Flood* album.

After that album, live performances of Sunshine were usually excellent. One good example is November 30, 1973, in Boston, Massachusetts. This performance is available on *Dick's Picks, Volume 14* (D2:T1). The Dead played Sunshine in the second set that night. That performance is also available here: (Sunshine #3). The jams are almost dreamy in this version, and Lesh's bass is particularly interesting. The band comes closer to the staccato style of "Row Jimmy" in this version than in others.

The Dead's performance of Sunshine on December 19, 1973, in Tampa, Florida, is probably the best live performance of the song. The Tampa performance was released on *Dick's Picks, Volume 1* (D1:T1)—yes, this is the first song on the first album in the *Dick's Picks* series. For the complete show as originally performed, visit this link for a matrix recording: (Sunshine #4). This recording is especially good for the clarity of Bob Weir's rhythm guitar work.

As mentioned earlier, for some reason Sunshine fell off the rotation after its last performance in 1974, only to break out after a gap of more than twelve hundred shows on December 6, 1992, in Chandler, Arizona, where Sunshine was the opening song. In this version (Sunshine #5), the song begins with an a cappella rendition of the chorus, which was not the case in earlier years. The jams are shorter in this nine-minute version, and they are less improvisational, until the outro, which shines. The new arrangement includes a half-time rendering of the chorus toward the end of the song. There's a sense of rustiness in this performance, especially compared to the Tampa show mentioned earlier; after all, the song was absent from the rotation for eighteen years.

So the mystery remains: why was Sunshine dropped from the rotation at all, let alone for so many years? And second, why was the arrangement downgraded in the breakout shows during the 1990s? We don't have answers for that, but we know that "Here Comes Sunshine" remains an essential song for understanding the Dead as they developed in the early 1970s. For that alone—not to mention the lyrics and the tight jamming—we hope you can enjoy the selections suggested.

"He's Gone"

"He's Gone" is a Garcia/Hunter tune that first appeared on April 17, 1972, at Tivoli Gardens in Copenhagen, Denmark, during the Grateful Dead's Europe '72 tour. With its languid tempo, gospel overtones, and therapeutic lyrics, "He's Gone" has long been one of our favorite Grateful Dead songs. The Dead played the song 328 times; its final performance was on July 6, 1995, just days before the Dead's final concert on July 9, 1995.

In 1972, when "He's Gone" first slipped into the rotation, it appeared in either the first or second set. But by late 1972, it had become firmly lodged in the second set. Prior to the Dead's touring hiatus in 1975, "He's Gone" often segued into "Truckin'." After the hiatus, more often than not, it segued into "Drumz." The Dead's performances of the song were remarkably consistent over the years: with the exception of the outro jams, "He's Gone" did not evolve dramatically, unlike many other songs in the repertoire.

Musically, "He's Gone" is relatively simple in structure, with its two verses, a repeated chorus, a short musical bridge followed by a solo, and a vocal bridge. The musical improvisation appears mostly in the outro section, especially in later years, when the subject of the song seemed to shift. It is generally accepted that the lyrics (Gone #1) for the song were aimed at Lenny Hart, a manager of the band who allegedly stole more than a hundred thousand dollars before fleeing, complicated by the fact that Lenny Hart was the father of Mickey Hart, one of the Dead's drummers. Mickey subsequently left the band but rejoined in late 1974, just before the Dead's touring hiatus. The opening phrase, "Rat in a drain ditch," evokes the band's feelings about Lenny. He could "steal your face right off your head," they sing.

Over the years, the narrative shifted away from the story of Lenny Hart, and "He's Gone" became something of a requiem. One performance played the song in honor of Bobby Sands, an IRA revolutionary who had recently died as a prisoner in Northern Ireland. The song also invoked the memory of the Dead's original keyboardist and front man, Ron ("Pigpen") McKernan, who died a few months after the song was first performed. Since Jerry Garcia's death, especially when the song is played by post-1995 bands like Dead & Company, most Deadheads think of the song as homage to Garcia.

Like many other Grateful Dead songs, however, "He's Gone" also includes hopeful and positive lyrics. The "steal your face" line always provoked a loud crowd response, as did Bob's favorite line: "nothin' left to do but smile, smile, smile." That and other lines in the song—for example, "the price wasn't anything"—might seem to disguise resentful bitterness, but we take these lyrics to be more upbeat—even in the face of calamity, we carry on. The repeated line, "nothin's gonna bring him back," sung in the outro, often with gospel flair, can help anybody grieving a loss. In short, the song originally chronicled a costly event in the Dead's history but evolved into a much more positive anthem.

The first performance of "He's Gone," on April 17, 1972, in Copenhagen, Denmark, is a faster tempo version than those in later years. This version is in the box set *Europe '72* and is also accessible here: (Gone #2). In this version, the band repeats the opening verse and chorus after the solo, but they do not sing the vocal bridge, nor is there a significant outro at the conclusion. This is a well-played but shorthand version of the song.

Less than a month later, on May 10, 1972, in Amsterdam, the Dead played the version of "He's Gone" that was released on the album *Europe '72* (D1:T2), also accessible here: (Gone #3). Already the Dead had modified the song: the opening intro notes are different, for example. The tempo slowed slightly, more akin to what we would hear in later years. The solo is shorter and the opening verses are not repeated; instead, the vocal bridge is included ("going where the wind don't blow so"). Finally, there's the hint of an improvisational outro before the song ends to polite applause.

The two earlier versions we highlighted timed in between six and eight minutes. The Dead's performance of "He's Gone" at the famous Englishtown, New Jersey, show on September 3, 1977, is longer, at more than fourteen minutes. This version was released on *Dick's Picks, Volume 15* (D3:T1) and is also accessible here: (Gone #4). This is one of the greatest performances of this song, even though Garcia reverses the lyrics in the second verse. About nine minutes in, the audience claps in time to the final verse and chorus, and the song evolves into a sweet gospel jam that continues to the end of the song, with "Ooo, nothin's gonna bring him back" repeatedly sung, mostly a cappella. At about 13:40, Lesh announces with a bass bomb that the instrumental outro is to begin. The band then improvises a jam that lasts until "He's Gone" segues into "Not Fade Away."

Finally, we recommend the performance on May 5, 1981, at Nassau Coliseum, another powerful version of "He's Gone." This is the version dedicated to Bobby

Sands, the Irish hunger striker, and was released on *Dick's Picks, Volume 13* (D3:T1). By now, the song is a sing-along—we recommend the audience recording cited here for maximum audience response: (Gone #5). If ever there was a performance of this song that captures the essence of the interactions between the Dead and their audience, this is it. In addition, the music is masterfully played—this is a classic, mature version of the song. After the outro, they segue into "Drumz" after a powerful foray into "Spanish Jam."

"He's Gone" is perhaps underrepresented in the pantheon of great Grateful Dead songs, yet we think it's one of their best. It is not as up-tempo as many songs, not as complicated as others, but there was always room at a Dead show for a ballad. The song's lyrics speak to those of us who have suffered loss—this song helps us carry on in the face of those losses and setbacks. It is definitely one of the essential Grateful Dead songs.

"High Time"

True love, back to the land, forget about politics, earn our own way, end the war, smoke some weed, drop some acid, false pretenses—the late 1960s and the early 1970s were complicated in many ways for those living through them. They were "high times" in many ways, but not so high in many others. The Grateful Dead's song "High Time," another Hunter and Garcia collaboration, speaks to many of these dynamics.

"High Time" is a languid ballad that first appeared on the *Workingman's Dead* album in 1970. Its first live performance was June 21, 1969, and its final performance was March 24, 1995. The Dead played "High Time" live 133 times in total. It remained in the repertoire off and on throughout the run, although it was never played frequently after 1971. It was not played at all from mid-1970 to mid-1976, a gap of 341 shows, and there were no performances of it at all in 1978, 1983, and 1989.

In its early life in 1969 and 1970, when it was performed sixty-one times, "High Time" was sometimes performed in the second set, but many of the shows during that period didn't follow what later became the standard two-set format. After the song returned to the rotation in 1976, it was more often a second set song until 1986. After that, it was always a first set song. Regardless of its placement, "High Time" was a good choice when the Dead wanted to slow things down.

"High Time" is another of Robert Hunter's love songs. The lyrics (High Time #1) focus on the day-to-day activities of our narrator, who is trying to make it on his own somewhere in the countryside. He's also trying to negotiate his relationship with a former partner. It begins with miscommunication: "You told me good-bye" but you "didn't mean good-bye." "How was I to know?" Love involves communication, as veterans of any love relationship agree, so our narrator has a problem to solve. At the beginning of the song, the miscommunication produces hard times, not high time, despite the song's title and chorus, so the song is more than a little ironic. Yet although there may be trouble and pain tomorrow, there is still optimism in the "high time" line sung repeatedly. By the end of the song, things look better: "we could have us a high time, living the good life." It's never clear whether the narrator's optimism is warranted, but at least he's trying, a familiar motif in Hunter's poems.

Musically, "High Time" is a slow ballad, often plaintive in tone. The level of instrumentation varies within the song: sometimes it's quiet and sometimes there's a lot of music going on. The end of the song is more abrupt than many Dead songs, with basically no outro at all other than a fade after the last chorus. The intro, on the other hand, often seemed to be a bit of an adventure. It often wasn't clear if the band was just noodling or perhaps searching for the right opening chords or improvising around the musical motif. There's a good vocal bridge in the song, where the energy level usually increases.

In the first performance of "High Time," on June 21, 1969, at the Fillmore East in New York City, Jerry Garcia sounds a bit like an old folk singer sitting on the front stoop straining his voice to get the high notes at the outset. The song starts slowly, as it does in many live versions of this song, but the energy soon picks up. This version illustrates the Grateful Dead's skill in raising and lowering the energy level repeatedly in the same song, unusually so in a first performance. You can hear this version here: (High Time #2).

June 9, 1976, is the breakout performance of "High Time" after a six-year break and a gap of 341 shows. This show, in Boston, has "High Time" later in the second set, but not in the "Jerry ballad" slot. This version was released on the album *Road Trips, Volume 4, No. 5* (D2:T7) and is also accessible as an audience performance (High Time #3). Perhaps because the tempo is quite slow in this version, we can better appreciate the complex sequence of chord changes in this song. The energy level by the last verse is remarkable—this has become a "power ballad," not a folk song about the back-to-the-land movement.

Headyversion.com's number one version of "High Time" is from May 17, 1977, in Tuscaloosa, Alabama, at the University of Alabama, when it was played in the middle of the first set. Listen to it here: (High Time #4). This recording lets you hear Keith's piano clearly, and the backing vocals are excellent. There's a bit of an outro before the fade. This is a sweet version to listen to, as is this later version, from August 11, 1987, which Barry recorded at Red Rocks: (High Time #5).

Finally, after skipping all of 1989 and with only one performance of "High Time" in 1988, the Dead broke it out again on June 8, 1990, at the Cal Expo Amphitheatre in Sacramento, California, where they played it in the first set. This version has a solid introduction, in which the band progresses through the chord sequence in a lilting, light version of the song's motif. It's a pleasant version to listen to, and you can access it here: (High Time #6). The Grateful Dead's tours in early 1990 were arguably the best of the late-year tours, and that's reflected here in this version.

The Grateful Dead's ballads and semi-ballads were famously rotated in the Jerry ballad slot toward the end of the second set. "High Time" never quite reached that status in the Dead's rotation, but instead became a regular if infrequent number in the first set. We recommend "High Time" as a ballad worth your consideration because of its lyrics and its complex music.

"I Need a Miracle"

"I Need a Miracle," (aka Miracle), written and composed by Bob Weir and John Perry Barlow, was a steady part of the Grateful Dead's concert rotation from its first performance on August 30, 1978, through its final performance on June 30, 1995. It was performed every year, usually more than ten times, for a total of 271 live performances. It occasionally appeared in the first set in 1978 and 1979, but Miracle resided in the second set from 1980 onward with only four exceptions. As the years passed, Miracle began to appear regularly right after the Drumz > Space segment of the second set. It served as a rousing return to the more structured musical portion of the second set, and it was often followed by a "Jerry ballad" a song like "Stella Blue," "Black Peter," "Wharf Rat," or "Days Between."

Lyrically, "I Need a Miracle" is an upfront ode to pleasure and excess: (Miracle #1). There are no cowboys, no outlaws, and no down-and-outs in this song. Our hero is looking for fun, preferably with a woman "twice my age," height, or weight, depending on the verse, and the song offers a clear summary: "too much of everything is just enough." On the other side of the coin, seeking with such intensity might mean you don't already have what you need, hence some angst and worry about the future (don't forget the song's title).

Deadheads certainly never forgot; the idea of the miracle has passed into Deadhead culture in two ways. First, Miracle is a great sing-along: the audience routinely sang out the chorus line, "I need a miracle every day." In later years, Bob Weir would *skip* this line so everyone could hear the audience singing it. Second, from around the time Weir introduced the song, people without tickets to a Dead show would stand outside the venue with one index finger upraised over their heads, signaling they needed a ticket, or a miracle. Anybody with an extra ticket would have no problem finding someone willing to take it. This concept is recognized by the Grateful Dead as well: the front cover of the album *Dozin' at the Knick* depicts this scene.

Musically, "I Need a Miracle" is a rocker. Garcia's guitar filled between lines of the verses, and Lesh played a clear thumping bass line. There's strong punctuation after many of the lines. The vocal bridge midway through the song where the band riffs on the phrase, "I need a miracle every day" is always fun to hear, to find out what new twist the band might add. For a good example, listen to the Dead's performance of Miracle at the Giza Theater in Egypt on September 16, 1978, which was released on the album *Rocking the Cradle: Egypt 1978* (D1:T7). This was only the fourth live performance of Miracle and is available here: (Miracle #2). In this early version, the solo is the song's outro. Voters at headyersion.com have deemed this the best overall performance of Miracle, but we think later versions are better.

On September 12, 1987, in Landover, Maryland, the Dead played a short version of Miracle, just over three minutes long. This recording, (Miracle #3), is particularly good for listening to the audience sing the chorus line along with Bob Weir. This version has the vocalizing improvisation after the last verse, with a short outro as the band segues into "Morning Dew."

The Grateful Dead's show on September 16, 1990, at Madison Square Garden in New York City, included an excellent version of Miracle. This show was released as *Dick's Picks, Volume 9* (D3:T4), the only version of Miracle that appears in the *Dick's Picks* series. It's accessible here: (Miracle #4). This performance is a good standard against which to measure other versions of Miracle. The tempo is up-beat, and the bass line has a lot of good improvising. The vocal bridge is short and excellent, and the outro is a good jam. Plus the audience gives it their all during the sing-along line.

March 21, 1993, saw the Dead play Miracle in the second set, after the Space segment. That version (Miracle #5) starts slowly with an extended intro but then begins to rock. On this audience recording, you can hear the audience virtually drown out Bob Weir when he sings the chorus line. Indeed, on the fourth iteration, he doesn't sing the line, leaving it to the crowd. After the outro, the band segues into the Jerry ballad, which on this occasion was "Days Between."

"I Need a Miracle" was a lighthearted, upbeat addition to the Dead's repertoire and never failed to get positive audience reactions, especially when it was played in the second set as a complement to, and in contrast with, "Space" segments. Part of the reason why this is an essential song for us in this book is this contextual point: as a standalone song, Miracle may not be the best number the Dead performed, but in the context of a good second set, it was a great song. We hope you enjoy listening to it.

"Iko Iko"

In this book we have included songs from the "traditional" songbook. "Iko Iko" (aka Iko) is one of these, although it was probably written by James "Sugar Boy" Crawford. The traditional songs we've chosen either have interesting histories or illustrate the Dead's talent of rearranging traditional songs. In this case, Iko is a good example of both.

Iko's backstory is interesting: the song is African in origin, in style, if not lyrics. It developed as a folk song in New Orleans, with lyrics that spoke to the history of the "Indian" tribes that organized in the African American community around Mardi Gras. There are many sources for the details of this history, including a summary by Oliver Trager (1997, 195–96) and the American Blues Scene (Iko #1). David Dodd's blog also has interesting insights into both the song and the ways it has passed into the culture of the Deadheads: (Iko #2).

When discussing Iko, most sources mention the Dixie Cups, a "girl group" from New Orleans that probably made the most well-known recording of Iko. That version is on the album *The Music Never Stopped: Roots of the Grateful Dead* (T3) and is also accessible here as a video: (Iko #3). If you are not familiar with Iko, it is worth your time to watch this short video as a benchmark against which to compare what the Grateful Dead did in their own arrangement.

The song is very simple, as can be seen in the Dixie Cups version. The lyrics are available here: (Iko #4). The Grateful Dead did not change the lyrics in any appreciable manner, so the question becomes: what *did* the Dead do with this song? In a word, they arranged it to sound like a Grateful Dead song. There's quite a contrast between the Dead's performances of Iko and that of the Dixie Cups. The Grateful Dead played Iko 165 times, in either set, with its final performance on July 5, 1995. As time passed, it became more of an early second set song, perhaps to get people up and dancing after the set break, but sometimes it was later in the set, to change the mood.

Iko's first performance was on May 15, 1977, amid perhaps the band's greatest touring season, and the Dead played Iko deep in the second set, with "Saint Stephen" > Iko > "Not Fade Away" (aka NFA) as one continuous medley of songs. That show was released in the box set *May 1977* (D3:T2) and is also available here: (Iko #5), where the first two minutes or so sound like the intro to NFA. But the Dead segue into Iko, if only for a minute or two, using the same tempo as NFA. After this quick excursion, the Dead segue back into NFA and carry on.

The Dead didn't play Iko that frequently, and our second recommendation, February 4, 1979, is almost two years after the 5/15/77 show, but it's only eleven performances after that first one. Here again Iko is deep in the second set, and the Dead play it coming out of the Drumz/Space segment, which surely helped the crowd transition to the rest of that set. The tempo is quite funky on this version: (Iko #6). It takes a while for the song to emerge from the intro, but when it does, the crowd gets to hear some excellent bass work.

The performance on November 2, 1985, in Richmond, Virginia, is also worth listening to: (Iko #7). At that show, the Dead used Iko as the opener for the second set, something that happened with some regularity in the mid-1980s. This excellent audience recording captures the crowd's excitement—if you've seen the Dead, you can imagine the crowd dancing. The tempo now is quicker, with typically excellent work by Lesh on lead bass. This version has a great outro: it takes the volume down and then back up.

Bob's personal favorite is September 16, 1990, at New York's Madison Square Garden, released on *Dick's Picks, Volume 9* (D2:T2) and available here: (Iko #8). What the Dixie Cups did in two minutes the Grateful Dead here turn into a ten-minute sing- and clap-along. "Hey now!" This is the Dead at their best: Dixieland-style improvisation with a hint of a reggae beat. The solos have the band exploring the motif in each player's own way, Dixieland style, coming back together for the next round of vocals. The crowd clearly appreciates Brent Mydland's work on keyboards. The outro

Grateful Dead—Alpine Valley, July 1989

Jerry Garcia—Sandstone Amphitheater, July 4, 1990

Phil Lesh—Sandstone Amphitheater, July 4, 1990

Bob Weir—Sandstone Amphitheater, July 4, 1990

Brent Mydland—Alpine Valley, July 1989

Grateful Dead—Laguna Seca Raceway, May 1987

Jerry Garcia—Telluride Town Park, August 1987

Phil Lesh—Telluride Town Park, August 1987

Bob Weir—Alpine Valley, July 1989

Brent Mydland—Telluride Town Park, August 1987

Grateful Dead—Greek Theatre, August 1987

Bob Weir & Bill Kreutzmann—Telluride Town Park, August 1987

Chris Barnes & Bob Weir—St. Louis, MO, July 4, 1995

Tapers Setting Up at Shoreline Amphitheater, May 1992

Crowd makes an unbroken chain at Sandstone, July 1990

in this version is particularly tight. Everything came together in this performance; it may well be the best you'll hear.

And then there's the April Fool's day show in the Nassau Coliseum on April 1, 1993. At that show, Barney the purple dinosaur sat in on bass during Iko. Definitely a special treat, and you can hear it here: (Iko #9). Barney was apparently recruited during the set break, as the Dead opened the second set with Iko. From the audience response, you can tell that this is a crowd who grew up watching Barney on television. He's not bad as a bass player, either, and he seems to have put on quite a show, if crowd responses are to be believed.

We selected Iko as one of the Dead's essential songs because of the Grateful Dead's arrangement of a simple folk song with a fascinating history. Readers new to the Grateful Dead experience can see in this song the way the Dead were able to adapt songs to their own playing style, always drawing from the many roots of the American music traditions. We hope you liked the recommended selections.

"It Must Have Been the Roses"

"It Must Have Been the Roses" (aka Roses) is sometimes attributed to the Hunter-Garcia partnership, but David Dodd (2005, 221) and Garcia himself attribute it solely to Hunter, who originally composed the song as a bluegrass number (Trager 1997, 205). Since the Dead played this song at a very slow tempo, as opposed to a typical bluegrass tempo, we can speculate that Garcia may have had more to do with the performance of Roses, perhaps enough to be listed as coauthor.

Roses was introduced on the album *From the Mars Hotel*, released in June 1974. The Dead had started to perform it live earlier that year, on February 22, 1974, at Winterland in San Francisco. They played Roses thirty-one times in 1974, its first year in the rotation. Altogether they played Roses 159 times over the years, always at least once or twice a year. The final performance for Roses was on June 22, 1995, in Albany, New York, at the Knickerbocker Arena.

In its early years, Roses was played mostly in the first set but also dozens of times in the second set. After 1982, Roses became a first set song and stayed there for its remaining performances. In 1980, the Dead played Roses in acoustic sets on ten occasions. Although slow and pensive musically, Roses was rarely, if ever, performed in the Jerry ballad slot late in the second set. Instead, it was usually played as a separate, self-contained song in either the first set or quite early in the second set.

It has been said that it's harder to play music well at a slow tempo than at high speed; Roses is evidence of how good the Grateful Dead were musically. Performances of Roses are typically well orchestrated and illustrate the Dead's tendency toward several "lead" instruments improvising around the basic melody. Just about any version of the song includes typical Grateful Dead–style ensemble music, with instruments playing off each other, with more or less emphasis on a staccato style, depending on the version. It's not unlike a good chamber quintet.

The lyrics are the key to Roses, and you can see them here: (Roses #1). This is a love song, one speaking to the beauty of commitment despite the vicissitudes of time. Our narrator, perhaps because of the roses, says he cannot leave his lover, but he does. He spends years at sea—perhaps a symbolic reference to confusion—but ultimately returns. In the final verse, the couple seem to be older and wiser, but as is often the case with senior citizens, "no one comes 'round anymore." In the end, Roses is a bittersweet tune—then again, so is life.

On February 24, 1974 (Roses #2), at Winterland in San Francisco, the second time the Grateful Dead performed Roses, it was the second song of the second set, after "Cumberland Blues," a fast-paced, bluegrass-sounding song. Roses, with its slow tempo, was certainly a contrast. The band followed Roses with "Big River," their cover of Johnny Cash's song, also quite up-tempo. The keyboards in this version show Keith Godchaux's tendency to play piano as a rhythm instrument. And we can hear Phil Lesh's high vocal backup, not a great asset in this case. Yet for an early version of the song, it's clear that the band was prepared, because the performance is tight.

From 1974 we jump to April 9, 1989, in Louisville, Kentucky (Roses #3), where Roses is played in the first set between "Walking Blues" and "Me and My Uncle," two songs with faster tempos than Roses. Again, Roses provides a contrast, in terms of both tempo and genre, even though "Walking Blues" is not significantly up-tempo. Here in mid-1989, Garcia's voice is strong. His counterpoint-style guitar playing is more evident than in the earlier 2/24/74 show. And there's now a Garcia solo before the final singing of the chorus. This is an excellent quality audience recording.

Finally, we refer you to July 24, 1994, at Soldier Field in Chicago, available here: (Roses #4). At this show, Roses was preceded by "It's All Over Now," a Shirley and Bobby Womack cover, also covered by the Rolling Stones. Roses was followed by "El Paso," the Marty Robbins cover. Both of these songs are up-tempo, relatively high-energy songs. This performance is worth listening to as a comparison with earlier, stronger performances of Roses.

Focusing narrowly on "It Must Have Been the Roses" shows us that this love song is an essential Grateful Dead song simply because of its lyrics, its message. But incorporating a little more context, particularly the songs before and after Roses, lets us see another aspect of Grateful Dead shows: while their most famous songs might be up-tempo rockers like "Sugar Magnolia," "Truckin'," "U.S. Blues," or "Touch of Grey," every Dead show had multiple changes of tempo and mood. Most of the ballads that appeared in the Jerry ballad slot near the end of the second set are obvious examples, but "It Must Have Been the Roses" also illustrates this dynamic, in either of the two sets at any given show.

"Jack a Roe"

"Jack a Roe" is a lilting, folksy song that the Grateful Dead performed either in acoustic sets in a series of shows in 1980 or in the first set of electric shows; it was played only one time in the second set in 115 performances. This is a traditional song, one that the Dead adapted from the treasure trove of American folk music as heard in the folk movement, the jug band music movement, and "old-timey" early country music movement in the 1960s.

You could say there's a marriage trilogy among the "folk songs" the Grateful Dead played. In "Cold Rain and Snow," as mentioned earlier, the hero has a nagging wife and he wishes he were elsewhere. In fact, in the original versions of the song—though not in the Dead's version—he murders her. "Peggy-O," coming later, also tells a tale of unrequited love: Peggy-O would wed "sweet William-O," but she fears her parents would reject him because of his relative lack of wealth: "your guineas are too few." Enraged, he declares war but is killed, leaving her to lament. Finally, we have "Jack a Roe," a folk song that again addresses the theme of love and marriage. For more on these thoughts, see Josephine McQuail's fine essay (1994): (Jack a Roe #1).

"Jack a Roe" is a song about a young woman in love with Jack the sailor; the lyrics are here: (Jack a Roe #2). In the original folk song, her father forbids her to pursue this relationship. In the Dead's version, she is prevented from pursuing it initially because Jack goes sailing off to war. She decides to follow him, "dressed in men's array." This is perhaps the only Grateful Dead reference to the theme of transgender behavior, a much more visible trend at present than it was in the 1970s. Our heroine sails away herself, finds Jack wounded, and gets a doctor to heal him. In the final verse, there's a happy ending: in a surprising twist, the narrator suddenly shifts from a historical tale to a seemingly current conversation with his listener, turning the song into a marriage proposal: "this couple they got married, so why not you and me?" Maybe the whole story is just a setup?

Musically, as mentioned earlier, this is a folk song performed something like Dixieland style with precise guitar playing and excellent musical support from the band. We particularly like the strong punctuation at the end of the song. "Jack a Roe" is a stable song and fairly short, so there was no serious improvisation, no extended jams. Like many other first set songs, it's self-contained, with a clear start and ending.

The Dead introduced "Jack a Roe" on May 13, 1977, in Chicago (Jack a Roe #3). With the exception of an extended intro as the band seemed to be getting their bearings, this version is not that different from others you will find. Garcia's solos, especially the second, are ringing. The performance on October 10, 1980, at the Warfield Theater in San Francisco, is an excellent acoustic performance that appeared on the album *Reckoning* (T8) and is also available as a soundboard recording (Jack a Roe #4). On March 19, 1990, in Hartford, Connecticut, the Dead performed an electric "Jack a Roe," a song that was released as part of the compilation album *Spring 1990: So Glad You Made It* (D1:T8). It is also available as an audience recording here: (Jack a Roe #5), better to hear the crowd's responses: clearly they liked Garcia's solos.

As you can hear in the selections referenced earlier, "Jack a Roe" is a great Grateful Dead song, but one without significant change or evolution during the years between 1977 and its final performance on July 8, 1995, the band's second-to-last performance in Chicago. So for a change of pace, we provide two links to other artists who have performed "Jack a Roe."

The first of these is Bob Dylan, who played "Jack a Roe" live on the *Late Show* on November 16, 1993, available here: (Jack a Roe #6). Note that Dylan simplifies the chord structure of the song. Early in the song, a banjo dominates, which may be historically accurate in terms of the song's origins. Later the mix has much less banjo and more acoustic guitar. And of course Dylan sings it in his trademark style, in which he approximates the correct notes. With all due respect to the Nobel laureate, this recording helps illustrate why we are fans of the Grateful Dead.

Finally, Joan Baez recorded the song on her live 1963 album *Joan Baez in Concert: Part 2*. This version predates the Dead, who likely listened to it at some point. Baez's version is true to the tune, its chord structures, and its lyrics, but she plays it at a very slow tempo: it's just this side of a dirge, which seems odd for a song with a happy ending. This version is available here: (Jack a Roe #7). If you've listened to those two selections by Dylan and Baez, you might like to conclude with Barry's excellent recording of the Dead doing "Jack a Roe" on July 21, 1990, at Tinley Park, Illinois: (Jack a Roe #8).

"Jack a Roe" is a traditional folk tune that the Grateful Dead adapted and performed to great success for almost two decades. Or maybe it's a love song wrapped in a proposal of marriage. It's "essential," in our thinking, because it illustrates the great variety of styles in the Dead's skill set. We love it.

"Jack Straw"

This song is one of the few written by Bob Weir with Robert Hunter. Weir sometimes changed the lyrics provided by Hunter, and this didn't lead to a long-term writing relationship like Hunter had with Garcia. In any case, "Jack Straw" was another mainstay in the Grateful Dead's repertoire that was played 473 times beginning on October 19, 1971 (Jack #1), at the University of Minnesota in Minneapolis. This was quite a remarkable show because it was also the debut of three new Garcia/Hunter tunes, "Tennessee Jed," "Comes a Time," and "Ramble on Rose." If that wasn't enough to excite fans, there were also two more new Weir tunes: "Mexicali Blues," this one with lyrics by John Perry Barlow, and "One More Saturday Night," with music and words by Weir. Finally, this was the first show with Keith Godchaux on keyboards, brought in to aid the increasingly frail Ron "Pigpen" McKernan. The last performance of "Jack Straw" was July 8, 1995, (Jack #2), at Soldier Field in Chicago, the next-to-last Grateful Dead show.

There seems to be a theme of "Jacks" in Grateful Dead lyrics. With this song, we have "Jack Straw from Wichita"; in "Ramble on Rose" we have "Jack the Ripper," "Jack and Jill," and "Wolfman Jack." Then there's the Dead's traditional song "Jack-a-Roe," with the line "They call me Jack-a-Roe." And finally there's the Dead's "Brown Eyed Women," with the line "Gently Jack Jones won't you come to me."

"Jack Straw" is another of Weir's "cowboy" songs, which include a cover of Marty Robbins's "El Paso," Weir's own "Mexicali Blues," and a cover of Johnny Cash's "Big River." These are all songs that typically appeared in the first set of a Dead show as the band warmed up for the second, more improvisational set.

"Jack Straw" is the story of a couple of thieves on the run after robbing and killing a watchman. Rather than a single narrator telling the story, the usual approach for Dead songs, this one is a conversation between Jack and his buddy Shannon. Weir sang as Jack and Garcia as Shannon. Surprising to us was that Weir wrote some of the lines of the song, those told by Jack. The killing of the watchman isn't enough, and before the song is over, Jack has killed Shannon for "moving much too slow." At least that's *our* take on it. You can find David Dodd's thoughts on it here: (Jack #3).

Musically, "Jack Straw" starts out slowly with an acoustic guitar–type riff followed by the vocal introduction to the story. The tempo picks up as Shannon tells his tale of theft and murder. Jack's response, in the same quicker tempo that remains throughout the rest of the song until the coda, repeats the opening refrain, "we can share the women; we can share the wine." The vocals are interesting, but it's Garcia's guitar that really aroused the crowd—as is so often the case, of course. On the vocal side, one of the great moments at any Dead show occurred when the band came out of one of those magnificent Garcia solos and the two sang the line "Jack Straw from Wichita, cut his buddy down." While "Jack Straw" is a short song, clocking in at only around six minutes, it's still a crowd-pleaser and deserves its status as "essential."

"Jack Straw" was never recorded for a studio album but made its first recorded appearance on the three-LP *Europe '72* album in 1973. (Barry sold this album in his record store in Kansas City at that time.) Since then, it's appeared on more the sixty official releases, and you can see a full list through 2016 here: (Jack #4). "Jack Straw" is also found on the more recent eleven-CD box set *May 1977: Get Shown the Light*.

Remember that this is a first set song with limited improvisation, so there won't be as much variation among versions as a second set song. With that in mind, here are some recommendations. Start with August 27, 1972, at the Old Renaissance Faire Grounds in Veneta, Oregon: (Jack #5). This is an excellent performance at the famous Sunshine Daydream show. This is from 1972, which was a terrific year for all Grateful Dead concerts. This "Jack Straw" is number two on the headyversion.com list.

January 11, 1979, Nassau Coliseum, Uniondale, New York (Jack #6), has a marvelous Garcia solo—how does Garcia squeeze in so many notes? Weir changes one of the lines to "we used to play for acid, now we play for Clive," referring to Clive Davis, head of Arista Records, the Dead's new record company. This version gets the highest ranking from headyversion.com. February 10, 1979, at Memorial Hall in Kansas City (Jack #7), is a lesser-known show from this same period, and Barry's fourth Dead show. It also has a Garcia solo that really gets the crowd fired up. You'll like it!

For our last recommendation, check out September 19, 1990, Madison Square Garden, New York (Jack #8), which shows a more mature Grateful Dead. It features Bruce Hornsby's singing and piano playing along with a very loud New York crowd: well-deserved support for the band.

"Lazy Lightnin'" > "Supplication"

This is another twofer: two songs that were nearly always played together and in fact were written as a pair by Bob Weir and John Perry Barlow in 1975 during the Dead's hiatus. It might be surprising that "Lazy Lightnin'" > "Supplication" is included here, since it was only part of the Dead's active list of songs from June 3, 1976 (Lazy #1), until October 31, 1984 (Lazy #2), when it was dropped after 111 performances. "Supplication" was played a few more times either with the lyrics or simply as a jam. The song pair appeared as a studio recording only on the *Kingfish* LP in 1976, with Weir playing with that band, which he occasionally did.

This is another of Barry's favorites, but like so many of his favorites, it's hard to articulate why. Much of it has to do with the transition from "Lazy Lightnin'" into "Supplication," as well as Garcia's guitar work throughout. At the same time, Weir's vocals are also a plus, especially during "Supplication," where he's pleading with the object of his affection to "heed my supplication." And the beginning of the song's musical introduction in the unusual 7/8 time signature makes what's coming next unmistakable. "Supplication" (with lyrics) was played by itself once on May 22, 1993, at Shoreline Amphitheater in Mountain View, California, and a "Supplication Jam" (without lyrics) was played thirteen times between 1985 and 1995, as well as once September 4, 1984, at the Civic Center in Providence, Rhode Island, a show Bob remembers fondly.

The lyrics for "Lazy Lightnin'" > "Supplication" tell the story of a man who is fanatical about a woman with "sleepy fire" in her eyes, and he has found that she is "messin' with my reason" to that point that it's become "an obsession but it's pleasing," despite that fact that she's "kinda fright'nin'." In spite of these mixed emotions, as the song shifts to "Supplication," he begins to hoot and holler for her to give him some "indication if all of this is real." You can read all the lyrics here: (Lazy #3).

Because of the relatively limited number of live performances of "Lazy Lightnin'" > "Supplication"—it was in the live repertoire for only eight years—and because it never appeared on a Dead studio album, there are a limited number of official releases for this pair of fine songs. In total there are only about twenty official releases, which you can see here: (Lazy #4).

Barry considers himself very lucky to have seen three versions of "Lazy Lightnin'" > "Supplication," as well as two versions of the "Supplication Jam." You may feel the same if you listen to a few of our suggestions and experience the energy build in this song. Here are some we recommend, including several of the versions Barry saw. Try October 28, 1977, from Memorial Hall in Kansas City (Lazy #5); July 7, 1981, from Municipal Auditorium, also in Kansas City (Lazy #6); or September 6, 1983, from Red Rocks, near Denver: (Lazy #7). To hear the "Supplication Jam," check out June 24, 1991, from Sandstone Amphitheatre in Bonner Springs, Kansas: (Lazy #8).

Of course, there are other notable versions worth listening to, as well, such as the one from New Haven, Connecticut, on May 5, 1977, in the *Get Shown the Light* box set and here: (Lazy #9). This show was just three days before the classic Barton Hall show at Cornell University. Or try the version from Nassau Coliseum on May 15, 1980: (Lazy #10). To hear a unique version of "Supplication," check out this version, where it's sandwiched in the middle of "Playing in the Band" at the College of William and Mary in Williamsburg, Virginia, on September 24, 1976: (Lazy #11). Finally, here's another fine audience version of "Supplication" from May 22, 1993, at Shoreline Amphitheatre: (Lazy #12).

As we often say in these song reviews, do be sure to listen to more than one version of "Lazy Lightnin'" > "Supplication" so you can see how the performances changed over time, as well as how the audience responds as the energy builds in each version.

"Lazy River Road"

"Lazy River Road" debuted on February 21, 1993 (Lazy #1), at the Oakland Coliseum Arena, one of the last three songs by Garcia and Hunter that were added to the Dead's repertoire. It was played sixty-five times, with the last performance at the Dead's final show in Chicago on July 9, 1995: (Lazy #2). It was played regularly during its three years of life, including twenty-nine times in 1993, twenty-four times in 1994, and twelve times in 1995, which was really only half a year of touring for the Dead. "Lazy River Road" is not a serious rocker nor a stretch-out-and-jam song. Instead it's a laid-back, easygoing song that shows how the Dead had matured after twenty-eight years of touring when it premiered. "Jaunty" comes to mind to describe it.

Hunter's lyrics for "Lazy River Road" provide a charming song for Garcia to sing about "love's sweet song." It's peppered with delightful words and phrases that only Hunter could write. Where else would we find the "Sycamore Slough," "Shadowfall Ward," or the "Seminole Square"? The story itself centers on the narrator's love for these unusual Hunteresque places, along with his willingness to meet her if she'll simply call for him. After all, he let all the others pass by because "I only wanted you." And how about "moonlight wails as hound dogs bay" or "stars fall down in buckets like rain"? Barry's favorite line is "night time double-clutches into today like a truck downshifting its load." Overall, the lyrics once again demonstrate Hunter's poetic genius, and you can find them here: (Lazy #3). Musically, "Lazy River Road" shows how well Garcia could write a simple and lovely tune to showcase Hunter's lyrics, part of their songwriting symbiosis. Despite the laidback playing and lack of improvisation, it's not a short tune, typically running seven to eight minutes.

The only official release of "Lazy River Road" is on the *So Many Roads* box set released in 1995, a studio rehearsal performance from February 18, 1993 (D5:T5).

This song, along with several other Garcia/Hunter compositions including "Liberty," "So Many Roads," "Standing on the Moon," and "Days Between," as well as some by Weir and by Lesh from this same period, were part of the never-completed album the Dead had been rehearsing before Garcia died. The lack of official releases is probably due, at least in part, to the decline of Garcia's voice and playing in 1994 and 1995.

Barry saw "Lazy River Road" thirteen times, the first on March 14, 1993 (Lazy #4), just three weeks after the debut. This was a memorable show in Cleveland because the show scheduled there for March 13 had been cancelled due to a blizzard, and Deadheads were grateful to have the second night's show to enjoy. Another version of "Lazy River Road" on May 20, 1995, was memorable to Barry for what came after the song finished. It was a hot, sunny day at the Silver Dome stadium in the Las Vegas desert, and people were literally passing out from the heat. After finishing "Lazy River Road," Jerry spoke from the stage, which he seldom did at that time in the Dead's career, and said, "Just go ahead and pass all the unconscious people up here to the front. They'll prop 'em up somewhere, and we'll stack 'em like logs. We're not doin' this for fun, ya know!" Of course that elicited a cheer from the crowd. Check it out here: (Lazy #5).

Despite the lack of official releases of "Lazy River Road," you can find some fine live versions. Here are two more that Barry saw and we both recommend: first a soundboard recording from Memphis on April Fool's Day 1995 (Lazy #6), and the second from Deer Creek Amphitheatre in Noblesville, Indiana, on June 23, 1993: (Lazy #7). Two other enjoyable versions are from the University of North Carolina, Chapel Hill, on March 25, 1993 (Lazy #8), and from Madison Square Garden on September 22, 1993, which features David Murray as guest on saxophone: (Lazy #9). Finally, here's one Barry recorded on May 20, 1995, in Las Vegas: (Lazy #10). This is a sweet version with that characteristic rolling sound the Dead perfected.

We've pointed you to several versions of "Lazy River Road" for your listening enjoyment. It's a lovely tune, so check it out, especially the versions from 1993. At that point Garcia was still in fine voice and plays it beautifully, although the performances from 1994 and 1995 sound much better than they're often give credit for. This song is a great window into what the Dead sounded like in their last years on the road.

"Looks Like Rain"

"Looks Like Rain" (aka LL Rain) is a Bob Weir and John Perry Barlow collaboration that was introduced to the Grateful Dead's live repertoire on March 21, 1972, at the Academy of Music in New York City: (LLR #1). The debut is a special treat with Garcia playing steel guitar. This was one of the seven shows that was a "warm-up" for the Europe '72 tour. LL Rain was an ongoing and regular part of live performances through the rest of the Grateful Dead's career except for 1974 and 1975, when it was not played at all. In total, LL Rain was played 417 times, with the last performance on June 30, 1995: (LLR #2). It was one of more than a dozen songs introduced in

1971 and 1972 that were not included on a studio album. However, it was recorded on Weir's *Ace* LP album in 1972 (LLR #3), which was an unofficial Dead album.

For some reason, it seems as if Bob Weir is not always given the respect he deserves by some in the Deadhead community. Part of it, we suspect, is because he was always in Garcia's shadow. The truth is that Weir is a unique rhythm guitar player and a fine songwriter. "Looks Like Rain" is another example of his songwriting ability, together with Barlow's lovely lyrics. This is a story about a lover whose partner has moved on, leaving him behind to continue to love her "and that's not gonna change," despite suffering "hurt again and again." Although Barlow's lyrics are typically more literal than Hunter's, they are still sweet and touching. The opening verse demonstrates this when the storyteller awakens to find his lover gone and "the covers were still warm where you'd been laying." He becomes filled with dread when he realizes "you might not be sleeping here again." He goes on about his love for her until the closing verse, telling her "I only want to hold you, I don't want to tie you down" and "my landscape would be empty if you were gone." It's a simple love song with a beautiful melody and powerful singing by Weir. One line remains a mystery, however: "I'll still sing you love songs written in the letters of your name." What does that mean? You can find all the lyrics here: (LLR #4).

Musically, LL Rain presents as a mid-tempo ballad. It opens with music that resembles the prelude to "Weather Report Suite," but soon shifts to a fuller sound. By the end of the first verse, a heavy bass line tells us that this is not exactly a folk ballad. There are breaks and pauses to punctuate the lines around the title, "it surely looks like rain." In most versions, Garcia's guitar lead hits an emotional high note just at the end of his solo after the second verse. This instrumental section generally is powerful, and Garcia's ending note masterfully transitions the tone back to the languid ballad style of the opening verses. Many Grateful Dead songs alternate between relatively quiet music and powerful, loud rock and roll, and LL Rain is a good example, as well as one of the best of the Weir/Barlow collaborations. Weir's vocals toward the end of the song, with repeated iterations of the "looks like rain, feels like rain, here comes the rain." line, with vocal improvisations, is particularly fun to hear. In many of the 1970s versions, Donna Godchaux's backup vocals complement Weir's intensity as the song ends.

There are many fine live versions of "Looks Like Rain" in the official releases, and you can see a full list through 2016 here: (LLR #5). One in particular that we recommend is on *Dick's Picks, Volume 33* from October 9, 1976, in Oakland. It can also be found here in an audience recording; unfortunately there is no soundboard version available: (LLR #6).

Here are some other excellent live versions of LL Rain that we recommend. One that ranks high on the headyversion.com list is from September 3, 1977, released on *Dick's Picks, Volume 15* (D1:T6), the Englishtown, New Jersey, show. Here's a nice matrix recording: (LLR #7).

Here's another matrix recording from a later show, March 28, 1990, at the Nassau Coliseum, New York. This version shows the later tone and MIDI effects of Garcia's guitar, along with a mature band, and it's from the Dead's "last great tour" in spring 1990. It was officially released on the *Spring 1990 (The Other One)* eighteen-CD box set. This one comes complete with thunder as Weir belts out "I can't stand the rain": (LLR #8).

Between February 1979 and June 1994, Barry saw twenty-eight performances of "Looks Like Rain." Of these, July 7, 1981, in Kansas City is another performance we recommend: (LLR #9). This very good matrix recording shows the Dead in the early 1980s, an often overlooked period. This LL Rain could change your mind about that. Listen to the wonderful use of sound dynamics as the band goes from a whisper to near roar depending on the lyrics being sung. The last version Barry saw was at Cal-Expo in Sacramento, California, on June 10, 1994 (LLR #10), and we recommend it. It starts out quiet and slow, and quickly gets approval from the audience. Weir's vocals are typically well done on this song, and that's the case in this version, as well. Given Garcia's declining health at this time, he sounds very good in this performance, as does Lesh, Welnick on keyboards, and the drummers in this ten-minute performance, which is a couple of minutes longer than most versions of LL Rain.

Regardless of the era or performance, "Looks Like Rain" is always a beautiful Grateful Dead song we're sure you'll enjoy.

"Loser"

"Loser," by Garcia and Hunter, is another of the Grateful Dead's songs about outlaws and marginal characters. "Loser" was a regular part of the Dead's rotation: they played it live every year after the song was introduced in February 1971, except for the 1975 hiatus. They performed "Loser" 345 times over the years, until its final performance on June 28, 1995. "Loser" was first recorded on the studio album *Garcia* in 1972 and was reissued as a CD in 1988 (D1:T4). Garcia played all the instruments on this album except the drums, which Bill Kreutzmann handled.

"Loser" is another example of the Dead's focus on the "dark side" of society. But unlike songs such as "Jack Straw," "Candyman," "Deal," or "Mexicali Blues," all of which include more upbeat music, "Loser" comes with heavier overtones. The tempo is moderate, almost plodding, as if chronicling some unstoppable force. It's a long, slow song, usually timing in around eight minutes. "Loser" is self-contained, not a song in which the Dead did much jamming, although Garcia did improvise during the solo, sometimes doubling its length, for example. The characteristic solo in "Loser" comes with barely controlled feedback, as Garcia turned up the volume. This is probably the Dead's one song in which the lead guitar dominated the scene so overwhelmingly and plaintively. The overall impression is one of heaviness. Over the years, with few exceptions, the Dead played the song in the first set of the show.

As for the lyrics, the title seems to tell it all, and you can see them here: (Loser #1).

Our narrator is in a game of poker, convinced that he'll win the hand because he sees that his next draw will be the queen of diamonds: ("by the way she shines"). He needs money and tries to cajole a companion into giving him "ten gold dollars" so he can add it to his bet. We can almost see his eyes growing wider with anticipation, even as he realizes he's lost more than he's won over the years: "If I had a gun for every ace I've drawn. . . ." At the end of the song, we don't know if our hero has won or lost the hand, so we are left to speculate, though he seems to live up to the title of the song.

The lyrics for "Loser" also contain a minor mystery, namely the identity of "sweet Suzy," a phrase Garcia sings at the end of the first line of the chorus. In 1971 and 1972, the phrase appears in most, if not all, live performances, and it is included in the studio album version of the song. After 1972, the phrase was almost never sung, although there are exceptions. David Dodd in his Greatest Stories series mentions this (Loser #2), also providing an excellent perspective on all the lyrics of the song. Peter Wendel's blog (Loser #3) adds perspective to this mystery.

Finally, "SimpleMannStann," whose comments appear here (Loser #4), documents that sweet Suzy was included at least two times after 1972. The first was on June 18, 1974, at Freedom Hall, in Louisville, Kentucky. Most of this show is issued on *Road Trips, Vol. 2, No. 3*, though not "Loser," which, however, is accessible here: (Loser #5). Garcia sings "sweet Suzy" in the first chorus, but not in the second. And on January 10, 1979, at Nassau Coliseum (Loser #6), a good quality audience recording, again Garcia sings the phrase in the first chorus but not in the second. Again, this kind of discussion probably tells more about Deadhead obsessiveness than anything else.

Dead performances of "Loser" are high quality. We have several recommendations for your listening pleasure. The first of these is from May 19, 1977, at the Fox Theater in Atlanta, which is available on *Dick's Picks, Volume 29* (D1:T8) as well as here: (Loser #7). The Dead's 1977 spring tour is generally rated at or near the top of their thirty-year run, and this version is a good example. Garcia's vocals and solo are strong in this performance: the guitar solo takes us right to the edge of feedback. This version of "Loser" might be the standard against which to measure others.

Second, we suggest September 3, 1977, at Englishtown, New Jersey, available on *Dick's Picks, Volume 15* (D2:T3) and here: (Loser #8), another example of the overall excellence of the 1977 tours. This is a rare instance in which the Dead played "Loser" in the second set, albeit early, and preceding "Estimated Prophet," perhaps another song about a "loser" of a different type, as we saw earlier. Here, the tempo for "Loser" is a fraction faster than the Atlanta show, and the solo is not quite as dominant.

Finally, for a later version, listen to March 24, 1990, from Albany, New York (Loser #9), a good audience recording, perhaps worth listening to for that reason alone. During the solo, listen for the Dead playing Dixieland jazz as only they could. Lesh's bass brings the crowd to a roar. Much of this show appears on the compilation album *Dozin' at the Knick*, released in 1996, but "Loser" is not included. This performance of "Loser" is the top pick of the fans at headyversion.com.

As we suggested earlier, "Loser" feels negative, almost overwhelmingly so: the title, the minor chords, the aggressive tone of the music, even the lyrics—the entire package is dark. But wait, there's more. We are reminded that we buy Powerball lottery tickets every week, against all odds. Are we "losers"? Or are we complex individuals with perhaps our own—hopefully minor—dark side? We think Hunter was speaking to this side of all of us, not just to one spectacular "loser."

"Lost Sailor" > "Saint of Circumstance"

"Lost Sailor" (aka Sailor), composed by Bob Weir with lyrics by John Perry Barlow, was first performed by the Grateful Dead on August 4, 1979. It was performed 145 times, with 112 of these occurring during the song's first three years in the rotation. Sailor's final performance occurred on March 24, 1986. Sailor was performed as a solo song only four times before being paired with "Saint of Circumstance" (aka Saint). Once that pairing (aka Sailor > Saint) began, on August 31, 1979, Sailor was performed 141 more times. Over the almost seven years that ensued, Sailor was *not* followed immediately by Saint only once. On that one occasion, November 1, 1985, Sailor segued into "Drumz," and after the drum solo and "Space," the band segued back into Saint, so even that performance paired the two songs. Listen to this pairing: (Sailor #1).

It is safe to say that the two songs formed a tight partnership and can be treated as a single essential entry, even though after March 24, 1986, Sailor's final performance, the Dead continued to play "Saint of Circumstance" as a separate song until the end of their run in 1995. Since the Dead performed Saint 222 times, this means that Saint was played some eighty-three times without Sailor, all after 1986. If all that seems confusing, just listen to the music play.

Barlow's lyrics for "Lost Sailor" (Sailor #2) describe a sailor lost at sea who can't find the moon, who has been at sea too long. But at a deeper level, the song is about any one of us, perhaps lost without direction as we are tossed on the sea of life. Not many of us have such singularity of purpose—not to mention resources—so as to be free from the confusion of life. In premodern societies, perhaps there was little confusion, as there were few choices in life for most people. But since modernity has arrived, we do have choices; sometimes we aren't sure which choices to make, and sometimes we make the wrong choices while we are "going on a dream." As Barlow writes and Weir sings: "There is a price for being free."

Like Sailor and many of the songs produced through the collaboration of Bob Weir and John Perry Barlow, "Saint of Circumstance" includes long and complicated lyrical phrases (Sailor #3). The story is a familiar one: an individual down on his luck, hoping for a better shot at life, thinking that shot might be at hand, but there's "rain falling down," not to mention "holes in what's left of my reason." Ultimately there's uncertainty about—well, everything that matters. In spite of this, he persists and continues pursuing his dream, whatever it may be: "Sure don't know what I'm going for"; "I'm gonna go for it, for sure."

In his blog series Greatest Stories Ever Told (Sailor #4), David Dodd points to many continuities between these two songs, even speculating that they might have been composed originally as a single song. Sirius, the Dog Star, is referenced in both. The line "goin' on a dream" appears in each. Both songs allude to the power of "sirens" that must be resisted. And both songs stress ambiguity and persistence, as the narrator faces the perils and pitfalls of life. In both, there's optimism in the face of uncertainty, if not adversity.

As mentioned earlier, the first performance of these two songs together was on August 31, 1979, in Glens Falls, New York, and is accessible here: (Sailor #5). (The songs are listed as separate tracks.) This version, performed toward the end of the first set, times in at just under twelve minutes. Garcia's first solo in the song is powerful and elegant at the same time. Weir's improvisational lyrics toward the end of the song raise the energy level, and Garcia's counterpoint makes for a powerful transition to the second song, "Saint of Circumstance."

Saint has a punchier tone, compared to Sailor, which is slower, more of a ballad. Weir misses some of the lyrics in this first performance and changes others, but the Dead's musical intensity doesn't waver. At approximately three minutes, there's the familiar musical bridge that leads to the heavy tempo of the coda section: "Sure don't know what I'm going for, but I'm gonna' go for it for sure." This performance has all the intensity of later versions, if not the polish. At the end of the song, the Dead segue into "Deal" to end the first set.

Although Sailor > Saint was introduced in the first set in 1979, the pairing gradually moved to the second set. On August 10, 1982, at the University of Iowa (Sailor #6), the combined songs timed in at more than thirteen and a half minutes. As we would imagine, after three years and dozens of performances, the musical quality is tighter than on 8/31/79, referenced earlier. This 8/10/82 version is as powerful a version of this pairing as one could expect to find. Garcia's solo is a little more free-form, again providing counterpoint to Weir's singing early in the song. By about 3:30 in Sailor, Weir's vocals riff on the song's motifs, improvising lyrics as the intensity increases, thanks both to Garcia's lead and the band's overall strength.

When the Dead segue into "Saint of Circumstance," we are treated to a faster tempo and a solid heavy bass line. Brent Mydland's vocal backup is a welcome addition. The short musical bridge is polished, as the band hints at the "I don't know" line before Weir sings the final verse. Then the "real" musical bridge commences, complete with the intense improvisation Deadheads have come to expect from the band. After about a minute or more of improvisation, the bridge resolves into the final section of the song, repeated iterations of "sure don't know what I'm going for" and "I'm gonna go for it for sure," again with vocal improvisation in the backup voices. At its conclusion, the Dead segue seamlessly into "Eyes of the World."

The final performance of these two songs as a pair took place on March 24, 1986, at the Spectrum in Philadelphia (Sailor #7) and is at just under fourteen minutes. By this point in time, the audience clearly recognizes "Lost Sailor" from the outset, and there's a strong response, although early on, many seem to think Bob Weir is singing "dark star" when he sings "Where's the Dog Star?" The crowd response at "there is a price for being free" is strong and sustained both times Weir sings the line. At about 4:15, Weir shifts from his singing voice to talking through the song before beginning a couple of minutes of vocal improvisation. Through its final minute or two, Sailor increases in intensity. Soon we hear the intro to "Saint of Circumstance," with its quick tempo. The long musical bridge into Saint turns into a free-form improvisation that lasts more than a minute, building until it resolves into the final coda section: "Sure don't know what I'm goin' for." Very high energy. The vocal improvisation in this section effectively ends the song, and the band segues into "Drumz."

At its inception, Sailor > Saint was born fairly complete. Over the years, the pairing evolved but only slightly. Listen for well-developed solos by Garcia, more scat and vocalizing by Weir, and extended musical bridges toward the end of "Saint of Circumstance." It's not clear why the Dead dropped "Lost Sailor" from the repertoire in 1986—perhaps Weir became impatient with slow ballads. At any rate, this pairing was a key part of dozens of shows in the early 1980s. It's essential for our appreciation of the Grateful Dead during this period.

"(Turn on Your) Love Light"

"(Turn on Your) Love Light" (aka Lovelight) is a treat to include on our list of essential Grateful Dead songs because it was another vehicle for Ron "Pigpen" McKernan to show off his remarkable blues talents as both singer and harp player. Grateful Dead biographer Dennis McNally referred to Pigpen as "Mr. Funk" and said he "could close a show like nobody's business." He also quotes Bay Area music critic Ralph Gleason, who said Pigpen could make Lovelight "into a one-man blues project" where he would stab "the phrases out into the crowd like a preacher" (2002, 300).

Lovelight debuted on August 5, 1967 (Lovelight #1), in Toronto, Canada, and stayed in the live repertoire until Pigpen's last version of it on May 24, 1972, in London (the only version of this one is on the *Europe '72: The Complete Recordings* box set). Shortly after, Pigpen stopped performing with the band on June 17, 1972, due to his poor health. Lovelight returned to the live performance catalog on October 16, 1981 (Lovelight #2), on borrowed instruments at a small club in Amsterdam with Bob Weir handling the vocals, but it did not become a consistently regular part of the repertoire again until July 7, 1984 (Lovelight #3). Then it remained until its last performance on June 19, 1995: (Lovelight #4). Including both Pigpen and Weir versions, there were 341 performances.

Lovelight was written by Joseph Scott and Deadric Malone and first recorded by Bobby "Blue" Bland in 1961. Pigpen recommended that the Dead begin playing it after he was impressed by a version that James Cotton played when he opened for the Dead, probably in late 1966. You can read the original lyrics here (Lovelight #5), but Pigpen brought his own special lyrical improvisations to this song. You'll have to listen to each of his performances to hear all his raunchy variations including the regular line: "She's got box-back nitties and great big noble thighs, working under cover with a boar hog's eye."

The first official Grateful Dead recording of Lovelight appears on the two-LP *Live/Dead* album from 1969. It's a fifteen-minute performance that takes up the entire side one of the second LP. Pigpen is in fine form, riffing with his own special lyrics to spice up the song and involve the audience. This album version was from January 26, 1969, at the Avalon Ballroom in San Francisco: (Lovelight #6). When Weir brought the song back to live performances, he didn't use Pigpen's riffs or lyrics, but he still did a pretty good rave-up himself.

Musically, Lovelight is a straightforward rhythm and blues tune, which the Dead could handle quite well, particularly during the Pigpen years. When Pigpen was the vocalist, Lovelight typically opened or closed the show. When Weir brought it back in the 1980s it was a bit more subdued, without the lyrical improvisation and long jams, and it was always in the second set or the encore. It was always a high-energy crowd-pleaser whether Pigpen or Weir handled the vocals. There are many official releases that include Lovelight. You can see them all here: (Lovelight #7).

So where should you start your listening to Lovelight? In addition to the links we've already provided, we recommend the performance from August 6, 1971 (Lovelight #8), at the Palladium in Hollywood, California. This is a hot version that runs nearly twenty-seven minutes on a matrix recording. This performance showcases Pigpen, of course, but also demonstrates what a great rockin' blues band the Dead could be. Pigpen is in top form with his vocal riffs as he creates hookups with the audience; headyversion.com picks this as the best performance of Lovelight. Next we suggest a 1969 Pigpen version from Tucson, Arizona, on March 11: (Lovelight #9). This is a good soundboard recording, and you'll hear Pigpen engage the crowd with his vocal improvisations, as well as the high-energy band at their early primal best backing him up.

Now we'll offer some recommendations for Bob Weir versions of Lovelight. As mentioned, these are shorter, with none of Pigpen's raunchy lyrics, but still powerful and fun. Let's start with two Weir performances Barry saw (alas, he never experienced a Pigpen performance). The first is from Alpine Valley in East Troy, Wisconsin, on July 19, 1989: (Lovelight #10). This was a seven-minute encore, and it's a very clear matrix recording with Weir doing his thing quite well, with nice backing from the boys—and the crowd loves it. Second, give a listen to one from the New Year's run on December 30, 1991, in Oakland, California: (Lovelight #11). Garcia uses his MIDI to add some fun sounds, and Phil is there with some good low end in this excellent Dan Healy ultra-matrix soundboard. Of course, Weir is in fine voice, consistent with his rock star persona. Our final recommendation is from Nassau Coliseum on Long Island, New York, on March 29, 1990: (Lovelight #12). This performance features guest Branford Marsalis on saxophone, and he gets the band all cranked up in this seven-minute matrix recording. Enjoy!

With more than 300 performances of Lovelight, it's not easy to pick the "best" version—or even twenty of them. Needless to say, listeners can have their pick of most of them thanks to streaming technology and Archive.org, so if you want more Pigpen or Weir, go for it!

"Me and My Uncle"

Although it's unlikely that "Me and My Uncle" (aka Uncle) is at the top of any Deadhead's list of favorite Grateful Dead songs, it is an essential part of their live performance repertoire. You might ask why, and the answer is simple: it was played by the Dead more than any other song, with a staggering 616 performances! It made its debut on November 29, 1966 (Uncle #1), and was played every year except 1968 and 1976 during the Dead's thirty-year career, until its last performance on July 6, 1995. Surprisingly, Corry Arnold in his amazing blog, Hooterollin' Around (Uncle #2), suggests that there may have been even more than 616 versions, since there are few extant recordings of the Grateful Dead in 1966.

"Me and My Uncle" is a cover song written by John Phillips of the Mamas and Papas fame. In his blog, Corry details the history of the song and how it found its way to Bob Weir and the Grateful Dead via "Curly Jim," an early 1960s "hippie" who seems to have been around when the song was written. The blog is definitely worth a read. After all, who knew that "folk" singer Judy Collins was the first to record the song on her 1964 album *The Judy Collins Concert*? She would have to remind John Phillips that he wrote the song, since Phillips was apparently drunk when the song was written.

Phillip's lyrics for "Me and My Uncle" perfectly fit Bob Weir's "cowboy songs" contribution to the Dead's repertoire. From its debut in 1966 until late 1974, Uncle could be found in either set; after September 1974, it was only played during first sets. The story is not unlike that of Weir's cover of Mary Robbins's "El Paso," Weir and Barlow's "Mexicali Blues," or even Weir and Hunter's "Jack Straw." Uncle is the story of two cowboys headed to west Texas who start a "friendly game" during a stopover in a Santa Fe barroom. Soon the narrator's uncle has been accused of cheating, which leads to murder, mayhem, and the narrator and uncle's quick departure to Mexico. Before it's over, the narrator, who is "as honest as a Denver man can be," has shown his true colors, killed his uncle, and "left his dead ass there by the side of the road." (Of course, he also grabs all the gold.) You can find the lyrics here: (Uncle #3).

Musically, "Me and My Uncle" is straightforward with a 4/4 time signature that's rocking but with little room for improvisation from Garcia and Lesh. It's also one of the shortest songs performed by the Dead, at about only three minutes or so. Often Weir paired Uncle with another song like "Mexicali Blues" or, more frequently, with a cover of Johnny Cash's "Big River," especially starting in early 1978. The combination of Uncle with "Big River" gave Jerry and the band room to stretch out and run a bit, as you'll see in nearly every version of that pair. Despite its lack of improvisation, Uncle is a naturally danceable tune and a good fit in the first set as the band warmed up for the second.

"Me and My Uncle" first appeared as an official recording on the 1971 two-LP live *The Grateful Dead* album (Uncle #4), more commonly known as *Skull & Roses*. Uncle has also appeared on many other official releases, and you can see a full list through 2016 here: (Uncle #5).

Barry saw thirty-six versions of Uncle, starting with his first show in Des Moines, Iowa, in 1974, and ending with his last show in St. Louis on July 6, 1995, also the last performance of the song. Given Garcia's failing health in 1995, this last performance is surprisingly good as you can hear (Uncle #6), although there's some musical confusion at the end of the song. Another performance we recommend, and one that Barry enjoyed, is the first night of the New Year's run of Dead shows on December 27, 1987, in Oakland, California. The band did a typically good job as you can tell here: (Uncle #7). Be sure to listen to "Big River," which follows Uncle, to confirm our earlier comment about "room to stretch out."

Most of the 616 performances can be found on Archive.org, and although headyversions.com describes a number of versions as "explosive" or "standout" or "one of the best," we think they all sound similar, which is to say excellent. Occasionally Weir changed the lyrics slightly in the fifth verse from "one of them cowboys, he starts to draw, well I shot him down, Lord" to "one of them cowboys, he starts to draw, well I grabbed me a bottle, cracked him in the jaw." You can hear that change on this "standout" version from Kezar Stadium in San Francisco on May 26, 1973: (Uncle #8).

Although we both agree that "Me and My Uncle" is not one of their *best* songs, it's still an essential part of the Grateful Dead's catalog, with 616 performances. Listen to at least a few versions before passing judgment.

"Mexicali Blues"

"Mexicali Blues" (aka Mexicali) is a short, up-tempo song composed by Bob Weir and John Perry Barlow. It was first performed on October 19, 1971, in Minneapolis, and the Grateful Dead performed it 435 times. Mexicali appeared on Weir's solo album, *Ace*, which has the rest of the Dead as backing musicians, in 1972 and on many other albums listed here: (Mexicali #1). The Dead performed Mexicali every year they toured except 1976. Mexicali might appear early in the second set on occasion, but much more often the Dead played it in the first set. Mexicali was last performed on July 6, 1995, only days before the Dead's final show.

Musically, Mexicali is as good an example as any of the Dead's repertoire of "cowboy country rock"—or at least of the California version of that genre. The tempo is upbeat, like a polka: you can almost hear the tuba in an "oompah band" arrangement, and you're expected to dance. Mexicali is one of the Dead's shortest songs, usually timing in at less than four minutes. It's a self-contained song with no extended solos. Instead, listeners should focus on Garcia's fills: he plays lead all the way through, so when Weir pauses between lyrical phrases, Garcia fills that space with a short riff. These riffs varied from performance to performance, but they always reveal Garcia's talent as a country music guitarist.

How then is "Mexicali Blues" the "blues"? The answer lies in the lyrics (Mexicali #2). Mexicali is not a lighthearted song, despite its lighthearted musical style. As with many Grateful Dead songs, the lyrics tell the story of an outlaw: our narrator is running away from "payin' dues" as well as from the law. He rides three days on horseback to get to Mexico, becomes involved with an underage young woman, and then kills a man coming for her. It seems obvious to us that he is responsible for his situation—he even admits that at one point—but the song ultimately blames women and their mysterious power over men. The song then concludes with our hero on the gallows while the narrator reflects about a different ending in which listeners find themselves "on horseback in the dark"—perhaps metaphorically—racing endlessly across the desert. There's not a lot to be cheerful about in this song. At the same time, the music is upbeat, and if you don't focus on the story, it's a great dance tune.

The Dead's first live performance of "Mexicali Blues," at the University of Minnesota in Minneapolis on October 19, 1971, is a good place to start our listening tour (Mexicali #3). This version has a solid bass line undergirding the song; the rest of the band is playing a Dixieland-style jazz arrangement rather than "cowboy rock." As often happened in Grateful Dead shows, the band altered the mood dramatically: this fast-paced Mexicali was preceded by "Brown Eyed Woman," played at a moderate tempo, and followed by "Comes a Time," one of the Dead's slowest ballads.

Mexicali soon became more polished, and there are dozens of performances from which to choose. We recommend several, listed here in chronological order.

- August 27, 1972, at Veneta, Oregon. This is the famous Springfield Creamery benefit show immortalized in the documentary film and album *Sunshine Daydream* (D1:T9), both released in 2013. This version is also accessible here: (Mexicali #4). This is a good version for listening to Garcia's constant lead: he emerges during the solos but then retreats to the background when Weir's vocals pick up. The denizens of the headyversion.com website deem this the top version of "Mexicali Blues." See their rankings here: (Mexicali #5).
- October 9, 1974, in London, England. This performance appears on *Dick's Picks, Volume 7* (D1:T2) and here: (Mexicali #6). This is an excellent version with Lesh alternating between a marching band–beat and improvising as a lead instrument during the solos.
- October 10, 1977, in Portland, Oregon (Mexicali #7). On this recording, it's easier to hear the individual instruments if you listen closely. This may be the best, most energetic version we've heard, with outstanding lead guitar by Garcia.
- Finally, March 20, 1992, in Hamilton, Ontario, Canada (Mexicali #8). This late version has a slower tempo and is one of the few versions that clocks in at

more than four minutes. Garcia's leads are stressed more in the solos than in the background, as in earlier versions. In this 1992 version, Garcia's leads are less prominent, and the arrangement becomes a jazzy ballad.

Like many other songs, "Mexicali Blues," one of the Grateful Dead's most frequently performed songs, illustrates how a song's performance varied throughout the decades that the Dead played it. The first version seems like a relatively undisciplined (and thoroughly enjoyable) Dixieland-style version. From there, most versions sound more like country rock, with Garcia's lead guitar filling all the pauses and rests. Perhaps the best version of this style is from Boston on April 2, 1973 (Mexicali #9), which also appeared on *Dave's Picks, Volume 21* (D1:T3). Here you can hear superb background filling and lead guitar by Jerry Garcia, great testimony to his talent, his country style, and his exquisite musical taste.

"Might As Well"

A true story: two friends are heading into Boston on Friday, June 11, 1976, to see the Grateful Dead at the Boston Music Hall. They have seats in the topmost row of the balcony, which is fine: what's important is that they are inside. They also have some LSD, which they've experimented with outdoors in various pleasant settings, but never indoors at a crowded Dead show. The big question: should they drop acid or not? The answer is addressed in that night's opening song, "Might As Well."

Most, if not all, Deadheads have had a "Grateful Dead experience" like that and are happy to recount the details. This anecdote's "experience" is heightened by the fact that although the Grateful Dead played "Might As Well" 111 times, it was used as the show's opening song only seven times. That 6/11/76 show was only the song's fourth performance, and only the second time they played it as the opener. The odds against having that big question "answered" in the opening song were steep. And yet, there it is.

The Dead performed "Might As Well" heavily in 1976, the year it was introduced, and again fairly frequently from 1983 through 1985. In other years, they played it relatively infrequently or not at all. Its final performance was on March 23, 1994; at that point they hadn't played the song since mid-1991, a gap of 187 shows. "Might As Well" was played in the second set only fifteen times, once as an encore. It was firmly a first set song.

Jerry Garcia and Robert Hunter composed "Might As Well" as a tribute to the well-known 1970 Festival Express train ride across Canada during which the Dead and many other famous musicians, including Janis Joplin, the New Riders of the Purple Sage, and the Band, partied between shows that played at scheduled intervals. The lyrics (Might As Well #1) are not nearly as complex as many of Hunter's poems: the song is about the party atmosphere of the Festival Express, the general absence of such in the places the train stopped, the fun during the ride, nostalgia for the ride, and the return to "normalcy" after the ride was over. Although the song is literally about the Festival Express tour, there's no question that one can interpret these lyrics for one's own purposes. We've often felt similar emotions after a vacation or after a Grateful Dead show. Or maybe the song is about the scale of human life?

"Might As Well" appears on Jerry Garcia's third solo album, *Reflections*, as well as on a few official recordings; you can see the list here: (Might As Well #2). Musically, for those who are not familiar with "Might As Well," let's just say that it's hard not to tap your foot as it plays. The song is an uplifting roust that takes you along with it. The vocal bridge, in particular, adds punctuation to the beat and raises the energy even more. The Dead played "Might As Well" with nearly the same arrangement throughout the song's run and with basically no variation in the tempo.

The June 11, 1976, performance at the Boston Music Hall is worth listening to for no other reason than the anecdote above, but this show hasn't been released by the Grateful Dead—yet. Listen to a good matrix version here: (Might As Well #3). Listen to the crowd when Garcia sings "never had such a good time in my life before." Garcia extends the repeated singing of the final chorus, typical of this song, and there's a moderately successful outro.

At Market Square Arena in Indianapolis on October 1, 1976, the Dead played "Might As Well"; a good-quality audience tape is available here: (Might As Well #4). On that night, the Dead opened the second set with this song. The instrumental outro on this version is worth listening to: it's extended with good improvisation.

The fans who voted at the headyversion.com website proclaimed October 29, 1978, at Dekalb, Illinois, as the best version of "Might As Well." Comments include "high energy version," "tons of energy in this opener," and our favorite: "Boys came out [of] the gate like a rabid dog. Jerry sounds like he is going to jump off the stage." You can listen to this version and read more comments here: (Might As Well #5). The crowd's responses are audible in this version.

For another version of "Might As Well" from 1977, see November 2, 1977, from Toronto, Ontario, which was released on *Dick's Picks, Volume 34* (D2:T6) and also here: (Might As Well #6). On that night, the Dead closed the first set with that song, and the outro is extended and rocking. This soundboard recording lets you hear Weir's work on rhythm guitar.

Finally, after a gap of 216 shows, the Dead played "Might As Well" as the first set closer on March 20, 1991, in Landover, Maryland. A good matrix recording is available here: (Might As Well #7). By the 1990s, the Dead's shows were not always consistently wonderful, but you'll hear no evidence of that in this version, especially in the powerful outro.

The Grateful Dead's "Might As Well" is a relatively simple, straightforward song that can help us make sense of our trajectory through life and its better moments/trips. At a more literal level, "Might As Well" captures the fun and dancing typical of a Dead show. This duality, typical of Hunter's poetry, makes this song essential.

"Mississippi Half-Step Uptown Toodleloo"

"Mississippi Half-Step Uptown Toodleloo" (aka Half-Step) wins the prize for the longest title of a Garcia and Hunter collaboration. It made its first concert appearance on July 16, 1972, in Hartford, Connecticut (Half-Step #1). Its studio recording is found on the Dead's first release on their own Grateful Dead Records *Wake of the Flood* LP in October 1973 (Half-Step #2). Half-Step was performed 234 times, the last one on July 6, 1995, in St. Louis (Half-Step #3). It was generally in heavy rotation in 1972 and 1973, with fifty-eight performances in those two years. Thereafter it averaged about eight shows per year, though it was not played at all in 1975, 1983, or 1984.

The lyrics for Half-Step (Half-Step #4), tell the story of a down-and-outer, as is often the case with Hunter's lyrics. When this storyteller was born, his "Daddy sat down and cried." You'll find biblical references such as his mark of "Cain and Abel" and gambling references like "loaded dice" and "ace of spades behind his ear," both themes that Hunter uses frequently. (See the lyrics for "Deal," "Loser," and "Me and My Uncle," for more examples of the gambling motif.) Despite his troubles, the storyteller is optimistic and forward looking in lines such as "I'm on my way—on my way" and "Lost my boots in transit, baby, pile of smokin' leather, I nailed a retread to my feet and prayed for better weather." After three verses and three choruses, the song ends on an especially upbeat note with a totally different lyric: "across the Rio Grand-eo, across the lazy river" that Garcia repeated at least twice but usually several more times.

This is a lovely song musically by Garcia; it's both jaunty and lilting. It's a standard 4/4 beat, which gives it a positive feel. Half-Step is not a rocker but nevertheless a highly danceable tune. Garcia's vocals bring out the optimism of the storyteller, as do his guitar solos. What's especially fascinating about this song is the ending coda, which almost evolves into another "river song" with the closing "Rio Grand-eo" lines. The tune changes dramatically at this point, shifting from the key of C to A, becoming almost a totally different song. The Rio Grand-eo lines, which could be repeated any number of times, are followed by a second fast-paced solo by Garcia supported by Lesh's power bass lines, along with the rest of the band building the energy before the ending.

In addition to the studio recording of Half-Step on *Wake of the Flood*, live performances have been issued on many official releases. You can see a complete list through 2016 here: (Half-Step #5). Half-Step is also included in the *May 1977: Get Shown the Light* box set. If you don't have access to any of the many official releases of Half-Step, we'll recommend some especially good performances to stream for your listening pleasure.

The second performance of Half-Step that Barry saw, at Starlight Theatre in Kansas City on August 3, 1982, is one of the few he didn't record: he couldn't get his recording gear past security, and there was no tapers' section then. It's a tasty rendition that's rated highly on headyversion.com, and can be heard here in a high-quality matrix recording: (Half-Step #6).

Perhaps the most memorable version of Half-Step for Barry was April 15, 1989 (Half-Step #7), at the Mecca in Milwaukee. He and his (not yet) wife, Chris, drove from Kansas City to Milwaukee to spend the weekend with Deadhead friends and to see the two shows there on Saturday and Sunday. Unfortunately, when they arrived in Milwaukee on Friday, they discovered that they had left their concert tickets in Kansas City—major bummer! What to do? It was too late in the day for special delivery via USPS or FedEx. Finally they discovered they could buy a counter-to-counter airline ticket for their Grateful Dead concert tickets! The Saturday flight arrived at the downtown Milwaukee airport just before the concert started, and it was a short drive to the venue. As they entered the Mecca, Half-Step was just beginning, and Barry started his recorder on the way to the seats. This version is also recommended on headyversion.com. Once again the "Rio Grand-eo" coda takes off. Another version Barry saw and recorded is from June 7, 1991, at Deer Creek Amphitheatre near Indianapolis. We agree with headyversion.com's recommendation. You can listen to an audience recording here: (Half-Step #8).

We also highly recommend the exquisite performance from May 12, 1977, at Chicago's Auditorium Theater. It's available as the bonus CD from the *Winterland June 1977: The Complete Recordings* box set, or you can listen to a good-quality audience recording here: (Half Step #9).

The absolute best performance of Half-Step likely happened on September 3, 1977, in Englishtown, New Jersey, at the Raceway. It's on *Dick's Picks, Volume 15* (D1:T5), and you can also listen to the full *thirteen minutes* (!) in a delightful matrix recording here: (Half-Step #10). Buckle your seat belts before Garcia, Lesh, Weir, and the rest of the band take you to places you didn't know existed, and that's even before "Rio Grand-eo"! Enjoying this one is nearly guaranteed—it's a truly fine demonstration of what the Grateful Dead could do better than anybody else—jam!

"Morning Dew"

Written by Canadian folk singer Bonnie Dobson in 1961, "Morning Dew" (aka Dew) is a post–atomic war song—not the most pleasant topic for a Grateful Dead song. But it's a cover song that the band managed to make work as one of their big songs, typically in the second set or encore, where it nearly always appeared after 1971. The first performance of "Morning Dew" was January 14, 1967, and the last was June 21, 1995 (Dew #1). With a total of 254 performances, it was one of the four songs most often performed by Garcia, exceeded only by "China Cat Sunflower" (554 performances), "Deal" (423), and "Black Peter" (343). Dew was played at least once every year after its debut except 1975. The studio version appears on the Dead's first LP, *The Grateful Dead*, released in March 1967 (Dew #2). Thus, it has a very long history with the Dead, which is why it's an essential part of their repertoire, even though we've limited the number of cover songs written by other artists.

Dew is a dialogue between the only surviving man and woman on Earth after a nuclear war. The conversation is depressing, as you might imagine, since "I can't walk you out in the morning dew today" and "you didn't hear no baby cry today." This continues with "where have all the people gone?" until the song concludes "I guess it doesn't matter anyway." You can find the lyrics to Dew here: (Dew #3); formal songwriting credit is given to Dobson with cowriting credits given to Tim Rose, although there's controversy over his role. Despite the dirge-like story and the relatively few lyrics, Garcia and the Dead made Dew an inspirational performance, stretching it out musically and vocally and continuing to build energy with Garcia's soaring guitar solos and the band's pounding dynamics.

In addition to the studio version of Dew on the Dead's first album, more than fifty live performances have been released officially, including the *Get Shown the Light* box set, with the May 8, 1977, performance most often considered the best. So there are plenty of fine official versions available. You can see a full list through 2016 here: (Dew #4).

We'll make several recommendations, starting with the live debut of "Morning Dew" at Golden Gate Park in San Francisco on January 14, 1967, which can be found on a remarkably good soundboard recording (Dew #5). There's no hesitation or first-time jitters from anyone in the band. They are really prepared, and it's a fine performance with strong vocals from Garcia. Given the crowd's cheers when the first notes are played, it makes us wonder if they might have played it before, though there is no documentation to support that.

Given the outstanding consistency of quality performances during the Dead's Europe '72 tour, we recommend one from the Strand Lyceum in London on May 26. It's a slower version than most, which reveals the deep sadness of the story Jerry sings. This is also the one that appears on the *Europe '72* album. Listen to it on this excellent soundboard recording: (Dew #6).

Because of overwhelming support for the May 8, 1977, Barton Hall performance on headyversion.com, we include this wonderful matrix recording that you can try out for yourself (Dew #7). It's a barn burner for sure, clocking in at more than thirteen minutes as it closes the second set. If this were the end of the world, this performance would be one helluva way to go.

It took several Dead concerts before Barry saw his first Dew at the Dead's three-show run for their twentieth anniversary in Berkeley, California, on June 14, 1985. We recommend this 6/14/85 rendition, where it opened the second set, in this crystal clear audience recording: (Dew #8).

Another version that Barry saw at Alpine Valley in East Troy, Wisconsin, on July 19, 1989, is one that we also recommend. At this stage of the Dead's career, the band and music are more mature, and Garcia is in good health. These factors make this another fine performance, with Garcia literally yelling the lyrics at times. Listen to

Barry's recording (Dew #9), and you'll understand why this version also ranks high on the headyversion.com list.

Continuing chronologically through our recommendations, our last is from 1995. This is a year the Dead did not always provide the best performances, given Garcia's declining health. With that said, don't write off the chance to hear this version from Las Vegas on May 20, 1995. It's the last Dew that Barry saw performed and the next to last version ever played. The band is prepared, and Garcia delivers the goods with his vocals and guitar. Here's a link to a clear audience recording: (Dew #10). The performance is extremely powerful, regardless of the year it was played, which makes us wonder why 1995 has gotten such a bad rep.

We've given you a good deal of information and recommendations here, which should make it clear how important "Morning Dew" is to the Grateful Dead's live repertoire and legacy. So you decide: do the Grateful Dead make Dew a dirge or an inspiration?

"The Music Never Stopped"

"The Music Never Stopped" (aka Music) is one of the Grateful Dead's most rousing and interesting songs. Bob Weir and John Perry Barlow composed the song, which debuted on August 13, 1975, in the famous Great American Music Hall show in San Francisco during the Dead's touring hiatus. The Dead played this song 234 times over the years. Its last performance was on June 28, 1995, in Auburn Hills, Michigan. Music appeared in different spots in the show: it could open or close either set.

As with many Grateful Dead songs, Music was played most frequently early in its run. This included thirty times out of forty-one shows in 1976, when the Dead resumed touring after their hiatus, and twenty-nine times out of sixty shows in 1977. Music was performed less often after 1978, though it was always in the rotation.

The lyrics to Music are cheerful and uplifting, at least after the beginning (Music #1). The song opens in a desultory town beaten down by summer's heat. Someone hears music at the edge of town, and a band comes marching through, lifting everyone's spirits. And not just any band, but "a band beyond description, Jehovah's favorite choir." The townspeople are soon caught up in the spirit: they clap, they hold hands, they dance, they laugh, they scream, and a rooster crows at midnight. Finally, even the weather changes: there's a cool breeze, and "the corn's a bumper crop." Perhaps most importantly, "the music never stopped."

Music's structure remained fairly constant throughout its rotation. The basic riff of the song is played repeatedly with breaks at the end of the verses. The early vocal bridge serves as a kind of chorus with a change of tempo and chord structure before the basic riff resumes for the next verse. The second vocal bridge follows the same pattern as the first, though with mostly different lyrics. After the final vocal line, there's a second instrumental bridge, with a different tempo—this is the section that the Dead extended throughout the song's existence, until it became a fairly free-form improvisation. The band then seamlessly concludes the song with an extended outro that repeats the song's basic riff with increasing intensity, bringing the crowd along with it, as suggested in the lyrics. The magic in listening to Music is the sequence of the changing sections and the rousing outro.

Music's debut performance, 8/13/75, was issued on the album *One from the Vault*, and a soundboard recording is available here: (Music #2). This version is beautifully played and sung but without the intense energy or extended jams of later versions. We recommend it here for the contrast, especially when Music ended a set.

On April 24, 1978 (Music #3), in Normal, Illinois, Music closed the first set. This performance is about three years into Music's run, so the band had developed a more refined performance. The song begins as a lilting melody, with the instruments playing off the drums. The vocals intensify as the song progresses, with Donna Godchaux taking the vocal lead during the third verse. The instrumental bridge after the vocals is soaring, with Garcia and Lesh both playing lead lines. The outro builds to a strong ending, with Garcia "mandolining"; this Music is definitely *not* a gentle, lilting melody by the coda. This is a good version to hear Music at its best, so turn up the volume!

For a later version, we recommend the performance on July 17, 1989, at East Troy, Wisconsin, released on the 1977 compilation album *Fallout from the Phil Zone* (D2:T1) and here: (Music #4). After years of hearing the song, the audience responds immediately to the first notes and often during the song. The vocals portion of the song is over at about 3:15, and the instrumental bridge kicks in. This bridge segues to the outro at about 5:45, and the outro lasts the remaining three minutes. Garcia's lead guitar takes everyone higher and higher: we can almost see the dancing.

For a still later performance, listen to September 25, 1991, at Boston Garden. This version was issued on the album *Dick's Picks, Volume 17* (D1:T9) and here: (Music #5). As with the two previous versions recommended earlier, this Music ends the first set. This recording is especially good for the audience responses throughout the song. Of particular note is the tempo shift in the outro: at about 5:20, the band suddenly goes to half-time, playing double measures for the notes in the song's basic riff, and stays in that meter until just before the song ends, when they switch back to the regular tempo.

Finally, listen to Barry's recording of Music from Cardinal Stadium in Louisville, Kentucky, on July 6, 1990 (Music #6). Phil's bass line is especially clear on this version, which has an extended section of the outro with double measures. What a great way to end the first set!

If you've listened to these versions of "The Music Never Stopped," you'll understand why we love this song. It has always been one of Bob's favorites, both because of the music itself and also because of the enthusiastic crowd responses. It was the Dead's way of leaving you a little higher at the end of a set. And it worked.

Many Grateful Dead songs take up serious topics, and life is not always wonderful for our narrators. Often the lyrics focus on people beaten down by fate or poverty, as we've noted in many of these entries. "The Music Never Stopped" is serious as well, if you look at the lyrics, but it's also uplifting: it's okay to let the magic of the traveling circus invade our towns and to let that magic make the world a better place. In this sense, it becomes important *not* to let the music stop, and this is perhaps the best role Deadheads can play in today's world.

"Not Fade Away"

Buddy Holly's "Not Fade Away" (aka NFA) is a cover song that demanded to be included in this book. The Grateful Dead used NFA as one of their signature songs, a rousing show closer that got the whole audience involved in both the vocals and the music. NFA, one of rock and roll's original great songs, was released by Buddy Holly in 1957. Listen to the original here: (NFA #1). The Dead adopted Holly's rhythmic clapping, the background vocalizing, and the fade-out coda.

As for the lyrics, NFA is both a longing lament and a celebration of love, not unusual for the Grateful Dead. The lyrics are here: (NFA #2). The narrator hasn't been successful in establishing a relationship with the desired—yet—but he persists because "love is real, not fade away." Both musically and lyrically, NFA seems too simple a song to be such a success, but the soul of a song lies in its performances. No less an observer than Jerry Garcia has said: "'Not Fade Away' is a fabulous song . . . and I loved it when it was a rock 'n' roll song—I mean I loved it when I was a kid, and doing it now almost always gives me a thrill. It stands my hair on end. It's just a great song" (McNally 2015a, 216).

The Dead played NFA 531 times beginning on July 19, 1968, in San Francisco. NFA was the Dead's sixth-most-played song overall, a mainstay in the rotation. Its final performance was July 5, 1995, the final week of the Dead's thirty-year run. NFA was almost always a second set song, and it was used as the encore on a few occasions in the 1980s.

What exactly did the Grateful Dead do to NFA to make it their own? Through the years, they adapted the song in three significant ways. First, they extended it with improvisational jamming, turning an AM radio song of 2:25 minutes into an FM song that easily could last ten minutes or longer. Second, the Dead combined NFA into medleys, usually with "Going Down the Road Feelin' Bad" (aka GDTRFB), especially in the early 1970s. And third, they incorporated the audience via active participation: toward the end of the song, as the Dead were fading out, the crowd clapped rhythmically and/or sang along on an adaptation of the last phrase of the song, "you know our love will not fade away." Often, the only sound heard for minutes was the audience. Hearing the song with full audience participation is to realize how far the Dead took NFA. They kept the basic ingredients but made it their own by using their strengths as a band: their skills at improvising, creating seamless segues, and their interactions with the Deadheads in the audience.

As mentioned earlier, the Dead's first performance of NFA was June 19, 1968 (NFA #3). On this soundboard recording, the voices are muted, unfortunately; we offer it only as an example of the early versions of this song. This performance finds NFA emerging from a "Drumz" solo and begins with a sing and response, with massive input from Lesh on bass. The tempo is quite fast, with a driving beat throughout. You get the energy and the style of the late 1960s Grateful Dead, but you don't hear the later adaptations that made the song more their own and less of a simple cover tune.

On April 5, 1971, in New York City, the Dead played probably the earliest easily accessible version of "Not Fade Away." This version appears on the Dead's 1971 album *Grateful Dead* (aka the *Skull & Roses* album) and is also accessible as a soundboard recording (NFA #4). This version is a good example of the Dead's expansion of instrumental improvisation. In the early 1970s, the Dead often ended shows with the combination of NFA > GDTRFB; this version is particularly good as an example of that. After GDTRFB, the band segues back into NFA for the end of the medley. We urge our readers to listen through GDTRFB as well as NFA for the full flavor of the performance, including the NFA "tease" at the end of GDTRFB. The version on the 1971 album isn't quite the same as the archive link above, incidentally: the album is more polished and slightly less authentic, since the band edited the original music for the album.

One of the occasions when "Not Fade Away" was performed as the show's encore took place in Oxford, Maine, on July 3, 1988 (NFA #5). With Brent Mydland on keyboards and vocal background at the high end, the sound in this version is much fuller than the performance from 4/5/71. When the audience kicks in, you can hear the uplifting chant from the assembled Deadheads, even as the band fades away and leaves the stage. The chant continues for quite a while—a glorious moment at any Dead show.

Bob was in attendance for a superb performance of "Not Fade Away" at the Atlanta Omni on April 3, 1990, where the Dead used NFA to close the second set. This show is part of the *Spring 1990: The Other One* box set, and an excellent matrix recording is available (NFA #6). This version has it all, including an intro segue, extended instrumental jamming, and great vocals with the audience singing along: GDTRFB > "Throwing Stones" > NFA. After the verses, the audience begins the rhythmic clapping and starts chanting back to the band, a very emotional moment—and for the last two minutes or so of the song, it's *only* the audience. As it turned out, the chanting and clapping lasted until the band returned to the stage for the encore.

Space limitations prevent us from giving you more recommendations, but a list of the dozens of albums that include NFA is available (NFA #7). We hope the versions we've recommended illustrate that whatever our feelings about the cover songs the Grateful Dead played, "Not Fade Away" had to be included in this book. To really hear and understand the Dead, NFA is essential.

"One More Saturday Night"

"One More Saturday Night" (aka Saturday Night) credits only Bob Weir as composer, with no assistance from lyricists Robert Hunter or John Perry Barlow. It was introduced to audiences on October 19, 1971 (OMSN #1), in Minneapolis at a show that was memorable for several other song debuts, as well as the introduction of Keith Godchaux on keyboards. The studio recording of Saturday Night was on Weir's May 1972, "solo" LP *Ace* (OMSN #2). The last performance of Saturday Night was on July 8, 1995 (OMSN #3), in Chicago, the next-to-last Grateful Dead concert. Saturday Night was played 340 times and was always part of the live song rotation.

Weir's lyrics (OMSN #4) are a simple outline of, and invitation to, a Saturday night party. The storyteller says there's a "mighty sign writ in fire across the heavens" to let us know there's "a party tonight." The dance party is "at the local armory" and at midnight "the whole place is gonna fly." The president even gets advice from his wife to "put on your rocking shoes" in order to get over his dissatisfaction with current events. Weir keeps the crowd engaged throughout the song and repeats the chorus, which emphasizes, "hey, Saturday Night!" multiple times at the end of the song to get everyone on their feet dancing, which they were typically happy to do during this rocker.

According to Dennis McNally (2015a, 394), Robert Hunter had a falling-out with Weir after their initial collaboration on the lyrics for Saturday Night. Weir reworked Hunter's draft of the lyrics, gave them back to him, and asked Hunter to call the song "U.S. Blues." This didn't sit well with Hunter, who found Weir's lyrics not at all to his liking, refused to change the title, and ultimately refused any credit for the song.

Saturday Night is a Weir rocker that's very much in the Chuck Berry style. It is written in a basic 4/4 time signature, which gives it a good beat. This makes it easy to dance to and sing along with. Saturday Night was most often played at Saturday concerts, and because of the song's high energy, it also closed shows nearly 150 times in the twenty-four years it was in the live repertoire.

The first official live version of "One More Saturday Night" was released on the Dead's three-LP album *Europe '72* in November 1972. Given the number of live performances, it's no surprise that many more live versions have been released. At the time of this writing, there are more than thirty-eight official releases, and you can see a full list through 2016 here: (OMSN #5).

Perhaps the best known or most appreciated version of Saturday Night is from the Ithaca, New York, show on May 8, 1977, which is included in the *Get Shown the Light* box set and was also released as an individual show on *Cornell 5/8/77*. It's certainly a great performance, ranked number two at headyversion.com. You can check it out here, in a very nice matrix recording, as it closes the show (OMSN #6). After you hear the Cornell version, try this one from the Europe '72 tour on April 8 at Wembley Empire Pool in London. It's the top pick on headyversion.com, and there's a tasty soundboard recording here: (OMSN #7). Next try this matrix recording from March 24, 1990, at Knickerbocker Arena in Albany, New York (OMSN #8), also highly ranked on headyversion.com.

Of the twenty-eight performances Barry saw, one of the more memorable was in Oakland on December 28, 1991. Saturday Night opened the show and also closed it! This is the only time the Dead did this in more than 300 performances, once again demonstrating their approach to always changing things up and never getting into a rut or routine. You can hear both of these versions here: (OMSN #9) and here: (OMSN #10). Headyversion.com also recommends it, as well as the performance on December 9, 1989, at the Los Angeles Forum, which Barry also saw when it closed the first set. There's a soundboard recording here: (OMSN #11).

The Grateful Dead played a wide variety of styles, as shown throughout this book. Some critics think the jamming is boring or "noodling," others might roll their eyes at the ballads. But the bottom line is, if you like straight-ahead rock and roll, "One More Saturday Night" fills the bill.

"The Other One"

Not many Grateful Dead songs from the first two or three years of the band's run survived until the end, but "The Other One" (aka TOO) is one of them. And survive it did, big time. TOO, attributed to Weir and Kreutzmann, was performed 583 times between October 22, 1967, and July 8, 1995—the third most played song in the Dead's repertoire. They played it on average more than twenty times per touring year starting in 1968, and they played it every year they were on tour. Add to that the five times the Dead performed "The Other One Jam," which is the music without the vocals, and you can see why TOO is one of the Dead's signature songs. If you went to a handful of Grateful Dead shows, there was a good chance that you would have seen a performance of "The Other One."

TOO has an interesting history, with a change of title and content. In its earliest performances until 1971, TOO was bracketed by Garcia's "Cryptical Envelopment" (aka Cryptical) and "He Had to Die," and the combo was called "The Other One Suite." The two verses we think of in TOO—beginning "Spanish lady" and "escaping through . . ." (or "skipping through . . .") were originally titled "The Faster We Go, the Rounder We Get." The lyrics for TOO (originally known as "That's It for the Other One") include two verses and a short chorus (TOO #1), which also includes the lyrics to Cryptical. The first of the two TOO verses may be referencing an LSD trip or another such magical experience. The second verse refers to Neal Cassady and the Merry Pranksters' bus, perhaps as part of the experience referenced in the first verse. We strongly recommend David Dodd's reflections on the history and background for this song (TOO #2).

TOO illustrates the Dead's ability to improvise during a song, to explore, and to take musical risks. Musically, it was a loud, up-tempo piece, usually played late in the show. On some occasions, an intro jam could extend several minutes before any vocals, sometimes a jam could take ten or fifteen minutes between the two verses, and at others a jam extended after the final verse—or all of the above could take place; there was never any single "official" arrangement. From the moment you heard "The Roll," Lesh's thunderous bass intro that often started the song, you were in for an amazing musical experience.

Perhaps as much as any song we have deemed essential, it's important to listen to TOO in its performance context. When TOO emerged out of "Drumz" or "Space," it brought the listener back to a more normal plane of existence, to the realm of dancing, perhaps. So when you listen to the following recommendations, keep in mind that listening to the preceding and following songs is a good idea.

February 13, 1970, at the Fillmore East in New York City is from a particularly famous run of shows, with TOO available on *Dick's Picks, Volume 4* (D2:T1) and accessible here: (TOO #3). In this version, TOO is bracketed by the two parts of "Cryptical Envelopment," and it also includes a drum solo. Note that the audience recording at the link provided includes the entire suite, so listen to four separate items; the link starts at Cryptical. TOO itself begins with a good roll by Lesh and then a fast-paced jam in which Garcia soars. This is an excellent early version of the suite.

September 3, 1972, at Boulder, Colorado, which is available on *Dick's Picks, Volume 36* (D4:T6), is a solid performance of TOO *without* the whole suite. It's also accessible here: (TOO #4). TOO is preceded by "He's Gone," and there's a short "He's Gone" instrumental coda that leads seamlessly into the first TOO jam. This version times in at just under thirty-one minutes, incidentally. It includes an extended intro with interesting musical explorations by both Garcia and Lesh. (At about 12:20, an audience channel on this recording intrudes into the mix, but better sound soon returns.) There's a short drum solo, Lesh plays the roll at about 15:25, and Weir begins the vocals a little later. There's a long jam and then the second verse with no outro as the band segues directly into "Wharf Rat." This is an excellent version for hearing the Dead explore and improvise.

On May 10, 1978, in New Haven, Connecticut (TOO #5), the song times in at 7:29, much shorter than the 9/3/72 version. This performance was released on *Dick's Picks, Volume 25* (D2:T4). There's no roll by Lesh at the outset, though there's a hint of one before the second verse. The jam between the two verses is relatively mellow, with a short outro jam before the band segues into "Wharf Rat." Finally, we suggest another shorter version, from May 9, 1987, at Laguna Seca, in Monterey, California (TOO #6), which times in at only 5:03. Again, there's no roll by Lesh. This version includes a short jam between the two verses.

"The Other One"—whether part of a longer suite or a standalone song—was a centerpiece of the Grateful Dead's repertoire for almost their entire thirty-year run. It is particularly interesting for Deadheads because of the way the song was adapted to reflect different stages of the Dead's career. Evolving from jam-infused suites to half-hour versions and then to shorter versions in later years, TOO is an important song for anyone trying to appreciate the Dead. Indeed, many Deadheads consider TOO the Dead's signature song.

"Peggy-O"

At any given Grateful Dead show, you might hear basic rock and roll; ballads; love songs; cowboy rock; spacey, improvisational jams; country; gospel; and even folk! "Peggy-O" is one of a handful of folk tunes in the Dead's repertoire. Called "Peggy-O" by the Grateful Dead, the song had an earlier life as a traditional folk song called "Fennario" and as a Scottish folk song before that. The Dead's arrangements and treatments of this traditional song always were crowd favorites. Like many songs by the Dead, the performances varied over time yet always seemed fresh.

"Peggy-O" debuted on December 10, 1973, in Charlotte, North Carolina, a show released as *Volume 8* of the Grateful Dead's *Download Series*. (There appears to be no other easily accessible version of this show.) It was played some 265 times before its final performance on July 5, 1995, in Maryland Heights, Missouri. "Peggy-O" was played at least once every year after 1973, including the 1975 hiatus.

The lyrics to "Peggy-O" (Peggy #1) tell the story of the romance between "pretty Peggy-O" and "sweet William-O," the captain of a marching group of soldiers. He will either "free all the people" or destroy the area, depending on whether Peggy accepts his offer of marriage. She is willing but fears that William's relative lack of wealth will anger her family, so she rejects the proposal. William subsequently perishes and is buried in "the Louisiana country-O." This line illustrates how the Grateful Dead appropriated and adapted songs as their own: it's hardly an English or Scottish folk song if the character is buried in the United States.

"Peggy-O"'s second live performance was on December 12, 1973, at the Omni in Atlanta (Peggy #2). You can hear Bob Weir's rhythm guitar more clearly here than in most recordings. The song appears late in the first set, which lasted more than an hour and a half. On this night, "Peggy-O" emerges as a calm, smooth song that sounds like a genuine folk song when compared to some later versions. The dynamics are outstanding: the Dead start very softly but pick up as the song progresses. Similarly, Lesh's bass starts out conventionally, but by the middle of the song, he's playing "lead bass," as was his wont. Yet the overall effect is one of peace and tranquility; this is a good early version.

On June 17, 1975, the Dead played "Peggy-O" at Winterland. "Peggy-O" was always a crowd favorite, and of this performance, a commenter—in June 2017!—states that it is so amazing that he wants this version played at his funeral. Listen to it and read other comments (Peggy #3). This was during the Dead's hiatus year and it was San Francisco, so the audience is particularly enthusiastic. The tempo is very slow, as slow a "Peggy-O" as any you'll hear, clocking in at more than nine and a half minutes, compared to the typical seven minutes or so. Plus, the band added a late solo between the final two verses. With this version, you can appreciate the Dead's uncanny ability to adapt and improvise with their music and to take risks before a live audience.

In spring 1977, the Grateful Dead were having one of their best, if not the best, touring seasons, and "Peggy-O" was no exception. At two shows, May 5, 1977, in New Haven, Connecticut, and May 7, 1977, in Boston, the Dead played outstanding versions of this song. Both are available in the box set *Get Shown the Light*, released in May 2017. Just hearing how Garcia pronounced the word "love" is by itself almost worth the price of admission. The solos soar, the lyrics ring true, the musical accompaniment is spot-on. These are excellent versions: you can hear New Haven as a soundboard (Peggy #4) and Boston as a matrix recording here: (Peggy #5).

Twenty years later, on July 5, 1995, the Dead played "Peggy-O" for the last time. You can listen here: (Peggy #6). The song starts more slowly: there are almost two minutes of tuning, noodling, and crowd noises before the song itself starts. We specifically chose this audience recording so you can experience the jubilant atmosphere at Dead shows. This version has a more upbeat tempo than most early versions. Garcia's voice is adequate, though a bit thin on some of the higher notes. At the same time, the musical backing is less complex than in earlier versions. Garcia's solos start slowly but improve, all of which is consistent with the general nature of 1995 shows.

We have pointed to only a few performances of "Peggy-O" here, but this song illustrates the trajectory of the Grateful Dead's thirty-year run, or at least since the early 1970s. But within that time frame, from 1971 through 1995, "Peggy-O" well illustrates the Dead's style of playing, especially for listeners willing to do the work and ferret out the nuances in style and quality of the music.

"Playing in the Band"

"Playing in the Band" (aka PITB) began life as an instrumental called "The Main Ten," because the song has ten beats to the measure. The Dead performed it under that title in 1969 and 1970, with Mickey Hart listed as the song's writer. You can hear "The Main Ten" from November 8, 1969, in San Francisco on *Dick's Picks, Volume 16* (D3:T2) and here: (PITB #1). If you are already familiar with "Playing in the Band," you'll recognize "The Main Ten" as a central motif in PITB.

When the Dead introduced "Playing in the Band" on February 18, 1971, it had acquired new authors, with Robert Hunter's lyrics and Bob Weir's music added to Mickey Hart's original instrumental. "The Main Ten" was incorporated into PITB, which became a favorite for Deadheads as well as for the band. PITB ranks fourth in the total number of performances of all Grateful Dead songs, with 582 performances, its last on July 5, 1995. PITB appeared mostly in the first set in the early 1970s, but after the touring hiatus in 1975, it became a steady second set song.

The lyrics for "Playing in the Band" (PITB #2) perhaps haven't the weight of other songs by Robert Hunter, although the distinction between people who "trust to reason" as opposed to those "who look for fights," certainly speaks to American political and social life in the early twenty-first century. Add to this the line about climbing up a tree "just lookin' at the sights" or "just lookin' for their kites," and you get the sense that the Dead were leaving politics behind.

To say that PITB's performance format was flexible is an understatement. The song is upbeat and powerful, with key elements that remained consistent throughout its history. These include the bell-like opening and closing riffs, the central motif from "The Main Ten," the instrumental bridge—one of the most powerful bridges in the Dead's entire repertoire—and the triumphant musical bridge just before the coda.

The overall performance structure of the song, however, changed dramatically over the years, probably more so than any other single Grateful Dead song. In the early versions of PITB, it was a self-contained song with little by way of improvisation. This classic version is from April 6, 1971, on the Dead's eponymous 1971 album *Grateful Dead* (aka *Skull & Roses*), also accessible here: (PITB #3). Most Grateful Dead extended jams do not appear on studio albums, but this is the exception. PITB appears on Bob Weir's solo album, *Ace*, from 1972. The only difference between this studio version and the *Skull & Roses* live version is the extended jam in the middle of the song.

Soon enough, the band began to include an extended instrumental section in their live performances, during which they played perhaps their best jazz. The pivot point for these versions occurs after the third verse: the band improvises on the central motif and then extends into a jam. At the end of the jam, the band reverts to improvising on the central motif again and then reprises the power bridge to bring the song back to the final chorus. This would become the characteristic pattern during the first few years of performance. There's an excellent live version on *Dick's Picks, Volume 1* (D1:T6) from December 19, 1973, in Tampa, accessible here: (PITB #4).

Besides the extended jam, PITB also provided a second, though minor, improvisational moment during the final bridge after the final chorus, where the number of iterations of that triumphal riff changed from show to show. In the Tampa show, for example, the Dead played this riff twelve times before ending the song. The Dead played another particularly high-energy version of PITB on November 18, 1972, at the University of Houston, available here: (PITB #5).

The Dead soon took PITB in a new direction, however. Instead of simply inserting an extended jazz segment into the song, the band began to insert a *song* into the jazz segment before returning to finish PITB with a flourish. One magnificent version in which the Dead inserted *two* songs into the jazz segment took place at UCLA on November 17, 1973. Issued on *Dave's Picks, Volume 5* (D2:T4–8), it is also available here: (PITB #6). On that night, the Grateful Dead opened with PITB, segued into "Uncle John's Band" (aka UJB), interrupted UJB with a segue into "Morning

Dew," finished "Morning Dew," segued back into "UJB," finished UJB, and then reprised PITB, ending the medley after almost fifty minutes of continuous music. This is definitely worth listening to.

On September 28, 1976, in Syracuse (*Dick's Picks, Volume 20* [D4:T1–10]), for example, the Dead opened the second set with PITB, segued into "The Wheel" and then several other songs. Some fifty-five minutes and eight songs later, they returned to PITB to end the second set. To hear this sequence, start with the audience recording (PITB #7). Enjoy the set.

Consider this: on March 31, 1991, in Greensboro, North Carolina, the Dead played PITB during the second set and went on to other songs without returning to PITB. At the same venue the next night, April 1, 1991, late in the second set, they reprised PITB and closed the song. These two shows are accessible here (PITB #8) and here (PITB #9).

But the Dead weren't through tinkering with PITB. In the two previous arrangements, the Dead "closed" "Playing in the Band" by returning to the song, whether from the jam or from a different song. But sometimes the Dead left PITB "open"— that is, they did not return to the song at all. At a show, you didn't know if the Dead would return to PITB once they went on to different songs: PITB may or may not be "closed." Here's an example of PITB left "unclosed," which Barry recorded at the Shoreline in Mountain View, California, on May 11, 1991 (PITB #10). There's some excellent jazz in this version.

What's a Deadhead to do under these circumstances? The moment after the jazz segment, when the band returns dramatically to the "Main Ten" motif and then the power bridge, is one of the great Deadhead moments at any show. But Deadheads usually agree that no matter how much one might yearn for the closing riffs of PITB, the best thing to do was enjoy whatever music was playing and to keep dancing.

PITB is a signature song for the Grateful Dead. Enjoy these performances.

"The Promised Land"

Like all Deadheads, we know that "Johnny B. Goode" by Chuck Berry was a frequent set closer or encore for the Grateful Dead. We also know that the Dead themselves loved the song; referring to "Johnny B. Goode," Jerry Garcia intones on the album *Fillmore: The Last Days*: "OK, folks, here's the one it's all about."

Why then are we including "The Promised Land" (aka Promised), also by Chuck Berry, as an essential song rather than "Johnny B. Goode"? First, we avoided cover songs that are still widely associated with their original composers, and "Johnny B. Goode" is still closely associated with Chuck Berry, more so than Promised. Second, the lyrics of Promised tell a more compelling story. Third, in a head-to-head battle, "Promised Land" is musically a more interesting song, even though both songs follow the same basic melodic structure of twelve-bar blues adapted to rock and roll.

"The Promised Land" was played 427 times between 1971 and 1995, very often as the opening song of a show and often as the closing song for the first set. With the exception of a gap of fifty-eight shows between 1971 and 1972, the Dead played Promised frequently: only a handful of times did they perform more than ten consecutive shows without putting it in the mix.

The story in "The Promised Land" is a familiar one; see the lyrics here: (Promised #1). A person searching for a better life leaves home to seek his or her fortune. In this case, the "poor boy" leaves Norfolk, Virginia, and travels by bus, train, and finally plane to get to Los Angeles. On the way, there are mishaps, but kind people materialize to help him. When he gets to Los Angeles, "the promised land" of the title, he phones home. At this point, Chuck Berry inserts a pun in the lyrics: "tell the folks back home the poor boy's on the line," which could mean the phone call itself or it could refer to "putting it all on the line" in terms of taking a big gamble in a new city. It's both, of course.

The Dead always played "The Promised Land" with an upbeat tempo. Bob Weir's vocals missed a line on occasion, but that never seemed to bother the audience, which invariably cheered him on. What variation there was usually appeared in the coda: after the last verse, the typical coda finished the song with perhaps one or two iterations of the final musical verse as a kind of short solo after the verses were sung. But the Dead extended the outro on many occasions.

On September 17, 1972, in Baltimore, a show released as *Dick's Picks, Volume 23* (D1:T1) and available here (Promised #2), the Dead opened with Promised and missed some of the lyrics. They played the coda verse only one time at the end of the song. On June 23, 1976, in Upper Darby, Pennsylvania (Promised #3), the Dead closed the first set with Promised and played the closing musical verse four times. On October 9, 1976, in Oakland, the Dead played an up-tempo version of Promised to open the show, which was issued on *Dick's Picks, Volume 33* (D1:T1) and is available here: (Promised #4). They played the closing musical verse three times. And on May 19, 1977, in Atlanta, the Dead slowed the tempo just a little and played the final verse four times with a big rock and roll ending, even though it was the show's opening number. This show was released on *Dick's Picks, Volume 29* (D1:T1), and you can hear it here: (Promised #5).

Englishtown, New Jersey, was the site of the famous September 3, 1977, show released on *Dick's Picks, Volume 15* (D1:T2), which you can listen to here: (Promised #6). The Dead launched Promised right after John Scher's famous introduction of "the finest band in the land." This is the version after which Bob Weir announced that Phil Lesh had broken a string because "he dug in maybe a little too hard." Weir goes on to announce that they would pause for a moment so they could get everything "just exactly perfect." Since he had muffed the vocals that afternoon, the announcement was perhaps appropriate. At any rate, it was the start of an auspicious show, one that has gained great fame among Deadheads. On this occasion, the band played the final musical verse three times.

December 29, 1977, issued as *Dick's Picks, Volume* 10 (D1:T9) (Promised #7), is a particularly lively version. The band played the final musical verse *five* times, with Garcia "mandolining" on the guitar between the fourth and fifth iterations of the coda verse. On December 26, 1979, in Oakland, issued as *Dick's Picks, Volume 5* (D1:T11) (Promised #8), the Dead finished the first set with Promised and played the coda verse four times at the end of the song. Finally, jumping ahead some fifteen years, the Grateful Dead played "The Promised Land" at their final show on July 9, 1995, in Chicago (Promised #9), where it ended the first set. They again played the coda verse five times during that show.

When listening to "The Promised Land," look for slight variations in tempo, for audience response when lyrics are flubbed, and for extended coda versions, which are always upbeat and exciting. Our selections give you a sample of the enthusiasm in the audience as well as the pleasure the band seemed to feel when playing Promised.

"Ramble on Rose"

Listening to "Ramble on Rose" (aka Ramble) suggests parallel interpretations in terms of the lyrics. On one hand, the song is a rolling history of American—and not-so-American—pop culture in the twentieth century with references to Jack the Ripper, Billy Sunday, Jack and Jill, Crazy Otto, Wolfman Jack, Mary Shelley, and Frankenstein. You can find the lyrics and annotations about these references, thanks to David Dodd, here: (Ramble #1).

But on the other hand, there's a relatively opaque subtheme regarding the difficulties of daily life and of persisting in the face of these difficulties. After all, according to the song lyrics: "the grass ain't greener, the wine ain't sweeter, either side of the hill." Moreover, we're complicated people—the lyrics would have us be like many of the individuals listed above, which would make us very complex folks, indeed, if it weren't all tongue-in-cheek. In the final analysis, it might make more sense not to try to make too much sense out of "Ramble on Rose." After all, it's hard to pin down a rambling rose—they go where they will. It might simply be better to let yourself be taken to the "leader of the band" as Garcia sings.

Musically, Ramble is a fun song, upbeat, easy to dance to, refreshing in tone, and inviting strong audience responses at certain points, as you'll hear. The Dead shuffled along with Ramble 316 times over the years, beginning on October 19, 1971, at the University of Minnesota show that introduced Keith Godchaux on keyboards and included six new songs, including Ramble. Ramble's final performance was on June 27, 1995. In its first two or three years, Ramble was more often than not a second set song, but after the 1975 hiatus, it was performed much more frequently (and starting in 1982 exclusively) in the first set. The Dead performed Ramble heavily from 1971 to 1973, and then anywhere from half a dozen to more than a dozen times a year after that.

Listening to our recommendations shows that "Ramble on Rose" was performed in much the same style throughout the song's run, although the tempo slowed down after its first years in the repertoire. There were no extensions or stretching out in this song: solos might vary in their specific content but were generally consistent from one year to the next. Even Phil Lesh, who famously plays lead bass, is relatively subdued in Ramble.

As we often do, let's start with Ramble's first performance on October 19, 1971 (Ramble #2). Right from the get-go, this Ramble has the Dead's characteristic staccato intro, which persisted through the song's run. This first version also has the relatively abrupt coda, also consistent throughout the performance life of the song. The vocal phrasing toward the end of the song is slightly different from later versions. Otherwise, this is a standard version.

Ramble's first appearance on an official album was *Europe '72*. The Dead played this version on May 26, 1972, at the Lyceum Theatre in London, England. Ramble was deep in the second set, and a soundboard recording is available here: (Ramble #3). This is a good version with which to compare others. On December 2, 1973, the Dead played Ramble in Boston midway through the first set. Here the tempo is slower. This version appears on the album *Dick's Picks, Volume 14* (D3:T7) and is accessible here, with more audience response, as well: (Ramble #4).

In spring 1977, the Dead were arguably touring at their best performance levels. On June 8, 1977, in San Francisco, they performed Ramble during the second set. This version was released in the box set *Winterland June 1977: The Complete Recordings* (D5:T3). You can also hear it here: (Ramble #5). Even in their 1977 prime, "Ramble on Rose" sounds much the same as the versions discussed earlier but again with that slower tempo.

Finally, we jump ahead to 1990, another year in which the Grateful Dead performed well. They played Ramble on March 18, 1990, in Hartford, Connecticut. This version is part of the box set *Spring 1990: The Other One* (D1:T9), also available here: (Ramble #6). At this point in the run, Ramble was always a first set song; this time it was the next-to-last song in the set, right before "The Music Never Stopped." This audience recording conveys the interaction between the band and the crowd, which cheers at the mention of New York City. If you sing along with this version, you clearly won't be the only one doing so.

"Ramble on Rose" was a steady, consistent, oldie but goodie throughout the Grateful Dead's post-1970 career. Played often with few surprises, along with lyrics evoking cultural roots, card games, and the power of a rock-and-roll band, Ramble is a Dead song that well captures the flavor of the experience.

"Ripple"

Ah, "Ripple"! Composed by Garcia and Hunter, "Ripple" is perhaps the best song ever written, a song held in tremendous esteem by Deadheads everywhere. As with "Unbroken Chain," which is discussed later in this book, at least some of our feelings regarding "Ripple" may be due to its relatively infrequent live performances:

absence makes the heart grow fonder. But more of our attachment to "Ripple" comes from the song itself: here you get a worldview and a recipe for living a good life without a threatening apocalypse if you don't behave. There are no avenging angels hovering in "Ripple."

"Ripple" made its studio appearance on the *American Beauty* album in November 1970. That album, along with *Workingman's Dead*, was part of the mother lode of new songs the Dead introduced around that time. Of the ten songs on *American Beauty*, eight became part of the canon and were played regularly throughout the Dead's run. Only "Til the Morning Comes" and "Operator" failed to become concert hits for the band, having been performed only five and four times respectively. Seven of the remaining songs on *American Beauty* were played hundreds of times apiece, but the Dead performed "Ripple" live only thirty-nine times.

How, then, is this the best song ever written? The music in "Ripple" is simple and straightforward, essentially a folk song. Although "Ripple" famously includes a chorus that is a seventeen-syllable haiku, the answer to the question is in the lyrics, which are available here, along with comments interpreting Hunter's poem: (Ripple #1). David Dodd's more lighthearted and personal feelings about "Ripple" are accessible here: (Ripple #2). In fact, there's probably as much "analysis" of "Ripple" as there is for any other Grateful Dead song. For some examples, see Beviglia (2015), Dowling (1997), and Greene (1988), and web pages at Quora (Ripple #3) and Song-Meanings (Ripple #4). For more examples, talk to any Deadhead.

"Ripple" offers a liberating view of life: How refreshing it is to hear the narrator of the song suggest that he does *not* know the one true path. How uplifting it is to gaze through a lyrical lens that shows life as a complex flow with both despair and pleasure: "dawn and the dark of night." In other words, we should live our lives with kindness and not waste time pursuing esoteric and complex theocratic lines.

Moreover, if you aspire to lead others, be careful, for "if you fall, you fall alone." And having adopted the "Ripple" approach to the universe ourselves, we suggest you study the lyrics and see what you think—we don't know *the* way, either, so we can't "take you home." We each have our own path. Indeed, rather than "I am the way" as an approach to life, consider that each of our own individual searches together constitute "Truth," as opposed to any one individual's answer.

As mentioned, there were only thirty-nine live performances of "Ripple." Of these, thirty-four were acoustic, and these were either from 1970 to 1971 or from acoustic sets in 1980 at the Warfield Theater in San Francisco. There are only five known electric performances of "Ripple." Though we suggest links later, we strongly urge listeners to begin with the studio version on *American Beauty*: (Ripple #5). This version is the gold standard against which to compare the live versions.

The first live performance predates that album by a few months and took place on August 18, 1970, at the Fillmore West in San Francisco (Ripple #6). Unlike many songs by the Dead, "Ripple" was born nearly in its mature form, as you can hear on this version. The most accessible acoustic version is probably September 26, 1980, at the Warfield, which was released on the acoustic album *Reckoning* and is also available here: (Ripple #7). This audience recording is excellent for both the audience's enthusiasm when they recognize the song and the quiet, almost reverential attitude during the singing. They cheer Otis, Bob Weir's dog, when he wandered on stage during the song.

The first electric performance of "Ripple" was on February 20, 1971, at the Capitol Theater in Port Chester, New York, available here: (Ripple #8). This is the only time the band played the song during the second set. Although electric, "Ripple" clearly has an acoustic style in this version. Even the electric versions don't differ much from the acoustic versions.

Finally, after a gap of seven years and 569 shows, the Dead broke out "Ripple" as the encore on September 3, 1988 (Ripple #9). Rumor has it that the Dead played "Ripple" in response to a request from the Make-a-Wish Foundation. Again, the audience is beyond enthusiastic when the song's intro begins and then reverentially quiet during the verses and chorus. This version hints at how the song might have matured had it been played more often.

It's hard to imagine any Deadhead leaving "Ripple" off his or her best-Dead-song list, so for that reason alone, "Ripple" is one of our "essential" songs. But if you meditate on the lyrics, you'll appreciate the song even more. We urge you to do so. If that's not enough, consider that this is the only song Bob has ever sung in public, or at least semi-publicly, at an Irish hooley. (The Irish guests had each sung songs, and they demanded one from "the Yank.")

As a parting suggestion due to its high status in the canon, we offer you the encore performance of "Ripple" by the surviving members of the band on July 3, 2015, at the first Chicago "Fare Thee Well" show commemorating the fiftieth anniversary of the Dead. Listen to Bob Weir singing it (Ripple #10).

"Row Jimmy"

In a stereotypical rock-and-roll band, one instrument plays the lead while the others back the lead. Sometimes, the lead rotates between two or more musicians, but at those moments, the rest of a band still plays rhythm. The Grateful Dead often played music as an ensemble, reminiscent of Dixieland jazz, in which multiple instruments take the lead simultaneously. The Dead did this in slow tempo songs as well as up-beat numbers. "Row Jimmy," a Hunter/Garcia masterpiece, is one example.

"Row Jimmy" was introduced on February 9, 1973, at the Maples Pavilion at Stanford University, a show with an early version of the Wall of Sound. The Dead played "Row Jimmy" 274 times over the years, including sixty-one times in 1973, and they played the song every year they toured. The final performance of "Row Jimmy" was June 21, 1995, in Albany, New York.

At every Dead show, the band played songs at a variety of tempos and in a variety of styles, from classic rock and roll and blues to psychedelic space. "Row Jimmy" was one of the slower, rolling songs. Among the Grateful Dead's ballads, "Row Jimmy" may be most notable because of the musical style the band follows, especially in the song's intro section, which might be called "staccato counterpoint." Each note is short and crisp, and each instrument plays a solo note and then rests while the other musicians each in turn also play a single note, sometimes on the beat and sometimes not. Some forms of classical chamber music play contrapuntal music, but usually at a faster tempo (think Vivaldi).

It is far easier to understand this style by listening to it than by describing it in words, so before we discuss the lyrics to "Row Jimmy," we recommend the September 9, 1974, London show, released on *Dick's Picks, Volume 7* (D1:T3), also available here: (Jimmy #1). Listen primarily to the first thirty seconds or so in order to identify the style of music we've been describing, but feel free to enjoy the whole song. Listen for the counterpoint in the fills around the chorus. Note that in the first solo Garcia shifts to playing sustained notes, no staccato here. The second solo has even more sustained notes, almost like a carillon ringing. Weir uses staccato-style phrasing throughout the song, and Lesh sometimes does and sometimes does not, shifting for some phrases to a more traditional bass line. Trager writes about Garcia's love for this song and calls it "a minor masterpiece" (1997, 324). We're not sure we agree with his use of the word "minor."

The lyrics to "Row Jimmy" (Jimmy #2) reflect a common theme in the music of the Grateful Dead, the struggles of poor and unfortunate individuals. In this case, the song takes place somewhere in the bayous of the south, someplace with levees and grinding poverty. The song contrasts moments of excitement—for example, catching a rabbit "by his hair" and the surprise of getting a half dollar—with the boredom of everyday life: "rock your baby to and fro, not too fast and not too slow."

Two other specific themes stand out in these lyrics. The "row, Jimmy, row" line in the chorus reflects not only the hardships of life but also persistence in the face of hardships and doubt: "gonna get there, I don't know." This motif is emphasized late in the song by being sung at a much slower tempo with minimal instrumentation. The second lyrical theme appears in the vocal bridge sung as a sort of summation near the end of the song. Here we see the social dimension of poverty: though you've been given a half dollar, it's not worth a lot because there's nothing to do in town, the juke box (i.e., a "juke" or noisy bar) having been torn down. In short, life is a slog, but you persist nonetheless.

The first performance of "Row Jimmy" took place at Stanford University on February 9, 1973 (Jimmy #3). Deadheads recall 2/9/73 as a significant show: seven new songs were introduced. "Row Jimmy" was the second song played. The tempo is a bit faster and the guitar solos were not as elaborate as they later became. The vocal harmonies are excellent, including during the a cappella bridge late in the song. Finally, although you can hear the counterpoint staccato style, it is far less developed than in later shows. This 2/9/73 Stanford show is a good version to use as a base point in your listening.

Many later versions rendered the contrapuntal staccato style a little less forcefully, much of the effort falling to Bob Weir to execute. We recommend listening, in chronological order, to the following three. First, try June 14, 1976, at the Beacon Theater in New York City, available here: (Jimmy #4). This is an all-around solid version. At this point in time, "Row Jimmy" was still a totally mellow song. The band puts great emphasis on the emotional content of the vocal bridge near the end of the song.

Second, May 28, 1977, in Hartford, released on the live album *To Terrapin* (D1:T5), also available here: (Jimmy #5), is a fairly mellow version with especially nice guitar solos. Finally, try April 12, 1978, Durham, North Carolina: (Jimmy #6). Garcia's second solo is particularly outstanding for raising the level of excitement far beyond the mostly mellow nature of the song. In later performances, the Dead often extended the song by repeating the final chorus with an emphasis on the counterpoint staccato style. This performance is a good example of the powerful coda the Dead used on "Row Jimmy."

These selections favor the 1970s, so we'll leave you with a performance of "Row Jimmy" from July 30, 1988, at Laguna Seca near Monterey, California, which Barry recorded (Jimmy #7). This recording captures the excellent bridge and the extended outro, with the Dead repeating the chorus.

"Row Jimmy" is one of the great songs in the Grateful Dead's repertoire. It exemplifies the musical talent of the band, specifically in the distinctive counterpoint staccato style described earlier. With its slow tempo, the song provided a counterpoint to the upbeat songs that often filled the first set. Finally, the lyrical themes are important in our reflections on contemporary society. Although it may be difficult to pin down Hunter's literal meaning in this poem, the overall theme—persistence in the face of obstacles, with no guarantees—is quite clear.

"Saint Stephen" > "The Eleven"

We pair "Saint Stephen" with "The Eleven" because of the intimate relationship between the two songs. The Grateful Dead performed "Saint Stephen" (aka Stephen), written by Hunter and Garcia, 165 times beginning in 1968 and ending in 1983, when it was retired from the rotation. From 1968 through the end of 1969, the Dead paired it with "The Eleven" during almost every performance. After mid-1970, "The Eleven" was retired, and from that point on, Stephen became an independent song. Stephen was almost exclusively a second set song. The Dead stopped playing Stephen in 1971, but they reprised it in 1976 after a gap of 224 shows, playing it with moderate frequency into 1978 and again retiring it until October 11, 1983, when they reprised it after a gap of 352 shows.

When we say "intimate relationship," it's because some of the lyrics for Stephen appear to be either a coda or an alternate set of lyrics to "The Eleven." Phil Lesh is credited with composing the music for this coda. In the lyrics to Stephen (Stephen #1), the final lines are in italics, as a coda; these lines are the "William Tell" verse. But AZLyrics.com (Stephen #2) attributes these lines to "The Eleven." Hunter himself places these lines in "Saint Stephen," and that should be definitive.

The lyrics to "Saint Stephen" are shot through with aphorisms Deadheads quote easily: "Talk about your plenty, talk about your ills; one man gathers what another man spills." "Can you answer? Yes, I can, but what would be the answer to the answer man?" "Been here so long he's got to calling it home." These are must-read lyrics in order to fully appreciate this song.

"The Eleven," composed by Phil Lesh and Robert Hunter, was a monster of a song from the early days of the Grateful Dead. The lyrics were difficult to hear in performance, as different members of the band sang different lines of the lyrics, which were distinct enough but still hard to follow without doing some work. Alex Allan has mapped out how the Dead actually sang the song and what they left out of Hunter's poem: (Stephen #3). The Dead do not simply hand you "The Eleven"; you have to make a bit of an effort here.

"The Eleven" is not a complicated song musically, although the time signature of eleven beats to the measure makes it more complicated to play. On the other hand, musically, "Saint Stephen" has changes, jams, and extended bridges. Blair Jackson describes it as "a cryptic rocker . . . with an unusual, irregular cadence, almost a combination of waltz and march rhythms in a rock motif" (1983, 94–95).

Stephen, without "The Eleven," first appeared on the *Aoxomoxoa* album in 1969, after its first live performance in 1968. "The Eleven" first appears on the two-LP album *Live Dead*, also in 1969. The pairing of Stephen with "The Eleven" on that album remains one of the signature performances of these songs. It's ironic, though, that the album uses songs from two different performances: Stephen is from February 27, 1969, and "The Eleven" is from January 26, 1969, both in San Francisco. These two performances are available here: (Stephen #4—fast forward to 23:20). An earlier pairing, from Los Angeles on August 24, 1968, was released on the album *Two from the Vault*, released in 1993 (D1:T2–3). This combo *is* from a single show; unfortunately, there's no recording available at the Archive.org web site.

On November 8, 1969, at the Fillmore in San Francisco, the Dead played the pair. This performance was issued as *Dick's Picks, Volume 16* (D2:T6–7) and here: (Stephen #5). This version opens with the coda notes from "Dark Star" and a longer-than-usual intro before the vocals begin. The William Tell verse is used as the intro to "The Eleven." Lesh's bass is prominent in this recording. The Dead let loose in this "The Eleven," as only they could in the late 1960s.

On April 26, 1969, in Chicago, the Dead played "The Eleven" but not Stephen, one of the relatively few performances from that period when the two songs were not paired. This version of "The Eleven" was released on *Dick's Picks, Volume 26* (D1:T7) as a jam: instruments only, no vocals. The following night, April 27, 1969, in Minneapolis, the Dead played both songs as a medley. This was also released on *Dick's Picks, Volume 26* (D2:T2–3) and here as a soundboard recording: (Stephen #6). The "William Tell" verse is the coda to Stephen on this recording. "The Eleven" in this pairing is a twelve-minute version.

Note that this version of "The Eleven" is totally different from the version played the night before, which was an instrumental jam, illustrating the different ways the

Dead might perform a song. Incidentally, for readers who might wonder why the band issued two versions of the same song on an album, this is why: though the title is the same, the arrangements are not. On this 4/27/69 version, the vocals are bracketed between an outstanding intro jam and an outstanding outro jam. We really like this version of "The Eleven."

On October 31, 1971, in Columbus, Ohio, the Dead played Stephen followed by "Not Fade Away," which was not uncommon after "The Eleven" was retired. This version is on *Dick's Picks, Volume 2* (D1:T3) and here: (Stephen #7). This was the last version of Stephen for five years; the Dead did not play it again until June 9, 1976, after a gap of 224 shows. This show, in Boston, was issued on *Road Trips, Volume 4, No. 5* (D2:T1) and is here as well: (Stephen #8). Nearly the first three minutes of this fifteen-minute audience recording are given to tuning and noodling, as the Dead prepare to open the second set. There's a loud crowd response when the crowd recognizes the song. This version has an extended jam after the early verses and bridge, and they finish it without the William Tell coda as they segue seamlessly into "Eyes of the World."

Finally, listen to Stephen from October 11, 1983, at Madison Square Garden (Stephen #9), when the Dead broke out the song after a gap of 352 shows. This audience recording captures the crowd's response when the Deadheads recognize the song after that long gap. Listen for the sing-alongs during the musical pauses. Could a band ever find a more enthusiastic audience? Grateful Dead shows didn't get much better than this moment in New York. Unfortunately, the Dead played Stephen only two more times and then retired it for good.

Stephen was one of the Grateful Dead's great early songs, one that showcased their versatility as a jam band, and its pairing with "The Eleven" was always a highlight of shows back in the day. We hope you enjoy listening to both songs.

"Samson and Delilah"

"Samson and Delilah" (aka Samson) is a traditional song for which the Grateful Dead, in this case Bob Weir, created a new arrangement. Like many traditional songs, there are older recordings by other artists going back to the 1920s under different titles. The Reverend Gary Davis recorded the song in a finger-picking gospel/folk song style that can be heard on the album *The Music Never Stopped: Roots of the Grateful Dead* and, from a different source, here: (Samson #1). Weir's arrangement of the song clearly shows the impact of this version by Davis. But as with many traditional songs they performed, the Dead's arrangement made the song their own.

The Dead introduced "Samson" in live performance on June 3, 1976, in Portland, Oregon. They played the song 364 times in nineteen years and every year after it was introduced. It was also included on the studio album *Terrapin Station*, released in 1977. In performance "Samson" was almost always a second set song—in fact, it was often the opener for the second set. On the rare occasions that it was a first set song, it often was played as either the show's opener or as the closer for the first set. After 1971 or so, when the Dead switched to the standard two-set show format, they usually played one or two self-contained songs early in the second set; "Samson" was often one of those songs.

Not surprisingly, the lyrics of the song tell the biblical story of Samson and Delilah. The complete lyrics are here: (Samson #2). We could assume that this song relates to the eternal "war between the sexes," but that interpretation didn't carry over into the Dead's performances. After the studio version, the Dead released some forty live performances of "Samson"; the list is available here: (Samson #3). Musically, "Samson" is a catchy, upbeat song, sure to get people dancing. One highlight of the live performances was the unusual—for the Dead—coda, which called for a full stop and reprise of the last chorus. As you'll hear later, whether or not the band successfully managed that was sometimes called into question.

The Dead had not yet recorded the studio version of "Samson" when they first performed it live on June 3, 1976, in Portland, Oregon. So you might expect something less than perfect, especially considering that this was the Dead's first show after the 1975 touring hiatus. On that night, the Dead opened the second set with "Samson." You can hear this performance here: (Samson #4), a matrix recording that combines soundboard and audience recordings. The tone for this performance is subtly funky, with a Dixieland style of instrumentation. Lesh plays lead bass throughout the song, which times in at about five and half minutes. For a first-time performance, this is a fine version, and they even nailed the outro.

On September 3, 1977, at Englishtown, New Jersey, the Dead played "Samson" deep in the second set. This show was issued as *Dick's Picks, Volume 15* (D2:T6) and is also accessible here: (Samson #5). The funkiness is gone, except perhaps for the drummers' intro. Instead, we have a danceable, high-spirited version with exceptional solos by Garcia on lead guitar. They flub the outro on this version, but who cares! This version times in at just under seven minutes.

For another 1977 show, check out May 22, 1977, at Pembroke Pines, Florida. This version of "Samson" reflects the high level of performance the Dead delivered in 1977 (Samson #6). Although the 9/2/77 version is slightly longer than other performances, "Samson" was, generally speaking, a contained song with a stable structure that featured shorter solos and less improvisation than other Dead songs. This 5/22/77 version has a longer intro, but apart from that, it's the standard structure.

For later versions, we recommend listening to March 22, 1990, from Hamilton, Ontario, and September 16, 1990, from Madison Square Garden in New York City. The first of these, 3/22/90, was released as part of compilation album, *Spring 1990: So Glad You Made It* (D2:T1). You can hear it here: (Samson #7). The New York City show, 9/16/90, opens the second set with "Samson." This show was released as *Dick's Picks, Volume 9* (D2:T1) and is accessible here: (Samson #8). It times in at about 7:30. Both of these versions are representative performances of "Samson" during the band's later years, and both have great guitar solos by Jerry Garcia, as well as lively bass lines from Phil Lesh. Feel free to dance along.

The Grateful Dead borrowed "Samson and Delilah" from the group of traditional songs that emerged in American music after recording music became more common in the 1920s. The Dead took the song to new heights, even without the improvisational jamming that characterized many of their songs. We hope you enjoy listening to the selections here.

"Scarlet Begonias" > "Fire on the Mountain"

This is one of a handful of song pairings that were often thought of by Deadheads as one unit. For this review we discuss both "Scarlet Begonias" and "Fire on the Mountain" separately, but our focus is primarily on the combination of the two.

"Scarlet Begonias" (aka Scarlet) is one of the many Garcia/Hunter collaborations, and perhaps Barry's personal favorite, with Bob not far behind. For both of us, it's a joyous song that always puts us in a good mood, bouncing around, and singing along—even when listening in the car. In his Grateful Dead biography, Dennis McNally says it has a Caribbean feel and calls it a "masterpiece" (2002, 471). We agree. Scarlet was first performed March 23, 1974 (Scar-Fire #1), at the Cow Palace in San Francisco and soon after appeared on the *From the Mars Hotel* album, released in June 1974 (Scar-Fire #2). The final performance was on July 2, 1995 (Scar-Fire #3), where it segued into "Fire on the Mountain" at Deer Creek Amphitheater near Indianapolis. Scarlet was played a total of 316 times between 1974 and 1995.

Like many Dead songs, Scarlet began as a relatively short song. The live debut was barely more than six minutes, which is longer than the studio version at slightly more than four minutes. Over time the live versions began to expand with some wonderful improvisational jams. In 1974 alone, there were twenty-eight performances, some of which were nearly twelve minutes long. In 1976, there was an epic fifteen-minute version (the longest) in Jersey City, New Jersey, on August 4, where it closed the first set (Scar-Fire #4). All of these are without "Fire on the Mountain" following it.

Robert Hunter wrote the lyrics, and he gave the listeners a taste of London in the opening line: "As I was walkin' round Grosvenor Square." This is an old, posh area of London with a lovely central park. David Dodd mentions this along with some other points linking the song to traditional British ballads and nursery rhymes. The song was written for Hunter's wife, Maureen; she's the woman who "was calling my eye," "had rings on her fingers and bells on her shoes," and "love . . . in her eye." Whether she wore "scarlet begonias tucked into her curls" is not clear, however. There are also references to card playing as well as bluffing and dealing. Card playing and gambling are a common theme in Hunter's lyrics, found in songs such as "Deal," "Loser," and "Candyman."

Other Hunter lines that resonated with Deadheads include "the wind in the willows played tea for two," "I ain't often right but I've never been wrong," and probably the most popular to sing along with: "Strangers stopping strangers just to shake their hand." You can read the full lyrics for Scarlet here: (Scar-Fire #5)—and you should since we can't include them all here.

Perhaps the most famous line in Scarlet—or at least the one that always makes the crowd roar—is "once in a while you can get shown the light in the strangest of places if you look at it right." Perhaps this enthusiastic crowd response is because Deadheads believe they were learning about life and values in a place discredited by most of mainstream society. This is just one of many Grateful Dead lyrics that generates this sort of crowd response.

"Fire on the Mountain" (aka Fire) began as an instrumental song, "Happiness Is Drumming" on *Diga* (Scar-Fire #6), a Mickey Hart collaboration with Zakir Hussein and a number of other musicians known as the Diga Rhythm Band. The *Diga* album was released in March 1976. On that album Garcia played on "Happiness Is Drumming," and he must have liked it because Robert Hunter wrote lyrics for it when the song later became "Fire on the Mountain." Hart and Hunter have the songwriting credit. The studio version of Fire appeared on the *Shakedown Street* album (Scar-Fire #7), released in 1978.

According to Hunter, he and Hart worked on the song at Hart's ranch, where Hart had his own recording studio. As they wrote, the surrounding hills were on fire, and it was approaching the studio—quite an inspiration and motivator! Hunter also comments in his book of lyrics that the Dead used only verses 1, 2, and 5 (1990). You can find the other two verses in his book or at Alex Allan's Grateful Dead Song and Lyric Finder (Scar-Fire #8).

Unlike "Scarlet Begonias," which was played by itself for three years, Fire made its debut as part of the "Scarlet Begonias" > "Fire on the Mountain" (aka Scarlet > Fire) pairing on March 18, 1977 (Scar-Fire #9), at Winterland in San Francisco. Fire was played as part of this pair 251 times, with the last performance of the two together on July 2, 1995.

After that first performance, Scarlet > Fire became the pattern for most of the next eighteen years. There were eight occasions when the band played Scarlet > "Touch of Grey" > Fire from 1984 to 1986. On a few other occasions Scarlet also segued into a handful of other tunes ("Playing in the Band," "Hell in a Bucket," "Little Red Rooster," "Samson and Delilah," "Women Are Smarter," "Sugar Magnolia," and "Estimated Prophet") from 1987 to 1990. But most of the time, it was simply Scarlet > Fire when it was played, and in total, there were only twelve performances of Fire without Scarlet as the lead-in. The pairing of Scarlet with Fire was truly a delight to behold, especially with the usually wonderful jam between the two songs—classic Grateful Dead improvisation.

Although the studio version of Fire runs just around four minutes, live performances ran much, much longer. For example, on July 4, 1990 (Scar-Fire #10), in Bonner Springs, Kansas, Fire runs nearly seventeen minutes thanks to one of those delightful jams out of Scarlet. Along with the preceding Scarlet, which is a bit over ten minutes long itself, we have a Scarlet > Fire that gives the audience more than twenty-seven minutes of blissful listening and dancing. Barry was in the audience taping this (literally) hot show, with temperatures over 100 degrees, and even Garcia was onstage in cut-offs. Barry was one of only a handful of tapers able to avoid a cassette-tape flip in the middle of this Scarlet > Fire. The link is to Barry's recording, by the way. Though many Scarlet > Fires were as long or even longer, this one was unexpected because it appeared late in the first half of the second set as they segued into Drumz > Space. His extra-long cassette made Barry a hero to his circle of taping friends when they copied tapes to share and trade. Of course, this was before downloads, streaming, and Archive.org, where Grateful Dead music is now so easily available.

Perhaps the most well-known Scarlet > Fire is from the famous Barton Hall show May 8, 1977 (Scar-Fire #11), in Ithaca, New York. It was released in 2017 as part of the *Get Shown the Light* box set as well as an individual show. Headyversion.org lists it as the best version of Scarlet > Fire. However, we think this is based on the fact that this particular show was one of the first quality soundboard shows available to tape traders in the 1980s. It's certainly a fine version but there are others that same week that are arguably as good or better. For example, you might want to check out Scarlet > Fire from May 5, 1977 (Scar-Fire #12), which Bob attended. (This performance was only two days before the Barton Hall show.) Or try May 11, 1977 (Scar-Fire #13), three days after the Barton Hall show.

The 1977 spring tour is sometimes considered the apex of Grateful Dead performances. Whether or not that's true, much of the tour has been officially released, and you can find outstanding versions of Scarlet > Fire on the more than thirty official releases. A complete list of Scarlet > Fire releases through 2016 are here: (Scar-Fire #14).

Then, of course, there's the almost mythical version of Scarlet > Fire played on June 12, 1980 (Scar-Fire #15), in Portland, Oregon. This was the night of a secondary Mount St. Helen's volcanic eruption, and fans were "treated" to volcanic ash falling from the sky as the show ended, even though the volcano was thirty-five miles away in Washington State. Michael Marlitt, a Deadhead friend of Barry's who was at the show, commented: "it was like a winter snowstorm, but warm!" The Dead's performance was hot.

Barry was fortunate to see Scarlet—without Fire—at his first Dead show in Des Moines, Iowa, June 16, 1974 (Scar-Fire #16). This performance was even more enjoyable since it was a Wall of Sound show. What a wonderful and amazing beast that was! Another memorable performance happened on April 15, 1988 (Scar-Fire #17), at the Rosemont Horizon in Chicago, when Scarlet > Fire opened the show. This was the only time that ever happened, and one of only three times Scarlet > Fire was played in the first set. Barry also saw its last performance at Deer Creek on July 2, 1995 (Scar-Fire #18).

The key to appreciating Scarlet > Fire, of course, is the jams, as is the case with all of the Dead's improvisational songs. The studio versions of Scarlet and Fire each ran less than five minutes long, yet live, the combination could run thirty minutes or more. There were jams in both of the songs when played live, usually with a long one as they segue between the two, morphing from Scarlet into Fire, and another as they wrap up Fire. And it's always good rockin'! So regardless of version, be it live or studio, "Scarlet Begonias" and "Fire on the Mountain" are both essential Grateful Dead music—separately or together.

"Shakedown Street"

"Shakedown Street" (aka Shakedown) is a nice rocker written by Jerry Garcia and Robert Hunter that was added to the Grateful Dead's repertoire in 1978. Along with "Stagger Lee" it's one of two Garcia/Hunter tunes that appeared on the album *Shakedown Street*, released on November 15, 1978 (Shakedown #1). Over time the title became synonymous with the Deadhead vending area found in the parking lot at most Grateful Dead concerts in the 1980s and 1990s.

"Shakedown Street" was first played in concert on August 31, 1978 (Shakedown #2), before the LP was released. It continued to be part of the live performance catalog every year until its last performance on July 9, 1995 (Shakedown #3), at the Dead's final performance in Chicago. Shakedown was played 163 times in those seventeen years, although its performance became less frequent, with only a handful each year after 1985.

Lyrically, "Shakedown Street" doesn't have much of a story to tell—or maybe it does. The narrator is responding to the listener who has complained that "this town ain't got no heart," "the sunny side of the street is dark," and "nothin' shakin' on Shakedown Street, used to be the heart of town." The narrator suggests the darkness could be because it's midnight, and if the listener would "poke around," he might see things differently. The narrator goes on to suggest the listener lived under a darkness that "crackled like a thunder cloud" perhaps because he "had too much too fast" and overplayed his part. This exchange could be interpreted as a conversation about the Haight-Ashbury area of San Francisco during and after the Summer of Love in 1969. When the hippie movement reached its peak and tourist buses began to roam the streets at this time, the magic of the counterculture movement in this area began to lose its momentum and became darker. Many in the area (and elsewhere around the United States) may indeed have had too much, too fast, and overplayed their parts due to too much sex, drugs, and rock and roll. You can read the complete lyrics here: (Shakedown #4).

"Shakedown Street" appears on a number of official releases, but not as many as one might expect given the number of times it was played and the energy the song brings to a concert. It was released as a 45-rpm single backed with "France" in 1979 and later as the B-side with "Alabama Getaway" in 1981. Overall, it's appeared on more than sixteen official releases, and you can see a full list of official releases through 2016 here: (Shakedown #5).

Musically, Shakedown is one of the many get-up-and-dance tunes from the Dead; you simply can't sit still when listening. As a result, it was usually a show or second set opener; early in its performance history it was even an encore. The vocals were always fun, with lots of give and take between Garcia—throwing out the line "just don't tell me this town ain't got no heart" and then "just gotta poke around,"—and Weir and Brent (or Vince, depending on the year it was performed) responding in kind. This could go on for quite a long time before the instrumental improvisation began, which, for both Barry and Bob, was where it really got fun! For example, listen to the June 30, 1985, performance from Merriweather Post Pavilion in Columbia, Maryland (Shakedown #6), which is the "best" version according to headyversion.com. This one clocks in at more than thirteen minutes and epitomizes what Deadheads like about Shakedown.

Barry saw Shakedown fourteen times beginning on February 9, 1979, when it was played as the encore. One he enjoyed and that we both recommend is from March 20, 1992, in Hamilton, Ontario, at the Copps Coliseum (Shakedown #7). Shakedown was only played four times in 1992, and this is a good quality matrix recording. It opened the second set and runs nearly thirteen minutes, with Weir and Vince Welnick doing the backing vocals and Garcia in fine form on vocals and guitar. He has his Mu-Tron envelope filter cranked up, jammin' it out, and you can hear the crowd show its appreciation.

Another wonderful version Barry saw that we recommend was at Starlight Theatre in Kansas City on August 3, 1982. This version is more than fourteen minutes long with delightful interplay between Garcia, Brent, Phil, and the rest of the band: (Shakedown #8); you'll like it too. The September 7, 1985, rendition from Red Rocks Amphitheatre is another we recommend (Shakedown #9). It opens the second set and gets everyone ready for more jumpin' music and improvisation. This is a tasty matrix version that includes more of the audience than a straight soundboard recording.

The last Shakedown Barry saw was from the Pyramid in Memphis on April 2, 1995: (Shakedown #10). For a show from 1995, this is a surprisingly strong performance, much stronger than the shows from May and July 1995. Garcia's singing and playing is quite good, and the band continues to pick up the tempo as the improvisation kicks in at about seven minutes into the twelve-minute performance.

Whatever versions of "Shakedown Street" you choose (and we recommend listening to more than one), we know you'll agree it belongs on the essential list.

"Ship of Fools"

Jerry Garcia and Robert Hunter wrote "Ship of Fools" (aka Ship), and the Grateful Dead debuted it in concert on February 22, 1974 (Ship #1), in San Francisco. Ship then appeared later that year on the LP *From the Mars Hotel* (Ship #2). Other than the 1975 hiatus from touring, it stayed in the Grateful Dead's live repertoire every year for a total of 225 performances, with the last one on June 25, 1995 (Ship #3).

This is perhaps the most overtly political song written and performed by the Grateful Dead. According to Dennis McNally, the Dead's official biographer, it was written as a reflection of the political atmosphere in 1974 surrounding the impeachment proceedings against president Nixon (2002, 470). Hunter's lyrics are relatively short but convey the message of distrust and the recognition of political lies in the repeated line: "It was later than I thought when I first believed you, now I cannot share your laughter, Ship of Fools." Of course, the message goes on, as you'll see when you read the lyrics here: (Ship #4). In a way, it's surprising for a song like Ship to be such a regular part of the Dead's catalog, since Garcia was apolitical, once saying something to the effect that he didn't vote "because it only encourages them." Nevertheless, the song was clearly meaningful enough to him and the band for it to be performed so regularly. As usual, Hunter leaves the lyrics wide open to many interpretations beyond the political. In any case, Ship is clearly a protest song.

At another level, Ship evokes a kind of revolutionary consciousness that is in many ways consistent with the writings of Antonio Gramsci, the Italian Marxist from the early twentieth century. Ship's lyrics are not simply about "dropping out" of mainstream society, nor are they about "consciousness" in the form of mind-expanding drugs or meditative techniques. Gramsci wrote about hegemony, a regime's hold over our political consciousness, and his writings stress the need for antihegemonic actions to change people's ways of thinking and believing. Interpreting Ship's lyrics on this level shows the song to be both powerful and political, easily their most serious statement about the 1960s counterculture as ideology.

Musically, Ship is a laid-back tune that always appeared in the second set, with a few exceptions from 1974 to 1976. It's written in 4/4 time and moves along slowly and quietly, more like a ballad than a political protest as the story unfolds. As it does, the energy builds up when Garcia delivers an impassioned plea, "I still might warn a few: Don't lend your hand to raise no flag atop no ship of fools," a Gramsci-inspired line if there ever was one. Nearly twenty different live performances of Ship have been released officially, and you can see the full list through 2016 at this link: (Ship #5).

Although Ship appears in the second set, it's one song that doesn't have much improvisation in it. This tends to limit the uniqueness of each performance, keeping them all relatively short. Keeping that in mind, we'll suggest a few versions for your listening pleasure. We've already provided a link to the debut version, so now we'll move ahead to May 9, 1977, in Buffalo, New York. This performance is from the famed spring 1977 tour, which is included on the *May 1977: Get Shown the Light* box set (D8:T3). You can stream a matrix recording here: (Ship #6). The energy shows why this tour is so well reviewed and appreciated.

Of the twenty-three performances of Ship that Barry saw, we recommend this one from August 11, 1987, at Red Rocks Amphitheatre in Colorado. The first of three nights at Red Rocks, this version of Ship is right on the mark, as you'll hear in this clear audience recording: (Ship #7). Garcia is in fine voice and his guitar solos get the crowd wound up in this high-energy performance that runs a bit more than eight minutes.

We also recommend a performance from the New Year's run in Oakland on December 30, 1991 (Ship #8). This is an awesome Dan Healy ultra-matrix recording with another solid performance from the band. Keyboards here are by Vince Welnick, and Garcia again sounds very good both vocally and instrumentally, along with a solid low end from Lesh.

Finally, we suggest one of the last performances of Ship from July 26, 1994, at Riverport Amphitheatre near St. Louis, Missouri (Ship #9). This is the last version Barry saw, and the Dead performed it only three more times after this. This is another audience recording that really brings out Weir's rhythm guitar, Welnick's keyboard, Lesh's bass, and, of course, Garcia's vocals and guitar.

Though Hunter's lyrics for "Ship of Fools" are not always understood as a political protest, the song itself is a lovely one that traveled well throughout much of the Grateful Dead's thirty-year history. Listen to a few we've suggested or check the list at headyversion.com (Ship #10), and you'll understand why.

"So Many Roads"

"So Many Roads" is another late entry to the Grateful Dead's catalog, with its first concert outing on February 22, 1992 (SMR #1), followed by a total of fifty-five live performances, ending with their last show in Chicago on July 9, 1995. This could be considered another "road" song in the Dead's canon, which is completely understandable given the amount of time the Dead were on the road throughout their thirty years of performing. Like all of the Dead's songs that debuted after 1989, "So Many Roads" does not appear on a studio album, although a studio rehearsal is on the *So Many Roads* box set released in 1995 (D5:T10).

"So Many Roads" is another fine song by Garcia and Hunter, and it's a real crowd-pleaser thanks to Garcia's powerful vocals, especially on the repeated closing line, "so many roads to ease my soul." Once again, Hunter's lyrics are a poetic delight with references and influences from past works by various sources including Jelly Roll Morton, Chuck Berry, Fats Domino, and others, according to David Dodd in *The Complete Annotated Grateful Dead Lyrics* (2005, 363–65). The simple story that unfolds is one of a world-weary "whinin' boy" who's "got no place to go." He's seen so many roads in so many places, spending too long "where the sun don't shine." His troubles worsen because "you don't seem to hear me when I call" and "you treat me so unkind." The many places he's been are described beautifully by Hunter with phrases like "land of the midnight sun where ice blue roses grow" and "roads of gold and silver snow." And though it's a slow ballad, Garcia winds it up with strong ending vocals, as mentioned, as well as exquisite guitar. The band also does a great job of backing his vocals as if they were a quiet church choir. You can find the complete lyrics here: (SMR #2).

Musically, "So Many Roads" is presented as an unhurried narrative that Garcia set to a simple but lovely tune. As is the case with so many Grateful Dead songs, it varies in length anywhere from six to twelve minutes depending on how long Garcia soloed, how long the two choruses lasted, as well as the last verse, which could be extended for many iterations, not unusual for the Dead. The ending is often reminiscent of "Knockin' on Heaven's Door," with the backup vocals subdued and quiet.

"So Many Roads" may be the song with the fewest official releases by the Dead. It appears on the *So Many Roads* box set as mentioned above, and its only other official release is as part of the *30 Trips around the Sun* eighty-CD box set that includes two versions: one from a performance in 1994 and the other from the last tour in 1995. To hear other versions of the song you'll have to visit Archive.org, which has all fifty-five versions.

Barry saw ten performances of "So Many Roads" and found it to be a wonderful new addition to the band's repertoire when he first saw it on March 21, 1992, a month after its debut. The version that struck Barry as particularly impressive was at Shoreline Amphitheatre in Mountain View, California, on September 18, 1994, where it appeared in the second set. Garcia's health was still good at this time, as was his voice and guitar playing. You'll agree if you listen to Barry's audience recording. Sit back and listen for Garcia's soaring guitar and vocal rave-up at the end of this nearly ten-minute version: (SMR #3). It's a delight—nearly enough to cause tears.

Other versions of "So Many Roads" that are worth listening to include the last performance at the Dead's last show in Chicago on July 9, 1995, mentioned in the introduction earlier. Garcia struggled on this tour both with his voice and his guitar playing. But in this last version, he manages to deliver the goods in a twelve-minute performance: (SMR #4). This is the version included in the *So Many Roads* box set, where it had a little extra help in the mixing.

An especially tasty version appears on the *30 Trips around the Sun* box set mentioned above from Boston Garden on October 1, 1994, also available here: (SMR #5). It's a particularly appealing seven-minute performance. The "So Many Roads" from Deer Creek near Indianapolis on June 29, 1992, is another that Barry saw and that we recommend. It's also a shorter seven-minute version, and Garcia and the band are all together; there's a sweet and quiet guitar solo after the first verse along with soft backup vocals. The crowd likes this one, too, as you can hear on this audience recording: (SMR #6).

Our last recommendation is from the Nassau Coliseum on Long Island, on March 23, 1994. Like all its performances, this one quiets the crowd as the song progresses, then winds them up as Garcia once again nearly shouts "so many roads to ease my soul." You can hear an audience recording here: (SMR #7). "So Many Roads" is a beautiful song that may not have had a chance to live up to its full potential. We are privileged to have the many recordings we do.

"Stagger Lee"

"Stagger Lee" is one of the Grateful Dead's "murder ballad" songs based on a recurring tale of murder, selective law enforcement, and a wronged and vengeful woman. Like other story songs in this book, including "Casey Jones" and "Dupree's Diamond Blues," the Dead played an original version composed by Jerry Garcia with lyrics by Robert Hunter.

As the story goes, Delia's lover, Billy, is murdered in cold blood for no apparent reason. She demands that the police arrest the shooter, Stagger Lee, and accuses Baio, the cop, of cowardice when he doesn't do so. She gets a gun, walks into a bar, lets Stagger Lee buy her a drink, and then "shot him in the balls." She drags him to city hall and turns him over to the police, saying: "see you hang him high." The song ends with the refrain: "The song that woman sang, was look out Stagger Lee." See the lyrics and information about the history of the song, including other lyrics and titles and a list of artists who recorded the song here: (Stagger Lee #1). There are also more than two dozen official recordings of "Stagger Lee" by the Dead: (Stagger Lee #2).

The Grateful Dead performed "Stagger Lee" 146 times beginning in 1978. They performed it only twice between 1980 and 1984 and then regularly for the rest of their run, averaging about eight performances a year. "Stagger Lee" was almost always a first set song. Musically, it's a mid-tempo song with a bouncy lilt to it, a great song to dance to. There was relatively little by way of improvisation or extended jams in most early versions of the song, but things got more interesting later on.

The Dead introduced "Stagger Lee" in live performance on August 30, 1978, at Red Rocks, Colorado. The only recording of that version is an audience recording of fair quality, available here: (Stagger Lee #3). We include it here because it is a relatively no-frills version of the song, which you can compare with later versions that developed in different musical directions.

The fans at headyversion.com chose as their favorite "Stagger Lee" the performance on December 16, 1978, in Nashville (Stagger Lee #4). Most of the comments at headyversion.com point to the great outro solo by Garcia on this version. It's worth noting that this performance is only four months after "Stagger Lee"'s first performance, so we can already hear changes. This is a slow, funky version.

From the 1980s, we have November 1, 1985, in Richmond, Virginia, which was issued as *Dick's Picks, Volume 21* (D1:T4). You can listen here: (Stagger Lee #5). This is a peppier version of "Stagger Lee." About two minutes in, Garcia starts one of his standard rolling solos, the kind of sound that helps you understand why folks say his guitar rings like a bell. And by the mid-1980s, the outros were more improvisational around the core riffs.

On September 16, 1990, in Madison Square Garden, the Dead performed a version of "Stagger Lee" that was released on *Dick's Picks, Volume 9* (D1:T4) that times in at about 8:30, compared to the 8/30/78 Red Rocks performance, which timed in at under six minutes. It's available here: (Stagger Lee #6). This show had two keyboardists: Bruce Hornsby and the newly added Vince Welnick. This version is played at a moderate tempo but less funky with a more rolling sound. Garcia's guitar work is excellent, his vocals less so. This version times in at about 7:30. The song has evolved a lot compared to earlier versions.

And for another show from the 1990s, we recommend March 24, 1993, in Chapel Hill, North Carolina, available here: (Stagger Lee #7). This version times in at under six minutes, so although we can see that "Stagger Lee" had grown longer over the years with the extended solos and the outro, the Dead still sometimes played shorter versions—this version is the second song in the show. We hope you enjoy this audience recording with lots of crowd responses.

"Stagger Lee" is best appreciated if you are familiar with the story, so do look up the lyrics for this song. Although there may be a band on the corner playing the old hymn "Nearer My God to Thee" in the final refrain, Delia herself is singing a different tune: "Look out Stagger Lee." There are other Grateful Dead songs with pointed endings like that, particularly "Me and My Uncle," where the narrator leaves his uncle lying dead "by the side of the road." Play "Stagger Lee" and keep dancing.

"Standing on the Moon"

"Standing on the Moon" (aka SOTM) is one of the last songs to be added to the Grateful Dead's live performance catalog. As such, it may not be familiar to all who listen to Grateful Dead music, even though it was released in 1989 on the Dead's last studio album, *Built to Last* (SOTM #1). SOTM made its live debut on February 5, 1989 (SOTM #2), and was last played in concert on June 30, 1995 (SOTM #3), for a total of seventy-five performances.

This is another lovely Garcia and Hunter slow ballad with a simple and unusual story to tell. The narrator/storyteller has a broad view of happenings on the Earth from his vantage point "standing on the moon." He sees the coast of California, the Gulf of Mexico, El Salvador, and Southeast Asia. He sees a "battle rage below," and there on the moon with him, he sees "Old Glory standing stiffly," "crimson, white, and indigo," left behind long ago by an astronaut. He hears children crying and "other songs of war." Yet even "with a lovely view of heaven," he's lonely and blue, with the simple desire to "be with you somewhere in San Francisco on a back porch in July." The last line of the song, "be with you," which Garcia repeated several times starting with 1993 performances, generated a real roar from the audience, who wanted nothing more than to be with Garcia, whether it be July in San Francisco or not. And, of course, we all knew Garcia himself wanted to be there with *us*, not just any generic "you." This is not a rocker nor a dance song; it's one to listen to and reflect on the emotion it evokes. Bob can't listen to SOTM without tears threatening.

One line late in the song leads us to an interpretive twist: "where talk is cheap and vision true." Bob sees this as a statement about government officials and others in the

United States who, during the violence in Vietnam and El Salvador, mouthed pious nonsense while standing on their moons, where "talk is cheap." Hunter's lyrics may have been clear and true, but not so the rhetoric of those helping to destroy Vietnam, for example. You can find the complete lyrics here: (SOTM #4).

"Standing on the Moon" was performed only four times in the first set early in its history, and then it moved on to the Jerry ballad spot in the second set. It was always an emotional performance, and every time Garcia sang it, he gave it his all—even in 1994 and 1995, when his health and voice were failing. Because there were fewer performances of SOTM than other essential songs from the Grateful Dead's repertoire, there are only around ten official releases available. You can see a complete list through 2016 here: (SOTM #5).

Barry saw seventeen versions of "Standing on the Moon" and was moved by each of them. Two in particular stand out. The performance he saw in Hamilton, Ontario, at the Copps Coliseum on March 20, 1992 (SOTM #6), is a real gem. This soundboard recording demonstrates the emotional power of the song, along with strong vocals from Garcia and commanding guitar leads during the last few minutes. The crowd loves it, and you will, too.

The last performance Barry saw, in Las Vegas on May 19, 1995 (SOTM #7), is another fine version with a slightly faster tempo. It's especially pleasing since Garcia had been struggling with his health, voice, and playing on this last Grateful Dead tour. But he's clearly up for it, as you'll hear in this audience recording.

All seventy-five live performances can be found on archive.org, and here are a few versions we recommend you check out. One of the best versions, if not *the* best, is from Eugene, Oregon, on August 21, 1993 (SOTM #8). It works on all levels with Garcia's voice and guitar really delivering the goods! No one in the audience could have been sitting during the rousing ending.

On July 17, 1989, at Alpine Valley in East Troy, Wisconsin (SOTM #9), the Dead gave the audience another excellent version of SOTM (this was the second time Barry saw it). Again Garcia plays and sings beautifully. He begins a vocal rave-up with the "be with you" line toward the end, but that didn't fully develop until 1993. You can hear a much fuller and well-delivered rave-up in the performance from March 23, 1994 (SOTM #10), at Nassau Coliseum on Long Island, New York. Barry saw this one, and it still gets to him now. This is an audience recording that will affect you, too!

The last recommendation for you is from the Buckeye Lake performance in Hebron, Ohio, from July 29, 1994 (SOTM #11). This is one of the longest versions of SOTM, clocking in at almost twelve minutes; typically, most versions last eight to ten minutes. Part of the reason for the length of this version is the extended introduction in which the band repeats the three-chord intro many times. Listen closely: is there a guest pedal steel guitar in the house? Garcia does some interesting guitar effects through most of the song and then in the last three minutes does the rave-up vocal that energizes the crowd, as you hear in this fine audience recording. Pay attention to Lesh's bass line during this ending rave-up.

Whichever version you choose, we know you'll enjoy "Standing on the Moon." We think this one is a song for the ages.

"Stella Blue"

So far, we've mentioned the "Jerry ballad" several times with short explanations. What better moment to provide a more complete description than with "Stella Blue" on the table? Late in the second set, usually right before the final song of the set, the Grateful Dead, with Garcia singing, played a Garcia/Hunter ballad, a slow, perhaps serious song that settled everyone down, at least a little bit, before the finale. Several songs could fill this slot—for example, "Black Peter" or "Wharf Rat." "Stella Blue" (aka Stella) was one of these, arguably the best, at least into the 1990s, when "Standing on the Moon" might have challenged for that accolade.

When the first notes of "Stella Blue" played at a Dead show, the atmosphere changed. There might be a quick roar of recognition, but then, as one Deadhead was heard to say: "It's time for church." Sure enough, what had been a raucous throng respectfully, if not reverentially, quieted as Garcia's simple intro riff launched the song. Listen for this shift in the recordings we recommend: could a Grateful Dead audience really become this quiet?

"Stella Blue" was first released on the album *Wake of the Flood* in 1973. The Grateful Dead played six of the seven songs on that album regularly. Stella was performed 328 times over the years, beginning on June 6, 1972, and ending on July 6, 1995. Early on, they played Stella a handful of times in the first set. Otherwise, it was firmly located in the second set, and as suggested earlier, usually in the Jerry ballad slot.

Robert Hunter's lyrics for "Stella Blue" (Stella #1) rank among his best poems. Like many Grateful Dead songs, there are multiple layers of meaning. On one hand, we see our now-familiar Grateful Dead protagonist, the struggling outsider trying to make a go of it, in this case as a guitarist. As in "Row Jimmy," the narrator doesn't know if he'll make it, but he must "dust off those rusty strings just one more time," and make them "shine." He persists, as we all must. The song seems autobiographical: is Garcia singing about his own life, or are we singing along about ourselves at the same time? Probably both.

Yet on the other hand, there is the song's worldview: our narrator realizes that the past is all a dream and that you can't hold on to it, so why not relax and let it flow, why not accept it as "vanished years"? This life is all that there is and accepting that is liberating. "Stella Blue" has inspired a lot of discussion over the years, including by David Dodd (Stella #2), and at Songmeanings.com here: (Stella #3). Trager calls it "extremely enigmatic" (1997, 355).

Listening to a performance of "Stella Blue" is always emotional. First, at the outset, there's the hush, as mentioned earlier. Second, it's a ballad, and not only is the tempo quite slow, but the volume seems to be lower, as if the Dead were attempting to quiet the audience for a few moments. Once that's achieved, the bridge verse ("I've stayed in every blue light, cheap hotel") turns the volume back up—the dynamics in a good performance of Stella are notable, especially comparing the singing verses with Garcia's solo after the bridge, not to mention the outro. Finally, listen to the way Garcia sings the words "Stella Blue," with just the slightest hint of a pause. There is no shortage of good performances of "Stella Blue" available. Deaddisc.com lists forty-four (Stella #4).

To listen to some good versions of Stella, we recommend the following, in no particular order. October 21, 1978, in San Francisco is available here: (Stella #5). This version also appears in the series *Road Trips, Vol. 1, No. 4* (D1:T7) and is headyversion. com's favorite. Note: this is an *audience* recording, so the fact that you can't hear the audience much is because the crowd was silent. This version has an outstanding outro.

We also like April 21, 1978, in Lexington, Kentucky, released in the box set *So Many Roads* (D3:T3) and available here: (Stella #6). In the liner notes, Garcia is quoted: "Ideally there's a song in there that's so delicate that it's got a moment in it of pure silence." Listen for that, perhaps right before he sings the phrase "Stella Blue." This is a soundboard recording, so you'll hear little audience input. There is another outstanding outro here, with a powerful coda, before the segue into Truckin'.

March 16, 1990, Landover, Maryland, released in the box set *Spring, 1990* (D3:T3) is really fine, and you can hear it here: (Stella #7). Spring 1990 was a good year for the Dead, reflected in this slightly shorter version of "Stella Blue." This audience recording lets you appreciate the dynamic interchanges between the Dead and the audience. It's hard to believe that Garcia is not singing about himself when he intones: "a broken angel sings, from a guitar." It's no secret that Garcia felt weighed down by his obligations to the industry that was the Grateful Dead—perhaps this song is about that.

Listen to March 9, 1995, at the Spectrum in Philadelphia, accessible here: (Stella #8). We suggest listening to this 1995 show for historical comparison. We know that Jerry Garcia was fading toward the end and the 1995 tours often reflected that. The music was fine, but Garcia's health was an issue, and it affected his voice. You can hear this in this audience recording. As usual, there's the huge audience response when the crowd recognizes the song and then relative quiet for the duration—that is, until the outro, which is again great. Garcia definitely rises to the occasion, as he nearly always did.

"Stella Blue" is simply one of the Grateful Dead's best ever songs. The lyrics are inspirational and important in their worldview: living in the present and accepting that the past is just "a dream." We all wish Garcia was still around to "dust off those rusty strings just one more time." As perhaps the best Jerry ballad, "Stella Blue" also illustrates the dynamics among different songs at shows as well as any single other song in the repertoire. Listen to songs that precede and follow Stella to see what we mean.

"Sugar Magnolia" > "Sunshine Daydream"

This review of "Sugar Magnolia" and "Sunshine Daydream" is sort of a "twofer." We'll discuss both of these together, as we've done with other song combinations such as "Scarlet Begonias" > "Fire on the Mountain." It's only "sort of a twofer," though, because the pair is really one song, "Sugar Magnolia" (aka Sugar Mag) with a coda called "Sunshine Daydream" (aka SSDD). It has music by Bob Weir with lyrics by Robert Hunter and Weir (more on this later).

Although it's commonly noted that "Sugar Magnolia" made its live debut on June 7, 1970 (Sugar Mag #1), listening to this first performance shows us an unfinished version of Sugar Mag that simply repeats the first three verses. This also occurs with the second performance on June 24, 1970 (Sugar Mag #2). Both of these versions are slow, tentative, and far from ready for live performance to such a degree that we don't even recommend listening to them! It's not until its third performance on August 18, 1970 (Sugar Mag #3), that the complete lyrics to Sugar Mag are performed, along with SSDD for the first time. This is the song Deadheads know and love in full bloom. The last performance of Sugar Mag with SSDD was July 9, 1995 (Sugar Mag #4), in Chicago, its 594th performance. This makes it the second-most-performed Grateful Dead song after "Me and My Uncle."

During the twenty-five years it was played, Sugar Mag and SSDD were nearly always played as one song. There were thirty-one exceptions in which Sugar Mag was played but SSDD was played later in the set—but this also has an exception! The first separation of the two was on December 10, 1973, when Sugar Mag was played close to the end of the second set. It was followed by "Goin' Down the Road Feelin' Bad" and then SSDD closed the set. At other performances, Sugar Mag opened a set and SSDD closed it. If that isn't surprising enough, there were other occasions, like December 31, 1989, when Sugar Mag opened the show and SSDD closed the first encore. The exception to the exception mentioned earlier took place in 1991, after the death of Bill Graham, concert impresario and great friend of the Dead. During a run of five shows that became a tribute to Graham, Sugar Mag, Graham's favorite Dead song, opened the first set on October 27, 1991, in Oakland, but the Dead did not play SSDD until it closed the second set on November 3, 1991, in San Francisco.

Regarding the "Sunshine Daydream" coda, Robert Hunter explained that Weir "just worked to death" on the song and would ask him for more or better lyrics. Finally, Weir "wanted some extravaganza to cap it all off," so Hunter wrote the lyrics for SSDD in the studio while they were recording the *American Beauty* LP (Jackson and Gans, 2015, 167). Because Sugar Mag and SSDD appear together on the *American Beauty* album released in November 1970, we'll simply refer to them as Sugar Mag hereafter, unless otherwise noted.

Weir was thinking of his longtime lady friend, Frankie Acardi, who worked in the Dead's business organization, when he wrote Sugar Mag. The lyrics don't always portray her in the kindest terms when Weir sings, "head's all empty and I don't care," though he goes on to say, "she's got everything delightful" and "everything I need." Frankie's history as a dancer is also touched on, "she can dance a Cajun rhythm" and "she can wade in a drop of dew." Even more, she can "make happy any man alive." You can find all the lyrics for this lively love song here: (Sugar Mag #5).

Musically, Sugar Mag is a delightful, highly danceable tune; perhaps "rollicking" is a better description. Weir wrote both parts in 4/4 time, and Garcia says, "I contributed the 'Sunshine Daydream' part, the chord changes at the end." So with the "extravaganza" described by Hunter now in place, the live performances became more robust, faster than the classic and lovely version on *American Beauty*, which features Garcia on pedal steel guitar. The energy of the live version now allowed it to open a show or close it, which it often did. You can listen to the studio version here: (Sugar Mag #6).

Weir and Hunter had been at odds over lyrics for a while, as noted earlier in our review of "One More Saturday Night." Their final falling out came after a performance of Sugar Mag at the Capitol Theatre in Port Chester, New York, in February 1971. Hunter saw the song as a "sweet country tune" when he and Weir finalized the lyrics in the studio, but now he heard it as a "ripping, show-closing rocker," which was not what he had in mind. This was the end of Hunter's collaboration with Weir. Hunter then told John Perry Barlow, "take him, he's yours," and Barlow became Weir's lyricist for the next eleven years (McNally 2002, 394).

Given the frequency of live performances of Sugar Mag, it should be no surprise to find many official live recordings: it's been released on more than fifty CDs or box sets. You can see a full list of official Sugar Mag releases through 2016 here: (Sugar Mag #7); there are also two versions on the more recent *May 1977: Get Shown the Light* eleven-CD box set.

If you don't have access to any of the above CDs or LPs or if you simply want to hear other live versions of Sugar Mag, here are some versions we recommend. We'll start with a few of the twenty-seven performances Barry saw. Because none of the later 1990s versions are on official recordings, check out this recording from the infamous Deer Creek show on July 2, 1995, after the gate-crashing episode and the death threat on Garcia. Given the circumstances, this is a surprisingly good nine-minute performance on an audience recording (Sugar Mag #8).

Now let's take a step back to December 30, 1990, for a New Year's run from Oakland. This one, also about nine minutes, is an ultra-matrix recording from Dead soundman, Dan Healy (Sugar Mag #9). Finally, from the shows Barry saw, we encourage you to hear this version from the Greek Theatre in Berkeley on June 14, 1985. This is from the three-show twentieth-anniversary run and it sounds wonderful in this matrix recording: (Sugar Mag #10). This one really rocks—look out for Phil!

Before ending this review of "Sugar Magnolia," we consider some earlier live performances; here are a few more highly recommended versions. First, try this very early version from February 18, 1971, at the Capitol Theater in Port Chester, New Jersey. You can hear Pigpen on organ, and Garcia has fun with his wah-wah pedal on this excellent soundboard recording: (Sugar Mag #11). This one rocks.

Next, enjoy a nice soundboard recording from November 24, 1972, in Dallas: (Sugar Mag #12). Turn this one up to hear Garcia going wild. Finally, we suggest a terrific October 10, 1981 version from a show you've probably never heard of: the Sports Palace in Barcelona, Spain. This is a long one at eleven minutes, and it's hot on this soundboard recording: (Sugar Mag #13).

In closing, we'll say this: though Robert Hunter was frustrated with Bob Weir for taking his "sweet country tune" and turning it into a "ripping, show-closing rocker," we're glad Weir did. If you check out our recommendations or almost any live version of "Sugar Magnolia," we think you'll agree. This may be *the* signature Grateful Dead song.

"Sugaree"

"Sugaree" is a song we're sure is on every Deadhead's essential list, and it certainly ranks high on ours. Once it joined the Dead's active repertoire on July 31, 1971 (Sugaree #1), this Garcia/Hunter collaboration was played 357 times, including its last performance in Chicago on July 8, 1995 (Sugaree #2). It was played every year after its debut, even at a show during the band's hiatus on August 13, 1975 (Sugaree #3), at the Great American Music Hall in San Francisco.

"Sugaree" is, according to Hunter, a "song, as I imagined it, . . . addressed to a pimp," as he explains in the liner notes for the 2004 Garcia box set *All Good Things: Jerry Garcia Studio Sessions* (47). Needless to say, this explains a lot when listening to the lyrics such as "how come you lay awake all night long?" and "in spite of all you gained you still have to stand out in the pouring rain." Then, of course, it also makes clearer the refrain, "shake it, shake it, Sugaree. Just don't tell them that you know me." You can find the complete lyrics here: (Sugaree #4). Hunter goes on to say he changed the original title from "Stingaree" to "Sugaree" because it "sounded better" after he became familiar with an Elizabeth Cotten song, "I've Got a Secret (Shake Sugaree)." Cotten was a folk singer and songwriter who was rediscovered in the late 1950s, and her album *Folksongs and Instrumentals with Guitar* influenced many contemporary artists, including Garcia and Hunter. Her most famous song, "Freight Train," was recorded by Garcia and David Grisman on their album, *Not for Kids Only*, in 1993.

Musically, "Sugaree" begins with a relatively laid-back, eight-bar intro before Garcia begins to sing. The song remains laid back as the song unfolds—until Garcia begins to unleash his guitar. Then, depending on the version, hold on! Both Bob and Barry marvel at what Garcia can do on this song. This is what makes Grateful Dead music so fascinating and always revealing: the power of improvisation. Each and every one of the 357 versions is unique, demonstrating the remarkable creativity—*in real time*—of Garcia and the band. This is a song that demands listening to more than one version!

The first official studio version of "Sugaree" was on Garcia's first solo LP, *Garcia*, released in 1972 (Sugaree #5). The first official Grateful Dead release was on the live *Steal Your Face* two-LP album in 1976, produced from the Dead's October 1974 run before their hiatus. This version was from their October 18, 1974, performance (Sugaree #6). After that, you can find "Sugaree" on more than *sixty* official live releases. You can see a full list through 2016 here: (Sugaree #7).

Barry saw twenty-seven performances of "Sugaree" and loved every one, including the version played at his first show on June 16, 1974, in Des Moines (Sugaree #8). This one is relatively short, less than six minutes, and there are brief public-address system problems at the beginning. Barry didn't see "Sugaree" again until August 17, 1980 (Sugaree #9), at the Municipal Auditorium in Kansas City. This was memorable simply because he had a front-row seat! For this one, Garcia unleashes that special guitar work described earlier, and it runs more than ten minutes. Garcia's guitar is a bit low in the mix, but it's still a good version. Then you might try April 11, 1987 (Sugaree #10), from the UIC Pavilion in Chicago, which is a nearly ten-minute version and a fine recording. This one shows off Garcia's kick-ass guitar work for sure, and the crowd agrees.

Though all of the versions Barry saw are enjoyable at the very least, to be blown away as described above, we recommend *any* version from the Dead's spring 1977 tour. The 2017 release of *Get Shown the Light* box set has a wonderful sixteen-minute version from May 5, 1977, in New Haven, Connecticut (D1:T2), which can also be found here: (Sugaree #11). Bob danced to that one in person.

There were many other truly great versions of "Sugaree" throughout the Dead's performing career, so we'll point you to a few more that rank high at headyversion .com. Try this fine sixteen-minute audience recording from October 17, 1983 (Sugaree #12), at the Olympic Center in Lake Placid, New York. Then check this nearly fifteen-minute matrix recording from June 21, 1980, at West High Auditorium in Anchorage, Alaska (Sugaree #13). Also be sure to listen to this sixteen-minute matrix recording from December 28, 1979, at the Oakland Coliseum: (Sugaree #14).

With that said, the *one not to miss* is from May 28, 1977, at the Hartford Civic Center. It was officially released on *To Terrapin: Hartford '77* (D1:T3) in 2009, and you can find that version of "Sugaree" here: (Sugaree #15). This is a nineteen-minute version in which Garcia nearly sets his strings on fire in multiple solos. It's astonishing! We dare you to put this on and *turn it up*! If you haven't heard this before, you will never be the same.

"Tennessee Jed"

"Tennessee Jed" (aka Jed) was composed by Jerry Garcia and Robert Hunter. The Dead performed Jed for the first time on October 19, 1971, in Minneapolis, and it was a regular part of the rotation from 1971 until its last performance on July 8,

1995, at Soldier Field in Chicago. The Dead played Jed 433 times over the years, making it one of their top twelve most-played songs. The first recording of "Tennessee Jed" appeared on the *Europe '72* album. There is no studio recording of the song: it lives only in live performances. Jed has appeared on several dozen released albums: there's a list here: (Tennessee #1).

The music in Jed doesn't much change from performance to performance, although the tempo varied from night to night. The principal solo in Jed comes toward the end of the song, with only a short chorus at the very end of the song before the quick coda. It was in that musical bridge that the Dead could raise the temperature of the song and generate audience response.

Some songs in the Grateful Dead's repertoire are fairly easy to label as to genre, from rock and roll to folk to blues, and so forth, but Jed is an exception. The tempo usually moves along at a steady beat, but the song at first glance is not a rocker. During the musical bridge after the final verse, the band brings rock-and-roll energy to the song. Jed is a difficult song to label, although "country rock" may be as close as anything. This song, like "Sugaree," is basically a sui generis Grateful Dead song.

The lyrics in Jed play to a familiar motif: the working-class narrator trying to make it through life in the face of difficult odds, accidents, you name it. Poor Jed begins the song a shackled member of a chain gang. To make matters worse, he falls down a flight of stairs, gets a black eye, cracks his spine, and even his dog gets kicked. He threatens the "rich man" that he'd better be ready to "butter my bread" when he, Jed, returns. The solution to his many woes? "Let's head back to Tennessee, Jed." His dog repeats the message, as does a slot machine. Who knows if Jed will ever return to confront the rich man, because there's "no place I'd rather be" than Tennessee. Consistent with other songs, this typical Grateful Dead character soldiers on.

The narrator is called Tennessee Jed, but—as most of the lyrics suggest—there should be a comma between the two words: "Tennessee, Jed." For most, if not all, of the song, Tennessee is Jed's (hoped-for) destination, not his name. We get the sense that if he gets there, Jed will never leave. Perhaps the song is simply a prisoner's dream.

October 19, 1971 (Tennessee #2), marks the Grateful Dead's first live performance of Jed at the University of Minnesota. This version is fast and the musical fills between the verses and the chorus are relatively spare. We like the staccato style throughout this version. This version of Jed was well received by the audience that night, considering it was a brand-new song. The song's essential ingredients are all present. This is a good version to listen to for comparison with later versions.

May 3, 1972, at the Olympia Theater in Paris, is the version of Jed that was released on the *Europe '72* album (D1:T13) and the *Europe '72* box set. This version is arguably the standard against which to measure others. A soundboard recording with very little audience response is available (Tennessee #3). Three years after Jed's first performance, the Dead played a version we like on October 24, 1974, at Winterland in San Francisco (Tennessee #4). The basic structure and playing style are not much different from most other versions. The tempo is slower than the shows discussed earlier. The bridge instrumental is particularly good.

Jed from October 10, 1982 (Tennessee #5), is excellent. On this night, the Dead have the staccato style down perfectly. As with the Winterland version, the musical bridge is excellent. Lesh's bass line is outstanding throughout the song. And to add a little (more) whimsy, Garcia ends the song playing the melody to "shave and a haircut, two bits."

For readers particularly interested in musicality, we recommend the performance from November 17, 1973, at Pauley Pavilion on UCLA's campus in Los Angeles. This show was released in 2013 as *Dave's Picks, Volume 5* (D1:T6) and is accessible here: (Tennessee #6). In this case, we intentionally provide a soundboard recording. Why? On many recordings, Bob Weir's work on rhythm guitar gets lost in the mix. But in this version of Jed, the recording lets you hear clearly what he plays throughout the song: listen to the left channel. Considering the fact that Tennessee is one of the Dead's more formulaic songs, hearing the variety of music Weir plays is particularly informative, especially compared to what one might expect of a rhythm guitarist. Moreover, the way Weir complements Garcia's lead guitar is amazing. It takes a little work to hear the beauty in the music, but it's worth the time investment.

In spite of the calamities visited upon our narrator, Jed is a lighthearted song. It's difficult to label, and it never changed significantly between its first and last performances. Yet it embodies the fun one encounters at a Grateful Dead show, and for that alone we deem it an essential Dead song. For seven or eight minutes, we dance, we sing along, and we forget our own calamities, at least for the moment. No harm in that.

"Terrapin Station"

Epic is the first word that comes to mind for this unique Grateful Dead song. It would be a mistake to categorize "Terrapin Station" (aka Terrapin) as rock and roll— or as part of most any other musical genre. Stories of its creation are mythical, as is the story in the song itself; more on this later. Terrapin made its live performance debut on February 26, 1977 (Terrapin #1), in San Bernardino, California, and its last performance on July 8, 1995 (Terrapin #2), in Chicago. In total there were 302 performances during the nineteen years it was played, and it was part of the live repertoire every year after its debut. The studio version was released on July 27, 1977, on the eponymous LP, *Terrapin Station*, and it took up the entire second side of the record at more than sixteen minutes.

Terrapin was given birth on a dark and stormy day when lyricist Robert Hunter was inspired by a storm he saw out the window over San Francisco Bay, and he began to write "let my inspiration flow." And it did, running to eight pages and more than a thousand words! Nearly simultaneously Jerry Garcia was driving not far from Hunter's home and heard a song in his head. The next day the two of them met and discovered how well Hunter's words fit with Garcia's music (McNally 2002, 498). The Grateful Dead version of Terrapin that emerged was reduced from Hunter's 1,000 words to about 400, which is what Garcia chose; as he often did, Garcia wanted the story to be left open-ended without a resolution.

The story in the song is mythical and ageless, and in three parts tells of a "Lady with a Fan," "Terrapin Station," and "At a Siding." The first part, "Lady with a Fan," is Hunter's version of an old English folk ballad, "Lady of Carlisle," dating from the fifteenth or sixteenth century. It's also known by the names "The Lion's Den" and "The Fan," both of which terms appear in Hunter's lyrics. The lady here has two suitors, a soldier and a sailor, and to win her hand, she asks both to retrieve her fan from a lion's den. The lyrics are filled with too many truly wonderful lines to include them here, but some examples are "while the storyteller speaks, a door within the fire creaks," "his job is to shed light, and not to master," and "faced with mysteries dark and vast, statements just seem vain at last." Read the full lyrics at David Dodd's wonderful Annotated Grateful Dead Lyrics site (Terrapin #3). Seriously, do read them, and you'll understand our choice of "epic" to begin this review.

Musically, Terrapin is a three-part suite with each of the three sections written in 4/4 time, but each is written in a different key. When played live, Terrapin was significantly different from the studio version, which included both lyrical and instrumental sections not played live. In particular, "At a Siding" was performed partially only once, and some of the instrumental sections—"Terrapin Transit," "Terrapin," and "Terrapin Flyer"—were never done live. In addition, record producer Keith Olsen added strings, horns, and chorus to the studio version, which annoyed some band members. But listen to it on a quality audio system, and it will impress you. You can hear the full studio version here: (Terrapin #4). More than twenty-five live Terrapin performances have been released officially, and you can see the complete list through 2016 at this link: (Terrapin #5).

Now for some listening recommendations for Terrapin. We've already provided a link for the debut performance, so next we suggest a version a month later at Winterland Arena in San Francisco, on March 18, 1977 (Terrapin #6). This is the only time they played "At a Siding"—or at least part of it—and also part of the rest of the suite, which was never played again. You'll need to listen to the next two tracks, listed as "Alhambra" (Terrapin #7), and "Drumz" (Terrapin #8), to hear it all. This was only the third performance of Terrapin; the two earlier versions did not include these, and since the studio version had not been released when this was performed, no one had any idea about "At a Siding" or the instrumental part preceding the drums! This is a fine soundboard recording that times in at more than fourteen minutes for all three parts.

Next, we recommend the first of the thirty-nine Terrapin performances Barry saw, this one on September 8, 1983 (Terrapin #9). This version is from the third of three shows at Red Rocks Amphitheatre, and it's a nearly thirteen-minute version on a nice soundboard recording. Our next recommendation, June 26, 1986, from the Metrodome in Minneapolis, is unusual. Barry saw this performance, as well, and it's memorable because he was one of only a small handful of tapers who managed to get their recording gear inside. No soundboard is available, and you can hear Barry's recording, one of the best available for this performance (Terrapin #10).

We move forward in time to July 4, 1989 (Terrapin #11), for a performance at Rich Stadium in Orchard Park, New York. This is a clear soundboard recording from a summer tour during a strong year for the Dead, and this performance ranks high on headyversion.com. Our next recommendation is another one Barry saw, at Deer Creek near Indianapolis on June 23, 1993 (Terrapin #12). This was the last of a three-show run, and Terrapin is played in the second set before "Drumz," as was often the case. This performance ranks high on the headyversion.com site. Listen to this audience recording and you'll hear why—it runs nearly twenty-five minutes! Needless to say, the crowd loved every minute of it and frequently roared their approval. For our ears, this is the best version; it's a monster!

Finally, we conclude our recommendations with the next-to-last performance of Terrapin from Three Rivers Stadium in Pittsburgh, Pennsylvania, on June 30, 1995: (Terrapin #13). As we've said regarding several of the 1995 performances, Garcia's health was declining, which affected his guitar playing and sometimes his voice as well. With this performance, although he's not at the top of his game, it's not likely you'll notice, either, however—unless you're one of those "picky Deadheads." This is a nineteen-minute version on a good audience recording.

"Terrapin Station" is a remarkable song for a rock-and-roll band to perform, and we all should feel blessed that the Grateful Dead wrote and shared this song with us and that we have their recorded legacy so we can hear this essential song today.

"They Love Each Other"

"They Love Each Other" (aka TLEO), composed by Robert Hunter and Jerry Garcia, is a cute, lilting love song that first appeared on Garcia's solo album *Reflections*, which was "solo" in name only, since the Grateful Dead were participants on half the tracks. Its first live performance was on February 9, 1973, at Stanford University. At that show, in addition to TLEO, six other original Grateful Dead songs were performed for the first time. TLEO's lyrics are simple and to the point and can be found at this link: (TLEO #1).

As a love song, there's probably none in the Dead's repertoire as straight to the point as TLEO. Many of Hunter's familiar themes are absent: there is no loss, no major struggle, no persistence needed in the face of mounting obstacles. The problems that appear in other songs, even in other love songs, don't materialize here. As the song goes, there's "nothing that you need to add or do."

It wasn't always that way. In its earliest performances, there were lyrics that were dropped after a few performances. The (now) missing lyrics did introduce some negative elements, but these were erased in the newer arrangement, resulting in a more positive tone. At TLEO's first performance on 2/9/73 (TLEO #2), you can hear both a faster tempo than in later versions and the bridge with the soon-to-be-dropped lyrics. In this version, Garcia doesn't quite follow the lyrics that appear at the lyrics link provided earlier.

TLEO was performed 226 times after that initial Stanford performance. In 1973, the year the Dead introduced the song, they played seventy-two shows and performed TLEO forty-six times. Subsequently, they played TLEO every year except 1995—TLEO's final performance was on September 27, 1994, at Boston Garden. The Dead almost always played TLEO in the first set with only a few exceptions, all of which took place in 1973, including the debut 2/9/73 show at Stanford. The Grateful Dead have issued at least twenty live versions of TLEO—a full listing as of 2016 is available here: (TLEO #3).

By December 12, 1973, at the Omni in Atlanta, Georgia, the Dead had modified TLEO only slightly, as you can hear at this link: (TLEO #4). In this performance, the tempo is lively and lilting, and the band seems eminently relaxed. Bob Weir's rhythm work is clearly audible—listen especially during the third ("diesel train") verse. Garcia's solo plays around the melody as only he could do it. The vocal bridge is still included here in late 1973, by the way.

Incidentally, on this specific recording from 12/12/73, you can hear the Dead's sound check for the show, consisting of the first seven items on this soundboard recording. The sound check starts with "Sleigh Ride," then "Rip It Up," the Little Richard rocker, and then "Blue Suede Shoes" before shifting to the more typical Dead repertoire with "Peggy-O." Among other things, that list hints at how the Dead, or at least Garcia, thought: At a mid-December show, "Sleigh Ride" makes sense. Little Richard was from Macon, Georgia, so playing "Rip It Up" in Atlanta makes sense. "Rip It Up" was covered by Elvis Presley, so Garcia continues with "Blue Suede Shoes."

The Dead's show on May 6, 1981, at the Nassau Coliseum on Long Island, New York, is on *Dick's Picks, Volume 13* (D1:T3), and TLEO is also accessible here: (TLEO #5). On this audience recording, you can hear the crowd's reactions to the song, and you can also hear Garcia flub the second verse. By 1978, the tempo is greatly slowed down, and TLEO has become more of a ballad than anything else, played with the smooth, rolling style the Dead were so good at. At the same time, Garcia's solo focuses heavily on the high end of the register, so this is not a totally mellow performance. The vocal bridge is gone, and the lyrics are realigned consistent with what we saw at the lyrics link provided earlier.

On September 8, 1987, more than a year later and after a gap of seventy shows, the Dead brought TLEO back into the rotation in Providence, Rhode Island, at the second of a three-show run that Bob attended and enjoyed immensely. There is a good audience recording at this link: (TLEO #6). This is a mature version of TLEO—it's all here: the ballad tempo; the rolling, staccato, smooth sound of the music; the bouncy fill riffs, including the coda riff; strong vocals; and excellent solos by both Brent Mydland and Jerry Garcia. Finally, give a listen to TLEO from February 26, 1977, in San Bernardino, California (TLEO #7). This version is the best-rated TLEO at the headyversion.com website. It's the Grateful Dead at their smoothest.

TLEO is a love song, played like a love song, with little except the basic song: not much by way of extended codas and such, for example. It did change over time, much for the better in our view, but you can come to your own conclusions if you've listened to the versions cited above. When you compare this song to others on the essential list, TLEO reveals yet another facet of the Grateful Dead's amazing versatility in style.

"Throwing Stones"

Rhythm guitarist Bob Weir and his frequent lyricist John Perry Barlow collaborated on "Throwing Stones," which made its live debut on September 17, 1982 (Stones #1), in Portland, Maine. During the next fourteen years, it was played 265 times, the last on July 5, 1995, at Riverport Amphitheatre near St. Louis. "Throwing Stones" was played regularly every year after its debut, with the most performances in 1983, when it was played thirty-two times. It was recorded in the studio and released in 1987 on the *In the Dark* CD (Stones #2). This was the first new album from the Dead in six years, and it also featured their one and only top-ten single: "Touch of Grey."

Stones is probably the most antiestablishment song written and played by the Grateful Dead during their thirty-year career; it was generally their practice to avoid anything political and to avoid lecturing the audience. One exception up to this time was "New Speedway Boogie," which was written in response to the tragic Altamont Speedway concert headlined by the Rolling Stones—another might be "Ship of Fools." With Ronald Reagan in the White House, Weir and Barlow felt they had to speak up, and "Throwing Stones" is the result. According to Dennis McNally (2002, 545), Weir called it "an 'anarchistic diatribe' against all manner of evil."

The lyrics are indeed a polemic, if not a diatribe. They open with a lovely description of Earth and the human race on it, "a peaceful place or so it looks from space," then tells of the fear that "we may lay our home to waste." This was the time in American history when the nuclear arms race escalated dramatically with Reagan's "Star Wars" space-based missile defense system. The lyrics go on to point out that "commissars and pinstripe bosses, roll the dice" with their focus on "selling guns 'stead of food today." Overall, it's a bleak portrayal of planet Earth and mankind under the thumb of politicians and businessmen. There are a few lines that always got the audience involved. First is "ashes, ashes all fall down" taken from the nursery rhyme "Ring around the Rosie." Another is "so the kids they dance and shake their bones," which is also descriptive of the Dead's audience. And finally, Weir's rant, "it's all too clear we're on our own" in which he repeated "on our own" over and over. You can find the complete lyrics here: (Stones #3).

Musically, "Throwing Stones" has some unusual characteristics: it opens on a dominant chord and Weir plays his chords on the third beat of the measure. There's also a jam in the middle, although it still remains "just a song" with limited improvisation. It does qualify as a danceable rocker, however. Because of the power of the tune and the lyrics, it nearly always appeared in the second set, and over time it stretched out musically from five minutes to eight or nine minutes.

Live performances of "Throwing Stones" appear on fifteen or so official releases. It also appears on a few official video releases, and it was also one of only six songs for which the Dead made an MTV video (Stones #4). You can see a full list of official releases through 2016 here: (Stones #5).

"Throwing Stones" didn't evolve much over time; it debuted in a mature form and little changed during the thirteen years it was performed. With that said, here are a few performances we recommend, including some of the forty-four Barry saw. We'll start with the "best" version, which, according to headyversion.com, was on October 10, 1982, not long after its debut. Here's the link to a very good matrix recording: (Stones #6). This one times in at nearly eight minutes, and the lyrics in the second verse are a bit different from later versions, which is not unusual for Weir. This is a good, jammy version.

Now we'll jump ahead to August 13, 1987 (Stones #7), at Red Rocks Amphitheatre. This is one Barry attended, at one of the most spectacular venues to see the Dead. More than eight minutes long, Weir extends himself vocally on this version. Next up is from Phil Lesh's fiftieth birthday, on March 15, 1990 (Stones #8), in Landover, Maryland. This show was officially released as the limited-edition *Terrapin Station* CD to help fund a place in the Bay Area of northern California for Deadheads to find all things Grateful Dead. This was intended to be "an interactive museum, sensory playground, and social/cultural laboratory," but that project never materialized (Metzger 1998). The link takes you to a soundboard recording with the boys kicking out a nine-minute version that comes late in the second set.

Next up, we recommend Richfield, Ohio, on March 14, 1993 (Stones #9). This one is memorable to Barry because the previous night's show was cancelled due to a blizzard, so the audience was ready for the Dead this second night. You can hear "Throwing Stones" near the end of the second set (a common place for it) in this very clear audience recording. It's nearly nine minutes long, and you'll hear the happy audience singing along throughout.

Finally, take a listen to the final performance of Stones on July 5, 1995 (Stones #10), near St. Louis at Riverport Amphitheatre. This was at the end of a long tour, and Garcia was at a low ebb due to his health issues. With that said, the performance is surprisingly good, so judge for yourself. Once again, the song appears near the end of the second set, and the band does an admirable job of supporting Weir—and Garcia—in this more than nine-minute performance. Once again, we find a surprisingly good performance from 1995.

"Throwing Stones" was one of Weir's and the Dead's major songs, nearly always found in the second set, where it wound the audience up before the show ended. Stones is clearly an essential part of the Dead's repertoire. Enjoy!

"To Lay Me Down"

"To Lay Me Down" is a beautiful ballad from Garcia and Hunter: they both did their job well on this one. Hunter again wrote a simple but heartfelt poem, Garcia matched it with a lovely melody and sang the lyrics with deep conviction. This song may seem contrary for a rock-and-roll band, but instead it adds another dimension to the Dead's ability to reach the audience. Sadly "To Lay Me Down" was played only sixty-three times, with the first performance on July 30, 1970, at the Matrix in San Francisco, and the last on June 28, 1992, at the Deer Creek Music Center near Indianapolis.

The Dead played "To Lay Me Down" only four times in 1970, and they were all acoustic performances. They didn't play it again until 1973, with three performances, and followed that with seven in 1974. After that it was not played again until 1980, which then saw the most performances in a year with sixteen. That year the Dead played a run of twenty-four shows in San Francisco, New Orleans, and New York with an opening acoustic set. This was an ideal setting for "To Lay Me Down," and they played it thirteen times in those acoustic sets. They played it two more times in 1980 in an electric set, and once more at the New Year's Eve 1980 acoustic set in San Francisco. After 1980, the number of performances became less frequent, if it was played at all.

The lyrics for "To Lay Me Down" can be understood literally, which is unusual for Hunter. In 2004, he elaborated on writing "To Lay Me Down" and the other songs on Garcia's 1972 first solo album, *Garcia*, in the booklet included with the 2004 Garcia box set *All Good Things: Jerry Garcia Studio Sessions*. Hunter says he spent some time in London in 1970, and he wrote the lyrics there. "The songs flowed like molten gold onto the page and stand as written." Inspiration for the lyrical images came from him lying on the grass and clover looking at clouds with an old girlfriend he'd not seen for many years (47–48). So we have "to lay me down with my head in sparkling clover," "to be with you once more," and "let the world go by like clouds a-streaming." Simple lines, but they are sweet and beautiful. The complete lyrics can be found at this link: (TLMD #1).

Musically, "To Lay Me Down" matches the simplicity of Hunter's lyrics. Garcia said in a 1981 interview with Blair Jackson and David Gans that it was the first song he ever wrote on the piano (Gans, 2002, 37). When asked about Dead love songs, Garcia makes it clear that "it's a love song. How could anybody miss that?" (83). It's played very slowly and quietly in 3/4 time. Though you might not think of it as a dance song, it is one that offers the opportunity for dreamy swaying if nothing else.

The first official Grateful Dead recording of "To Lay Me Down" appeared on the two-LP *Reckoning* album in 1981. This was a collection of songs taken from the acoustic sets at the 1980 shows mentioned earlier. The first official electric performance, from June 28, 1974, in Boston, appeared on *Dick's Picks, Volume 12* (D2:T6). You can also hear an audience version at this link: (TLMD #2). Altogether, there have been only about ten official releases of "To Lay Me Down," which is a shame for such a sweet love song.

Fortunately, we can recommend some performances to stream. The debut acoustic version from July 30, 1970, at the Matrix in San Francisco sounds good on this soundboard recording: (TLMD #3). Next you can check out this electric version, which is still very quiet, from July 31, 1974, in Hartford, Connecticut, a show Bob attended and that also was issued on *Dave's Picks, Volume 2* (D3:T1). This audience recording demonstrates how much respect the audience gives to the Dead's music on a quiet song like this: (TLMD #4).

Barry was lucky enough to see "To Lay Me Down" performed six times, beginning on July 7, 1981, and ending with its last performance on June 28, 1992. The second one Barry saw is this performance from Starlight Theatre in Kansas City on August 3, 1982. It's a nine-minute gem, and you can hear a fine matrix recording at this link: (TLMD #5). Another version Barry saw is from Los Angeles on February 10, 1989. This soundboard recording shows Garcia with a deeper, almost aching voice and quiet harmony from Brent Mydland and Bob Weir. Mydland's soft keyboard also adds a nice touch (TLMD #6).

We also recommend one from Madison Square Garden on September 18, 1990. This has Vince Welnick on electronic keyboard and Bruce Hornsby on piano, which offers a richer backing to the performance. Listen at this link: (TLMD #7). Finally, you can hear the last performance of "To Lay Me Down" on June 28, 1992, from Deer Creek, near Indianapolis (TLMD #8). This is a matrix recording.

"To Lay Me Down," as these recommendations show, is a truly beautiful love song. Despite the limited number of performances and official recordings, it will always remain an essential Grateful Dead song.

"Touch of Grey"

The first performance of "Touch of Grey" (aka Touch) was September 15, 1982, in Landover, Maryland, and the last was on July 9, 1995, in Chicago at the Dead's last concert. During those twenty-three years the song was played 213 times, and it was part of the song rotation every year. It peaked in number of performances in 1987 with thirty-two, due in large part because it had become a hit single that year.

In July 1986, Garcia nearly died due to previously undiagnosed diabetes. After he recovered, the Dead played for the first time again on December 15, 1986, and they opened the show with Touch. When Garcia sang the line "I will get by, I will survive" the crowd went nuts with nary a dry eye in the crowd. It got even wilder with the line "we will get by, we will survive," and this continued to fire up the crowd every time Touch was played thereafter. At this point, the song became a true anthem for the Dead and Deadheads.

This song may be considered both a blessing and a curse for the Grateful Dead. It was a blessing for them since it brought them fame and fortune, but it was also a curse because—it brought them fame and fortune, something they were never pursuing. Although the fortune was nice, the fame brought a multitude of problems after the song was released as a single and an MTV video in 1987 (Touch #1). Those problems were primarily due to the huge influx of Touch fans who were otherwise unfamiliar with the Grateful Dead and the culture of the Deadhead fans. For the Deadheads, a concert was all about listening to the music; for many of the "Touch-heads" it was about the hit single and the party. This led to larger venues and problems of crowd control, among other difficulties.

"Touch of Grey" is a Garcia and Hunter composition that has some clever lyrics with a lot of irony in them. For example, the opening line is "must be getting early, the clocks are running late" and later it's "the shoe is on the hand that fits." Hunter wrote both music and lyrics for Touch but never recorded it. Later Garcia found it and saw an opportunity for a "big" and "optimistic" song because of the "we will survive" line. When Garcia wrote his own melody for Touch, it became a bouncier, more "celebratory" song than Hunter's. And Hunter found it to be "a hell of a hot little tune" (Jackson and Gans 2015, 312, 329). You can find the complete lyrics at this link: (Touch #2). Throughout its history, Touch was the encore of the show thirty times, but more often it was the show opener, which happened eighty-nine times. It was a song that was guaranteed to get the crowd dancing and happily singing along with "we will survive."

The studio recording of Touch was first released as a 45 vinyl single (your choice of black or gray) in June 1987, and it became the Dead's first and only top-ten hit. When the album *In the Dark* was released in July 1987, Touch was the first track, and the album was also a hit. Many official recordings have followed, including a two-CD *Eternally Grateful* collection that was available only at Starbucks. Surprisingly few performances of Touch have been released officially, but it has been released on a few videos including *View from the Vault*, *View from the Vault III*, and *Truckin' up to Buffalo*.

Even though there are just a few officially issued releases, fortunately for us, *all* the live performances of Touch can be found online, and we'll recommend some for you now. Certainly the most obvious choice is the December 15, 1986, version when the Dead took the stage for the first time after Garcia's diabetic coma in July. You can hear this Touch here: (Touch #3). Needless to say, the crowd was already pumped before Touch opened the show. The crowd reaction to "we will survive" late in the song comes out nicely on this matrix recording. Barry, in attendance at that show, can vouch for the energy and emotion with this performance!

Next up, give a listen to the debut of Touch on September 15, 1982. This is an excellent audience recording of Touch's first performance as the encore (Touch #4), and it's played at a faster tempo. Follow up next with a rockin' version from Hartford on March 27, 1987, before it was a hit single or album. This is a superb soundboard matrix from the Dead's soundman Dan Healy (Touch #5). Next, try this tasty performance from July 18, 1989, in Alpine Valley in East Troy, Wisconsin, which Barry also saw. This one is recommended by both of us and by headyversion.com as well.

You can stream it here: (Touch #6). Our last suggestion is from the performance of Touch on December 18, 1994, in Los Angeles. This is the last one that Barry saw, and it's one of the last seven performances of Touch by the Dead. It's a nice audience recording you can stream here: (Touch #7).

"Touch of Grey" was always a crowd-pleaser, and it became an anthem for Deadheads, especially after Garcia's near-death experience in 1986. We think you'll understand why when you listen to our recommendations. And as a final thought, here's the link to a thirty-minute video on the making of the "Touch of Grey" official video, which catapulted the song into the top ten. It's fun (Touch #8).

"Truckin'"

"Truckin'" is likely the most well-known Grateful Dead song. After all, it did "go straight to the top of the charts, number one, numero uno, in Turlock, California," according to Bob Weir in his introductory comments to the audience before the band played "Truckin'" in their first performance on the Europe '72 tour on April 7, 1972. And it was one of the few Dead songs that got any radio airplay in the 1970s, along with "Casey Jones." You may be surprised to know that in 1997, "Truckin'" was recognized as a "national treasure" by the Library of Congress.

The very first performance of Truckin' was on August 18, 1970 (Truckin' #1), at the Fillmore West in San Francisco. It was played every year thereafter until its last performance on July 6, 1995 (Truckin' #2), at Riverport Amphitheatre near St. Louis. It was played a total of 519 times, which makes it one of only eight Dead songs played more than 500 times live. Its first recorded performance was on the *American Beauty* LP in November 1970 (Truckin' #3).

The first three live performances of "Truckin'" in 1970 were acoustic, but after those three it was played only in electric sets, even when the Dead revisited acoustic sets in 1980. It started its performance life in the first set but soon became mostly a second set selection, although it was occasionally played in the first set as late as 1990.

Songwriting credit for "Truckin'" is shared by Garcia, Lesh, Weir, and Hunter, and it contains the line that has truly become part of American culture: "what a long strange trip it's been." This is a line that's been used in numerous book titles, including Dennis McNally's official biography of the band; movie titles including the four-hour 2017 *Long Strange Trip* Grateful Dead documentary; and in newspaper and magazine headlines that have nothing to do with the Grateful Dead.

Robert Hunter's lyrics tell the "absolutely autobiographical" story of the Dead's early time on the road, according to Weir in an interview that appears in *Anthem to Beauty*, a 1997 DVD. Hunter is also interviewed, and he tells that it "was written over a long period of time," and there were "lots of verses." He went on to say he and the band thought they might continue to add verses over time, but that didn't happen because "once you get it down, it is down, and you don't go back and revisit it." You can find the lyrics here: (Truckin' #4).

Musically "Truckin'" is another rocker that gets the crowd on its feet dancing and singing along with the familiar lines—even though Weir *often* messed them up. Admittedly, there are some tough lines to sing at such a fast tempo such as, "arrows of neon and flashing marquees out on Main Street." The crowd often cheered Weir if he flubbed it! The crowd also typically joined in to sing "sometimes the light's all shining on me, other times I can barely see," and if they hadn't been singing up to this point, they definitely would with the next ever-so-familiar line, "what a long strange trip it's been." "Truckin'" undoubtedly wins the championship for being on the most official album releases. You can see a complete list of official releases through 2016 here: (Truckin' #5).

Besides being a rocker, "Truckin'" was another open-ended song that was ripe for improvisation. Whereas the studio version on *American Beauty* clocked in at just over five minutes, live versions could stretch out as long as sixteen minutes, as on May 19, 1974 (Truckin' #6), in Portland, Oregon, or eighteen minutes on July 31, 1974, Dillon Stadium in Hartford, a show Bob attended that you can hear on this soundboard recording: (Truckin' #7). (Note that this link also gives you the "Mind Left Body Jam" and "Spanish Jam.") If that's not long enough for you, then fasten your seatbelt for the more than thirty-minute version (yes, *thirty minutes!*) from the Philadelphia Convention Hall Auditorium on August 5, 1974 (Truckin' #8), where the boys take "Truckin'" to outer space before seguing into "Stella Blue." It's insane.

Barry saw "Truckin'" at his first show on June 16, 1974 (Truckin' #9), and we recommend giving it a listen even though we've pointed you to several other versions from 1974. This version is short, at only seven minutes, but it ranks high on the headyversion.com list. And here are some more recent versions Barry saw that we recommend. First, listen to July 15, 1989 (Truckin' #10), at Deer Creek Amphitheater, near Indianapolis. This is an audience recording that runs eight minutes. Next give a listen to Truckin' from Boston Garden on September 26, 1993 (Truckin #11), another clear audience recording that runs about eleven minutes. All of these later performances, although not necessarily "outstanding," are full of energy and show how the song matured over the years. With that said, the Dead's last performance of Truckin' on July 6, 1995 (see the link in the second paragraph), was clearly a struggle for Garcia. And it was tough to watch and hear despite the band's best efforts.

"Truckin'" started as a simple autobiographical song about the band's life on the road, became a real monster for outstanding improvisation, and then settled back into a comfortable but still satisfying routine during its twenty-five-year performance history. And the "long strange trip" catchphrase has passed into popular culture.

"Unbroken Chain"

"Unbroken Chain" (aka UBC) is the least performed of our essential Grateful Dead songs. It was written by bassist Phil Lesh and his good friend, poet Bobby Petersen. Petersen also wrote lyrics for three other Grateful Dead songs: "New Potato

Caboose" recorded on the 1968 *Anthem of the Sun* LP, "Revolutionary Hamstrung Blues" performed live once in 1986, and "Pride of Cucamonga." Both "Unbroken Chain" and "Pride of Cucamonga" were recorded on the Dead's *From the Mars Hotel* LP, released in 1974. Even though UBC was recorded in 1974, it remained absent from the Dead's live performances for twenty-one years, until March 19, 1995! And then it was played only ten times before its last performance on July 9, 1995, the last performance of the Grateful Dead's thirty-year career.

The lyrics to "Unbroken Chain" tell a powerful story, with words as lovely as any of Robert Hunter's lyrics, and that's saying a lot. It's a sweet song, with Phil's beautiful melody providing the perfect musical setting for it. The storyteller is on the road and a bit down and out (as is the case with narrators in several of the Dead's songs), and he's struggling to live a good life but finds himself frequently stymied. He wonders why folks are told to "love your brother" when "you'll catch it if you try." Yet there's always the "unbroken chain" of "sorrow and pearls" or "sky and sea" or "the western wind" or, most hopefully, "of you and me." One of the lines, "searching for the sound," became the title of Phil's autobiography in 2005. For an outstanding discussion about the lyrics to "Unbroken Chain," read the Dead.net blog by Nicholas Meriwether (UBC #1). David Dodd's discussion of UBC in his "Greatest Stories Ever Told" series is also worth reading (UBC #2).

Many Deadheads consider "Unbroken Chain" to be the *best* Grateful Dead song of all despite having been performed live so few times. Without a doubt, the studio version found on *From the Mars Hotel* is a true masterpiece. Sadly, no official live versions of UBC have been released, and many of the ten live performances are far from the Dead's best work, mostly due to Garcia's failing health in 1995. With that said, all ten live versions can be found on the Archive.org web site.

Two things are especially notable about its first performance in Philadelphia on March 19, 1995, available here: (UBC #3). Keep in mind that this is a song that was familiar to Deadheads since its original release in 1974 but *never* heard live. We've specifically selected an audience recording so you can hear the reaction of the crowd at the Spectrum for the song's first performance in the twenty-one years since its original release. To say the audience was excited is an understatement in the extreme. What is amazing is that so many people seemed aware that it was the first ever performance of a well-loved song none of them had ever heard live before. We're sure they also considered themselves very lucky as well.

That being said, the Dead themselves weren't familiar enough with the song to simply pluck it out of their arsenal for that 3/19/95 show. And so they rehearsed UBC two nights earlier at their sound check in Philadelphia. There is a recording of at least part of that rehearsal available here: (UBC #4). This recording is heavily mixed toward Lesh, which is probably appropriate since it's his song—Garcia doesn't seem to be involved until later in the recording. The entire "rehearsal" lasts about thirty minutes, and there's a lot of banter between Phil and the other band members as they play chord changes, ask him questions, and play parts of the song as well as one complete version. One fun highlight: Phil, becoming frustrated with the progress, asks, "What are the stumbling blocks right now?" to which Garcia replies: "Not knowing it!"

Perhaps the best live version of "Unbroken Chain" is the second one they performed on March 23, 1995, at the Charlotte Coliseum in Charlotte, North Carolina. Phil's singing is spot-on, and Garcia's guitar is better than on some of the other versions. You can judge for yourself here: (UBC #5). With this said, the final version of "Unbroken Chain" at Soldier Field in Chicago on July 9, 1995 (UBC #6), is not bad, despite the reputation of performances in 1995. Garcia's guitar during the instrumental portion toward the end is better than on many of the live versions, and he and Phil play a fine instrumental duet.

Barry considers himself extremely fortunate to have seen three of the live versions of "Unbroken Chain." His first on April 2, 1995, in Memphis was a good performance and can be heard here: (UBC #7). It closed the show as the encore, and that certainly sent Deadheads home with a big smile given what they had been lucky enough to hear. Barry also was at Las Vegas on May 21, 1995 (UBC #8), although it's not perhaps as strong as the 4/2/95 version. The third version Barry heard was at the Riverport Amphitheatre in Maryland Heights, Missouri, on July 6, 1995. This is the longest version of all at more than seven minutes. Although the band is really jamming, Garcia's guitar playing is a bit weak, as it was in many of these performances. You can hear Barry's recording of this performance here: (UBC #9).

Barry remembers leaving this show and thinking about all the problems the Grateful Dead had encountered on this last tour: there were way too many people at the Highgate, Vermont, shows; fans were struck by lightning at the RFK Stadium show in Washington, D.C.; gate crashers and death threats at Deer Creek; and more storm casualties in St. Louis. So if this Riverport show happened to be his last Grateful Dead show, that would be OK—he'd enjoyed a remarkable run of 194 shows. As it turned out, it *was* his last.

We can thank Phil Lesh's son, Grahame, who at age seven encouraged his dad to play "Unbroken Chain" in concert after hearing the version on *From the Mars Hotel*. As Phil points out in his autobiography, Grahame's enthusiasm for a live performance couldn't be denied (2005, 313). Despite UBC being "complicated and difficult to play," Phil added it to the set list for the Philadelphia show and continued "slotting it into . . . sets" for the rest of 1995.

Although none of the live versions of "Unbroken Chain" fully demonstrates the Grateful Dead's remarkable performance abilities, you definitely can hear it on the truly outstanding studio version on *From the Mars Hotel*. Find a copy or listen here: (UBC #10).

"Uncle John's Band"

The Grateful Dead performed many songs one could call "signature" songs, and the contents of any list would be debated by Deadheads old and young. Yet it's hard to imagine any set of signature Dead songs that would *not* include "Uncle John's Band," (aka UJB). UJB, written by Jerry Garcia and Robert Hunter, first appeared on the album *Workingman's Dead* in 1970. The first live performance was in late 1969, before the studio album. The Dead played the song 323 times over the years, and they played it almost every year of touring.

As Deadheads know, the Grateful Dead played many different songs in their shows. Even their signature songs were not played often enough for listeners to be able to count on their performance. The Dead were not a "greatest hits" band. For example, from 1981 through 1985, the Dead performed about 350 live shows but played UJB only about thirty times, so you had less than a 10 percent chance of hearing the song. And remember that this is a "signature" song.

The Grateful Dead played UJB at any point in the show and in any structural fashion they cared to pursue. UJB was played in the second set more often than not, but there are plenty of first set performances. It was often the encore, but it was used to open shows as well. The Dead performed the song acoustically as well as electrically. It was sometimes played from start to finish, sometimes it bracketed an intervening song. Though it always had a folk or bluegrass tone, it also included changes that led to jams and improvisations that were nothing like folk or bluegrass music. Whatever the label or structure, UJB was always danceable, always a treat.

The lyrics (UJB #1), as in many of Hunter's poems, are open to multiple levels of interpretation. The song could be a simple story of someone trying to recruit followers for a band, but it also could be about life and its many complexities. It could be about political intrigue, it could be a paean to aspects of the countercultural movements of the 1960s. Or it could be a love song about a longstanding relationship—or all of the above. Deadheads have all experienced hearing a phrase or two of the song in a different light because of some daily life experience—in other words, the song's maxims could take on new meaning. This song, with its many aphorisms, is as close to a "biblical" anthem as we get from the Dead.

The first live performance of UJB with vocals was December 4, 1969, in San Francisco, a good reference point for later versions (UJB #2). This performance is basically just the core song. UJB's characteristic intro riff is absent, and what later became a lively outro with a cappella vocals is also still to come. And listen to an early acoustic version at Harpur College in Binghampton, New York, on May 2, 1970, on *Dick's Picks, Volume 8* (D1:T11) and here: (UJB #3). This version does have the familiar intro riffs and the a cappella bridge before the coda.

The November 17, 1973, performance at UCLA in Los Angeles, released as *Dave's Picks, Volume 5* (D2:T5,T7) and available here (UJB #4), is one of the great performances of UJB. This is an example of the song being played in two separate pieces, with "Morning Dew" bracketed by UJB. With "Playing in the Band" as the opener and closer of the medley (Playing > UJB > "Morning Dew" > UJB > Playing), this is one of the greatest medleys the Dead ever played—it even has a name: "Playin' in Uncle John's Dew." Readers with an hour to spare will love this set of songs.

Another segmented version of UJB happened on December 26, 1979, in Oakland, California, and is on *Dick's Picks, Volume 5* (D2:T1 and D3:T8) and here: (UJB #5). The Dead opened the second set with UJB, then segued into "Estimated Prophet" and did not return to UJB until the second part of the encore, almost an hour and a half later. The first segment times in at about ten minutes and has two extended jams before the band moves into the next song. The second segment (UJB #6) picks up UJB at the coda section and extends this with another jam to end the show.

Bob's favorite performance of UJB took place in Hartford, Connecticut, on July 31, 1974, when UJB was the encore, played sometime around midnight outdoors on a hot summer evening. Picture the Wall of Sound behind the band, and as UJB begins, a cloud of dust rising up from the area to the right of the stage as a large circle of people, including Bob, danced the rest of the show away. Unfortunately, no video that we know of exists, but the show was released as *Dave's Picks, Volume 2* (D3:T8), and you can also listen here: (UJB #7). Feel free to kick up a little dust.

For fun, try this version from Atlanta, Georgia, on May 19,1977, released on *Dick's Picks, Volume 29* (D3:T3) and here: (UJB #8). This performance is notable for two reasons. First, the Dead *started* the song with the closing chorus at the start of the coda: UJB was a segue from Playing, and the jam apparently led them in a different direction than they expected. They recover nicely, though, don't you think? And second, most bands don't issue official recordings of their goofs, but here it is. Finally, we recommend you listen to Barry's recording of UJB at the Oakland Coliseum on December 27, 1987 (UJB #9). This later version has a relaxed feel to it. Barry's recording captures the audience responses very nicely.

We think "Uncle John's Band" is one of the Grateful Dead's truly special songs. We hope you can appreciate that from the recordings we've recommended. Perhaps more than any other single song in the repertoire, UJB may symbolize the shift in the Dead's style from the no-holds-barred psychedelic jamming of the 1960s toward a more song-based style from around 1970 onward. On the *Fillmore: The Last Days* album, from San Francisco, Jerry Garcia said, "Okay, folks. This is the one it's all about," before the band launched into "Johnny B. Goode." But with all due respect, we think "Uncle John's Band" is what it's all about.

"U.S. Blues"

One of the greatest Grateful Dead songs, "U.S. Blues," started its performance life with a different title: "Wave That Flag." The Dead were flexible: if it doesn't work one way, do it another way. Except for the chorus refrain—the "wave that flag" line—these songs have almost totally different lyrics, although the musical structure remains essentially the same. "Wave That Flag" is clearly the predecessor to "U.S. Blues," and we're treating the separate pieces as one entry here. Both iterations were written and composed by Robert Hunter and Jerry Garcia.

"Wave That Flag" was performed only fifteen times, all of them in 1973. After its final performance on June 10, 1973, the Dead retired the lyrics, which you can see at this link: (USBlues #1). We refer you to just one performance of "Wave That Flag," so you can hear both the lyrical contrast and the musical similarity with "U.S. Blues." Listen to March 28, 1973, in Springfield, Massachusetts (USBlues #2), a show that Bob attended that has been released as *Dave's Picks, Volume 16* (D1:T4). The lyrics on this version more or less resemble the lyrics at the link provided earlier. The chorus and the song's arrangement, however, are familiar to us as "U.S. Blues." "U.S. Blues" itself was performed 323 times, beginning in 1974, and it was in the rotation for the rest of the run. The Dead even played it twice in their four shows during their 1975 hiatus, once as an encore and once in the second set.

The lyrics to "U.S. Blues" are filled with critical social commentary, unlike most Grateful Dead songs. The lyrics (USBlues #3) target the U.S. social structure in the early 1970s. This may be the Dead's major countercultural "assault" on the mainstream: the U.S. government is equated with P. T. Barnum and described as an institution that will happily "run your life," "share your wealth," and even "steal your wife." At the same time, Hunter has Uncle Sam "hidin' out in a rock-and-roll band," which makes us wonder if Hunter saw the Grateful Dead, and rock and roll in general, as a modern-day analogy to the "bread and circuses" the Romans used to pacify the masses.

In any case, according to the song, we are living in a society filled with "back-to-back chicken shacks," and we need to "change our act" as a society. To us, the chorus of the song is both ironic and sarcastic: the latter is the line "wave that flag," a predilection of all sorts of pseudo-patriots. And the line "summertime done come and gone, my oh my" is certainly not about the seasonal cycle. It's about a decaying society, one apparently replete with flag-waving buffoons. "Ship of Fools" is probably the only other Grateful Dead song that rises to these heights of critical social commentary, though that song can be interpreted as focusing on an individual leader rather than society as a whole.

To watch part of a performance of "U.S. Blues," check out the *Grateful Dead Movie*. The music is from October 18, 1974, when the Dead played it as the encore. Deadheads who have seen the movie will recall the young man in the front row, singing along in total ecstasy. (One wonders whatever happened to that young man.) At any rate, you can see the show here: (USBlues #4). Incidentally, the version of "U.S. Blues" that appears on the album *Steal Your Face* is from the next night, October 19, 1974, which is a complete version available here: (USBlues #5).

An excellent performance to listen to is from May 7, 1977, in Boston (USBlues #6), the second of the four shows released in the box set *Get Shown the Light* (D3:T6). This is a soundboard recording, and as was often the case, "U.S. Blues" was the encore. This version is the standard against which to measure other performances. Listen for that big rock-and-roll show-ending flourish, and turn up the volume.

For the vast majority of the performances of "U.S. Blues," the Dead played it more or less consistently, along the lines of the 5/7/77 show mentioned earlier. One of our very favorite versions, however, comes from June 23, 1974, in Miami, where the Dead segued into "U.S. Blues" from a "Dark Star" jam and a "Spanish Jam." This version is part of the Dead's box set *So Many Roads (1965–1995)* (D2:T6). On the album, all three pieces are included as a single track. "U.S. Blues" is also available at this link: (USBlues #7). At the Archive.org website, each song is an individual link, so you can listen to what's played before or after the songs we highlight. In this case, you definitely should listen to what comes before—to "Spanish Jam," at least. If you like lead bass, you'll love this "Spanish Jam." Two things stand out here: first, the smooth segue into "U.S. Blues," some of which is hinted at in "Spanish Jam," and second, "U.S. Blues begins with a jam, unlike most versions. After the first verse begins, at about 2:45, this "U.S. Blues" matches the standard version.

The Grateful Dead issued dozens of live versions of "U.S. Blues"; a complete listing is available here: (USBlues #8). So there are many, many versions you can listen to. And headyversion.com (USBlues #9) lists fan favorite versions; note that our 6/23/74 favorite is headyversion.com's second favorite. Try any of the versions listed there. This is a great song, to be savored. Enjoy!

"Viola Lee Blues"

When the Grateful Dead formed in 1965, the band was already bringing together several strains of American music, particularly bluegrass, jug band music, folk music, rock and roll, and—Ron McKernan's (Pigpen) favorite—the blues. Perhaps because of Ken Kesey and the Acid Tests, however, the Dead were blending all of the above with psychedelic rock. Voila! We give you "Viola Lee Blues."

"Viola Lee Blues" (aka Viola) was written by Noah Lewis who, with his jug band, recorded the song in 1928. The early Grateful Dead were firmly committed to "old-time music," which you can learn more about here: (Viola #1). The Dead included this song on their first studio album, *The Grateful Dead*, released in 1967. That album had a total running time of about thirty-five minutes. Of that, Viola clocked in at more than ten minutes, almost a third of the whole album. This studio version can be heard here: (Viola #2). On an album with mostly short, quick tempo tracks, the Dead made a clear statement with Viola. We believe that this jam, on a studio album no less, is what separated the Dead from the rest of the bands in San Francisco back in the mid-1960s.

The Dead did not change the lyrics from Noah Lewis's original. The lyrics are hard to understand when the Dead sing them, but they can be found here: (Viola #3). The lament in the song concerns a prison sentence the singer is serving—it's the blues. Jailhouse blues is a motif in several songs the Dead performed, including, for example, two Merle Haggard covers, "Mama Tried" and "Sing Me Back Home." According to the available records, the Grateful Dead performed "Viola Lee Blues" thirty-two times between 1965 and 1970, when it was retired from the repertoire, but they most likely performed it many more times in the early years.

On July 16, 1966, at the Fillmore in San Francisco (Viola #4), the Dead performed an elegant and straightforward version of Viola. The musical passages between the sung verses are fun to listen to, with an almost funk-like tempo and rhythm. The three verses occupy just over the first three minutes of the song, leaving some six minutes for the extended jam that follows. Once the jam starts, the tempo picks up dramatically. At about 8:20, they perform a seamless segue back into the third verse before ending with a short coda. Considering this recording is only about one year into the performing life of the Grateful Dead, it's an amazing performance. A comment at this same link noted: "For a show this old, the sound is spectacular, and the playing is top shelf. Gives us 2nd generation [Dead]heads a chance to peer into a time that was magical."

That 7/16/66 performance, however, was relatively tame compared to others. Often, the Viola jam developed into a seemingly out-of-control improvisation only to end tightly at one precise moment. August 4, 1967, in Toronto, provides a good example: (Viola #5). The Dead begin the song with a longer intro, a habit that became common on many songs throughout their run. There's a hint of the jam to come between 3:00 and 3:30, in which the solo stops suddenly prior to the third verse. The jam proper starts after that verse, at about 4:15, and features both Lesh and Garcia. The long jam in this version times in at about fifteen minutes—lots of time for a Deadhead to float away with the band as they explore the far reaches. At around nine minutes, the tempo picks up speed and continues to do so, giving us a tremendous example of Garcia's virtuosity. At about fourteen minutes, there are hints of the free-for-all to come. A minute later, it's in full swing, and it continues to the exact moment (15:32) when it stops abruptly and the earlier tempo resumes. The third verse is repeated at 18:10 after a few more minutes of jamming. After the third verse, Viola dissolves into feedback. This is an outstanding version of Viola; it's a window into what the Grateful Dead were doing so well in the late 1960s.

There are many other outstanding versions. For example, headyversion.com (Viola #6) recommends May 2, 1970, the Harpur College show released by the Grateful Dead as *Dick's Picks, Volume 8* (D3:T4), available here: (Viola #7). This is a seventeen-minute version that dissolves into feedback. And listen to April 26, 1969, in Chicago. This Viola was issued on the compilation album *Fallout from the Phil Zone* (D1:T3) (Viola #8). In the liner notes Phil Lesh says of Viola: "The definitive early GD jammin' tune, the first one we ever really stretched out beyond all recognition." This one times in just over ten minutes and is quite funky—at least until the heavy stuff begins after about seven minutes.

We would never take a side in the enduring debate between those who say the Grateful Dead were "better" in the old days and those who prefer the "modern" Grateful Dead. We love the Dead's music from start to finish. However, "Viola Lee Blues" supports those who got off the bus when the Dead stopped playing songs and jams like Viola and "Caution (Do Not Stop on Tracks)," around 1970. The Grateful Dead's musical corpus may not have been the same after that, so "Viola Lee Blues" is clearly an essential song for anyone wanting to grasp the whole Grateful Dead trip.

"Weather Report Suite"/"Let It Grow"

The "Weather Report Suite," (aka WRS) is a series that includes "Prelude," "Part 1," and "Part 2," which is also called "Let It Grow." Of these, "Let It Grow" is by far the most played component of the triad. "Prelude" is not one of our 100 essential songs, but it is part of the suite. Both WRS "Part 1" and "Let It Grow" are most certainly among the essential. Even though these three compositions were not played together many times, we've decided to combine them into one discussion here.

WRS "Prelude" is a short instrumental that Bob Weir, its composer, originally played on acoustic guitar, usually with minimal participation from the rest of the band in the intro. It is a lovely piece of music and served to tone down the energy level at Dead shows whenever it was played. Prelude was played only fifty-two times, all between 1972 and 1974. (If you listen to the Dead's show on August 6, 1971, however, you might hear a hint of "Prelude" in the jam after "Me and My Uncle," primarily via Phil Lesh's bass.) Prelude was dropped from the rotation when the Dead began their hiatus from touring in late 1974.

WRS "Part 1," the second component of the suite, was composed by Bob Weir and Eric Anderson. The Dead played "Part 1" even fewer times than "Prelude," only forty-seven performances. In all of these, "Part 1" was preceded by "Prelude," and followed by "Let It Grow." All forty-seven performances took place in 1973 and 1974. "Part 1," like "Prelude," was dropped from the rotation on October 18, 1974, the final performance for both of these songs.

By contrast, "Let It Grow," composed by Bob Weir and the lyricist John Perry Barlow, did survive the Grateful Dead's hiatus. It was performed 276 times in all, which comes to about 230 solo performances after the hiatus. Its final performance was on July 2, 1995, the same week as the Dead's final show. "Let It Grow" was performed every year the Dead toured after the hiatus, for twenty years.

Much has been said about the lyrics in the "Weather Report Suite," and you can find them here for both "Part 1" and "Let It Grow": (WRS #1). The lyrics in "Part 1" read like a love song tied to the cycles of nature: things happen, for good or ill, even in a wonderful relationship. "Let It Grow" raises the level of thought from a romance to the nature of the universe—this is another of the Dead's "humanist materialism" songs. The lyrics at one level are romanticized observations; for example, a young woman is "as brown as the banks" of the river where she is gathering water. This while the "plowman," "broad as the back of the land he is sowing," does his work. All love what they're doing. But when it comes to putting a name on all this, Barlow avoids deities and has the thunder singing "I am!" The nature of reality is our material plane, not an idealized divinity. Musically, WRS goes from gentle beauty, to a romantic folk tune, to a dancer's delight. "Let It Grow" is the rocker of the three pieces, even with its relatively quiet coda.

We recommend six samples for your listening. Three are the complete suite, which means they take place between 1972 and 1974. The remaining three include "Let It Grow" alone, "Part 2" of WRS, from a later time. This lets you compare three versions of the first two segments of WRS and six versions of "Let It Grow" over its twenty-year span.

The first performance of WRS was on September 8, 1973, at the Nassau Coliseum on Long Island, New York, where the Grateful Dead played it during the first set. This performance is the first with WRS as a complete suite. Start listening here: (WRS #2), an audience recording that lists the suite as two tracks: there is no break between "Prelude" and "Part 1," which starts when Garcia's lead begins. This is not a superb recording of the show in terms of sound quality, but it does show that the suite emerged as a coherent whole from its first performance.

On December 19, 1973, the Dead played the whole suite at a show in Tampa, Florida (WRS #3), where WRS is listed as two separate tracks. Most of that show was released as *Dick's Picks, Volume 1* (D1:T4). On the album, the suite is listed as one single track. In this version, the tempo in "Part 1" is slower than in other versions. (This link also accesses the "Remember Your Hippie Training" instructions from the stage.)

The final performance of the complete WRS, as noted earlier, happened on October 18, 1974, in San Francisco at Winterland. You can hear a beautiful soundboard recording here: (WRS #4), where again you have to listen to two tracks—"Let It Grow" is a separate track on this recording. As you might have concluded from these three examples of WRS, the "high" comes from "Let It Grow," the loveliness of "Prelude" and "Part 1" notwithstanding. The Dead occasionally played "Let It Grow" in the second set, but after 1976 it was overwhelmingly a first set song, usually toward the end of the first set, as is the case in our next two versions.

On September 25, 1976, in Landover, Maryland, the Dead played "Let It Grow" as the next-to-last song of the first set. This show, except for one song ("It's All Over Now," by Bobby and Shirley Womack), was released as *Dick's Picks, Volume 20* (D1:T9), and "Let It Grow" is available here: (WRS #5). This is a soundboard recording, so you hear less of the audience's interaction with the band. This version does let you hear Donna Godchaux's vocal backup more clearly, as well as Keith Godchaux's piano. The jams show a lot of complementary improvisation, and there's a short drum solo before the band returns to the final singing of the chorus. The outro is exploratory: you might think that nobody in the band is playing "Let It Grow" any longer, except perhaps the drums, until the very end, when the characteristic riffs of the coda end the song. It's a beautiful jam.

For a slightly more classical version of "Let It Grow," listen to Barry's recording from May 19, 1992, from Cal-Expo in Sacramento, California: (WRS #6). This rocking version ended the first set. Listen for the syncopated phrases during the improvisational jams, as well as Lesh's great bass line.

As our final recommendation, try "Let It Grow" from December 16, 1992, at the Oakland Coliseum, where the Dead played it as the last song of the first set, a powerful ending at that. This show is available as *Dick's Picks, Volume 27* (D1:T7) and is accessible here: (WRS #7). (Note that at this Archive.org recording, there are no titles for the tracks on this audience recording: you are listening to track seven, which times in at 13:02.) We've covered eighteen years since the earliest performances of "Let It Grow." The structure here is still remarkably similar to the earlier versions. The band turns down the volume toward the end; it's a very quiet coda. This is an excellent end to a first set.

We hope you've enjoyed this excursion into these three songs that sometimes were—and sometimes weren't—played as a single suite. "Let It Grow," in particular, was a highlight song for the Dead from the mid-1970s onward. These selections illustrate the high energy, versatility, and improvisational skill of the Grateful Dead, as do many of their songs. Particularly notable in WRS, though, are the dynamics of the three pieces, which take us from quiet guitar through to rocking improvisation.

"West L.A. Fadeaway"

"West L.A. Fadeaway" (aka West LA), written by Garcia and Hunter, joined the Dead's live performance repertoire in 1982, along with a couple of their other songs, "Touch of Grey" and the less-appreciated (and *not* essential) "Keep Your Day Job." The studio version of West LA appeared on the Dead's *In the Dark* album, released in 1987 (West LA #1), which was their first album in six years. The first concert performance was August 28, 1982 (West LA #2), in Veneta, Oregon, almost ten years after the Dead's famous Sunshine Daydream show at the same venue. From that first live performance, West LA continued to be part of the live repertoire and was played a total of 140 times until its last outing on June 30, 1995 (West LA #3). In the debut performance, it was played in the second set, and then it quickly became a regular part of the first set, being played in the second set on only two other occasions.

The storyteller in this song tells a dark tale about "looking for a chateau" on the seedy side of LA where he can get a room "for an hour or two." This becomes darker when you realize that Hunter was referring to the Chateau Marmont in Los Angeles, where actor John Belushi died from a drug overdose in 1982, according to David Dodd (2005, 311). The tale continues with references to an old girlfriend—"I met an old mistake"—about whom he has nothing good to say and to "hauling items for the mob." Hunter reports a verse that Garcia sang only a few times in 1982 (1990, 239). It's in the first performance mentioned earlier, and you can hear the verse at 3:10, about Ginger who "tries to live by the golden rule" and suggests that "you treat people all right, other people will probably treat you cool." You can read all the lyrics including this extra verse here: (West LA #4). Garcia sings this verse in all eight of the 1982 performances.

Not mentioned in Hunter's book or on Dodd's site is that Garcia also plays around with several other lines in the song, particularly in regard to the number of rooms in the chateau. In the lyrics it's twenty-one, but sometimes he sings "forty-two rooms," "twenty-four rooms," or even "twenty-five rooms." Then on March 31, 1983, after the song hadn't been played since October 9, 1982, Garcia drops the "Ginger" verse and settles on "twenty-one rooms." Yet there's another line he continues to play with:

rather than "little red light on the highway, big green light on the speedway," he sings "big red light on the highway, little green light on the speedway."

Musically, West LA is a mid-tempo, funky rocker that benefits from Garcia's fuzz guitar effects and Brent Mydland's Hammond organ, as well as Lesh's powerful bass lines and Weir's unique rhythm playing. Garcia's lead solo before the final verse can really stretch out and crank up the energy, depending on the performance. There are surprisingly few official releases of "West L.A. Fadeaway," given its number of performances and steady presence in the repertoire. In addition to *In the Dark*, it was released on CD and video on *Downhill from Here* in 1997, *View from the Vault III* in 2002, and *View from the Vault IV* in 2003. It also appears as audio in both the *Spring 1990* box sets. And that's about it for official releases.

Barry saw West LA performed thirty-five times from September 7, 1983 (West LA #5), at Red Rocks Amphitheater through May 21, 1995, in Las Vegas (West LA #6). He really liked that 1983 Red Rocks version, and you might agree if you listen to that good audience recording at the link above; headyversions.com lists it as one of the best. Another worthy version is from Alpine Valley on July 19, 1989; we agree with headyversion.com that this might be the best. You can hear it in a fine matrix recording here: (West LA #7). Another performance we recommend is from December 17, 1986 (West LA #8), which is the second of the three "comeback" shows after Garcia's recovery from a diabetic coma that July. Listening to this, it's hard to believe that he had to relearn the guitar as part of his recovery.

For something different, check out these performances. The first is from December 31, 1988, in Oakland and features Clarence Clemons (from Bruce Springsteen's E Street Band), a headyversion.com pick and another performance Barry saw and enjoyed. This is an audience recording: (West LA #9). The second is from March 31, 1991, in Greensboro, North Carolina, and features Bruce Hornsby on piano while Vince Welnick plays electronic keyboard. This is a nine-minute version on a fine soundboard: (West LA #10). Finally, give a listen to West LA on July 1, 1992, from Buckeye Lake Music Center in Hebron, Ohio. This one includes Steve Miller on guitar and Norton Buffalo on harmonica. We recommend this excellent audience recording: (West LA #11).

West LA is another Grateful Dead song that's great fun to hear and dance to. Although it's featured on only a handful of official recordings, there are many performances available at Archive.org. We've pointed you to several versions from throughout its tenure in the repertoire. Despite being a "seedy love song" according to Garcia in a band conversation promoting the *In the Dark* album, it's still a funky, slinky, fun song with many enjoyable performances.

"Wharf Rat"

"Wharf Rat" was composed by Robert Hunter and Jerry Garcia and is one of the greatest of the Grateful Dead's songs. It has it all: intriguing lyrics (including a good story), musical flexibility, and a long performance history. The Dead played it

394 times between 1971 and 1995 and played it every year except for 1975, during the band's hiatus. Moreover, they played it regularly; that is, the gap between performances of "Wharf Rat" rarely exceeded ten shows. So if you saw more than a few Dead shows over the years, chances are you heard "Wharf Rat" somewhere along the line.

Except for a handful of early performances of "Wharf Rat," the Dead played the song exclusively during the second set. They often paired it with "The Other One," usually but not always with "Wharf Rat" second in the pairing. Because the Dead normally alternated vocals between Garcia and Bob Weir, the Dead usually followed "Wharf Rat" with a Weir tune—for example, "Not Fade Away," "Throwing Stones," "Sugar Magnolia," or "(Turn on Your) Lovelight." The endless variety of sequences in these last three or four songs in a typical Dead show always excited the audience.

The lyrics to "Wharf Rat" (Wharf Rat #1) initially seem to be a downer. Our narrator is wandering "down down, down by the docks of the city," when he encounters a "wharf rat," August West. West asks for a "dime for a cup of coffee." Our narrator doesn't have a dime, though he does have "time to hear his story." West's story is a depressing tale to be sure: he's lost Pearly Baker, his girl, and his sobriety; he's spent most of his life in prison "for some other fucker's crime"; and he has even been rejected by own family as well: "everyone knew I'd come to no good."

But Hunter inserted an optimistic vocal bridge filled with hope about getting "a new start" to "live the life I should." It's optimism we can barely believe, and yet at the same time it embodies the hope we all have for ourselves as we face life's challenges. Following that bridge, the story refocuses on our narrator, who first encourages August West and then subsequently wanders around the docks convinced (or convincing himself) that his own girlfriend, Molly Lee, will have been "true to me." We aren't sure, of course, as is often the case with Hunter's poetry, if our narrator is delusional in this or not. David Dodd's blog on "Wharf Rat" is particularly interesting and insightful (Wharf Rat #2).

Musically, "Wharf Rat" is a slow to mid-tempo song with minor chords to complement the lyrics. The bridge mentioned earlier is perhaps the Grateful Dead's best musical bridge. It breaks the plaintive tone completely, while shifting the time signature as well. Vocally, it adds a gospel tone, usually with great audience responses. "Wharf Rat," as a musical piece, usually had improvisational jams, whether before the song, during it, or after the last verse, before the Dead segued into the next song. And so we emphasize, as we have for other songs, that it is important to listen to the context, the sequence of songs in which "Wharf Rat" appears.

"Wharf Rat" is easily accessible for listening. According to Deaddisc.com, there are some sixty versions on various albums and box sets (Wharf Rat #3). "Wharf Rat" first appeared on an album in 1971, the live eponymous album *Grateful Dead* (aka *Skull & Roses*). That performance, from April 26, 1971, at the Fillmore East in New York City, is here: (Wharf Rat #4).

The Dead's first live performance of "Wharf Rat" was on February 18, 1971, just a couple of months earlier than the 4/27/71 version just mentioned. That debut, at the Capitol Theater in Port Chester, New York, also featured first performances of five other songs, which were recorded for but never used on the *Skull & Roses* album. This is one of the rare appearances of "Wharf Rat" in the first set, and you can hear a remastered soundboard recording here: (Wharf Rat #5). At this performance, the Dead bracketed "Wharf Rat" with "Dark Star." Be sure also to listen to the "Dark Star" jam that follows "Wharf Rat." Part of that jam, called "Beautiful Jam," was issued as part of the Dead's box set *So Many Roads* (D2:T2).

Some six years later, on May 25, 1977, one of the Dead's best touring seasons, the band played "Wharf Rat" in Richmond, Virginia, during the second set, bracketed before and after by "The Other One." This version is available on *Dave's Picks, Volume 1* (D3:T2), as well as here: (Wharf Rat #6). This matrix recording gives you a chance to hear the crowd responses. There's an imaginative intro to the song in this version, and the outro jam illustrates how the Dead varied the energy in a song that starts as a fairly subdued dirge. This performance is a good standard against which to compare others.

On November 3, 1991, in Golden Gate Park in San Francisco, the Dead played at a memorial concert for Bill Graham, their friend and concert impresario. At that show, they performed "Wharf Rat" as the next-to-last song of the second set, a typical spot for the song. There's a great outro worth listening to. You can hear this performance here: (Wharf Rat #7).

No review of "Wharf Rat" could be complete without mentioning the Wharf Rats, a group of Deadheads who adopted a twelve-step program model, à la Alcoholics Anonymous, to encourage sobriety during Dead shows for those so inclined. Much has been written about the drug scene at Grateful Dead shows, but it should also be noted that the Dead supported the Wharf Rats by giving them table space at shows, where Deadheads could meet before the show, during the set break, and after the show.

In sum, "Wharf Rat" is essential for its lyrics, its music, and its message for Deadheads and anybody else struggling with life. If you are down, try to soar with the bridge in this song.

"The Wheel"

"The Wheel" (aka Wheel), introduced on Garcia's eponymous solo album *Garcia* in 1972, was composed by Jerry Garcia and lyricist Robert Hunter. Many of the Dead's songs were played live prior to their release on studio albums, but that was not the case with Wheel, which the Dead did not perform live until 1976. The Dead performed Wheel 258 times before its last performance in 1995. Wheel was a steady part of the rotation; most years they played it about a dozen times or more, except for 1978 and 1979, when it was hardly played at all.

For its first performance, the Dead played Wheel as the encore, but after that, it was always a second set number. Most typically, Wheel followed Drumz > Space:

once the drum solo was finished, the band played a fairly unstructured, often spacey jam and then segued into Wheel when the drummers returned to the stage. The Dead performed Wheel with nearly the same musical structure and lyrical phrasing for its entire run, although the song's intros and outros could vary, depending on the song sequence during the second set of the show.

Wheel has a slow to mid-range tempo, but the pattern of chord changes lends a heavier tone musically. It's reminiscent of "Playing in the Band" when that song shifts into its power bridge. There is less emphasis on the instrumental solos in Wheel, perhaps intentionally so, in order to highlight the lyrics. Typically, since Wheel was often the first song after "Drumz," the band would segue into—well— just about any song that they normally played in the second set. After the space jam that usually followed "Drumz," Wheel was a great reentry song.

Wheel's lyrics *seem* straightforward (Wheel #1), but like many of Hunter's poems, there are multiple possible levels of interpretation. At that site, take a moment to read the comments about the meaning of these lyrics; they range from an interpretation based on drugs—thunder is weed; lightning is LSD—to religious interpretations— one comment claims Wheel is "the devil's music." Another comment claims the song evokes the noble goal of the Merry Pranksters; that is, always pushing oneself further, as implied in "Furthur," the name of the Pranksters' bus, and the post-1995 Weir and Lesh band. Ultimately, we may take Wheel as a symbol of life, as in Buddhism, as well as the need to persist in the face of obstacles in life. In this sense, we are like the song's robin, who is told to "run around, gotta get back where you belong."

On June 3, 1976, in Portland, Oregon, the Dead performed Wheel live for the first time, the only time Wheel was an encore, hence with no segue into or out of the song, perhaps the only time that ever happened with Wheel. This version starts with a solo drumbeat to set the tempo and ends with a short jam that lasts about a minute before the simple coda. There are clearly no first-time jitters for this performance: a high standard for this song is set already. A quality matrix recording is accessible here: (Wheel #2).

On September 28, 1976, in Syracuse, New York, Wheel did *not* appear as the first song after the drum solo and jam. Instead, at this show, issued on *Dick's Picks, Volume 20* (D4:T2), the Dead opened the second set with "Playing in the Band," and during that song's jam, they segued into Wheel and then continued without stopping to the end of the second set, which ended with the reprise of "Playing in the Band." Listen to this version here: (Wheel #3). This is a standard performance of Wheel—it's not a long song; usually it's bracketed by a longish introduction and an improvisational segue into the following song. Again, we recommend spending a little time listening to the preceding and following songs. In this recording, there are interesting crowd responses to the line, "if the thunder don't get you then the lightning will," and dur- ing the stop for the second iteration of the line "bound to cover just a little more ground." This is a fun version to listen to.

In the early 1980s, Wheel usually segued into a "major" Grateful Dead song, like "Truckin'," "Sugar Magnolia," "Uncle John's Band," or "Playing in the Band." Which is to say that the Dead followed the relatively slow tempo Wheel with a rocking up-beat song. An exception happened on March 10, 1981, at Madison Square Garden, when the Dead segued out of Wheel into "China Doll," one of the Dead's slowest laments, a very introspective song. This version is available on an audience tape (Wheel #4). On this recording, Brent Mydland's vocals lend a different accent to the lyrics.

On July 7, 1987, in Roanoke, Virginia, the Dead segued from Wheel into "Gimme Some Lovin'," a combination that occurred regularly in the late 1980s until that song was dropped from the rotation in 1990. Catch a good audience recording at this link: (Wheel #5). If these crowd responses don't get your juices flowing, we'd be very surprised.

On June 26, 1994, in Las Vegas, the Dead segued into Wheel from Drumz/Space, as they often did, and segued out into Dylan's "All along the Watchtower," a frequent pairing with Wheel in the 1990s. There's a good intro in this version. Here's a sound-board recording: (Wheel #6). Finally, listen to Barry's excellent audience recording of "The Wheel" from Laguna Seca Raceway, near Monterey, California, on July 29, 1988 (Wheel #7). Brent Mydland's vocals are strong in this one.

These last three performances illustrate the point we made earlier, that Wheel was performed with more or less the same musical structure over the years, unlike the many Dead songs that evolved in different directions. For the Dead, "The Wheel" was a relatively short song, usually played without extended solos or serious impro-visational jams, but Wheel brings some interesting lyrics to the table. It's a short masterpiece nestled within the Dead's commonly magnificent second sets.

Bonus Tracks

There you have it—the Grateful Dead's 100 essential songs. We had many, many discussions about what constitutes the essential Dead playlist, and now you've seen—and hopefully listened to—the list we agreed upon. Finishing this discussion of the Dead's music, it's important to remember that there's no objective list of "best" or "essential" songs or concerts. Listening to music is a purely subjective experience. This was clear after every live Grateful Dead concert, as fans left and the discussions among them began. Although there was often agreement on the overall performance or even on specific songs, it was never unanimous—never! So having listed our "essential" songs, we know we'll be asked why "Day Job" wasn't included (just kidding!) or why we *did* include "Days Between." We've given it our best shot. Now it's time for you to join the discussion.

But before that discussion picks up speed, we're adding a few "bonus tracks," as the band did on many official releases after 1995. These are songs that almost made the top 100 but were left out for one reason or another. Many didn't make the cut because of our earlier decisions about cover songs, for example, which we outlined in the introduction. Others, original songs, may have been pushed out because of the cover songs we did include or because their performances were limited.

So here are twenty bonus tracks that you might enjoy. As usual, we recommend searching for the lyrics for these songs before listening.

1. "Around and Around"
   A classic rock and roll song by Chuck Berry performed by the Dead 418 times, usually as the rousing finale of a set. Listen to this second set gem from December 19, 1973, in Tampa, Florida: (Bonus Track #1).

2. "Big Railroad Blues"
Big RxR Blues was written by Noah Lewis of the Cannon Jug Stompers and
first recorded in the 1920s. The Dead played it 175 times throughout their
thirty-year run, usually in the first set. Here's a version from May 6, 1981, at
Nassau Coliseum on Long Island, New York: (Bonus Track #2).

3. "Big River"
Johnny Cash's great song about unrequited love along the Mississippi
River. The Dead performed it 397 times, usually in the first set, with great
Dixieland-style instrumentation, as only the Dead could do it. Here's a mas-
terpiece from August 13, 1975, in San Francisco: (Bonus Track #3).

4. "Blow Away"
Brent Mydland put his soul into singing this heavy love song that he cowrote
with John Perry Barlow. The Dead played it only twenty-three times between
1988 and 1990. When Brent died, this song's performance life died with
him. Here's a good one, from March 26, 1990, Albany, New York: (Bonus
Track #4).

5. "Corrina"
This song was a late (1992) addition to the Dead's repertoire written by Weir/
Hunter/Hart. The Dead played it seventy-seven times, usually in the second
set, and usually with extended improvisation. Listen to a good version from
March 31, 1994, in Atlanta: (Bonus Track #5).

6. "Cosmic Charlie"
The Dead, tongue firmly in cheek, played "Cosmic Charlie" forty-one times,
mostly in the late 1960s. It's another Garcia/Hunter composition, definitely
a throwback to the early days of the band. If you're a person with pretensions,
this is aimed at you. Here's the May 2, 1970, performance with a great intro
from Binghamton, New York: (Bonus Track #6).

7. "Death Don't Have No Mercy"
A gospel lament written by the Reverend Gary Davis and played by the Dead
forty-nine times, mostly before 1971. The song prospered mightily when
Brent Mydland joined the band, so here's a powerful 1989 example from
late in the second set on September 2, 1989, at Mountain View, California:
(Bonus Track #7). Garcia sings the first verse, Weir the second, and Mydland
the third, after a soaring Garcia solo.

8. "Easy Wind"
Originally on the *Workingman's Dead* album, this Pigpen classic with music
and lyrics by Hunter had built-in tempo shifts. After Pigpen died, the Dead
did not play the song again. Here's a good version, from the Capitol Theater
in Port Chester, New York, on June 24, 1970: (Bonus Track #8).

9. "In the Midnight Hour"
Wilson Pickett and Steve Cropper wrote this great R & B hit in 1965, and
the Dead covered it forty-six times over the years. This early, thirty-minute
version opened the show on September 3, 1967, in Rio Nido, California,

and includes a classic Pigpen vocal rave: "Get yo' hands outta yo pockets": (Bonus Track #9).

10. "It Hurts Me Too"

Elmore James composed this blues tune, which Pigpen delivered with great soul. The Dead covered it forty-seven times, and the song left the rotation when Pigpen died. Pigpen could sing the blues! This audience recording is from the Europe '72 tour, April 14, 1972, in Copenhagen, from early in the second set: (Bonus Track #10).

11. "It's All Over Now"

This sprightly country rock song speaks to having the last laugh after love has gone bad. Bobby and Shirley Womack wrote the song and the Dead played it 160 times, almost always in the first set. The performance from July 17, 1989, at Alpine Valley in East Troy, Wisconsin, has it all: (Bonus Track #11).

12. "Let the Good Times Roll"

The great Sam Cooke composed this bouncy song, which the Dead performed forty-two times during the 1980s Brent Mydland era. Listen to this version, from the same Alpine Valley show as "It's All over Now." Good Times was that show's opener: (Bonus Track #12).

13. "Little Red Rooster"

A classic blues song composed by Willie Dixon and sung by Bob Weir, accompanied by throngs of howling Deadheads. The Dead played this song 272 times, mostly during the Brent Mydland era. Here's a good audience recording from July 7, 1989, at RFK Stadium: (Bonus Track #13). Surprise: Brent vocals.

14. "Loose Lucy"

A Garcia/Hunter original that's funky in most of its ninety-eight performances. It has a catchy sing-along line, plus a life lesson: "don't shake the tree when the fruit ain't ripe." Listen (and sing along) to this March 14, 1990, audience recording from the Capitol Center in Landover, Maryland: (Bonus Track #14). This version was a breakout performance after fifteen years and a gap of almost 1,000 shows. To the Dead, you will say—as we do—"Thank you for a real good time."

15. "Man Smart (Woman Smarter)"

Woman Smarter is a Caribbean-style calypso written by Norman Span ("King Radio"). The Dead played it 199 times. Pay careful attention to the lyrics: women may be smarter, but what is it exactly the women are leading the men toward? Listen to this one from the Fourth of July, 1989, in Buffalo, New York, with Brent Mydland sharing the vocals: (Bonus Track #15).

16. "My Brother Esau"

A Weir/Barlow antiwar classic, both biblical and political, usually played in the first set. Find the lyrics before listening. The Dead performed it 104 times, all between 1983 and 1987. We like this performance with its longer intro from October 28, 1985, at the Fox Theater in Atlanta: (Bonus Track #16). Weir's outro vocalizing is reminiscent of Pigpen's raves in the late 1960s.

17. "New Minglewood Blues"

    Sometimes titled "All New Minglewood Blues" or "New New Minglewood Blues" but usually known simply as "Minglewood," this is another old-time song written by Noah Lewis in the 1920s. The Dead, with Weir on vocals, performed it 435 times from 1966 to 1995, nearly the band's entire run. This version is the opener at the famous Cornell (Barton Hall) show from May 8, 1977: (Bonus Track #17).

18. "New Speedway Boogie"

    Garcia and Hunter's take on the Altamont Racetrack concert in which the Hell's Angels notoriously provided "security" for the Rolling Stones, who headlined. The Dead performed the song frequently in 1969 and 1970 and not again until 1991, with Garcia on vocals. This was a gap of 1,369 shows, the longest gap of any original Dead song. Listen to this early semi-acoustic version from September 20, 1970, at the Fillmore East in New York City: (Bonus Track #18). "One way or another, this darkness got to give."

19. "Sing Me Back Home"

    A gospel lullaby by Merle Haggard, this is a death row song about nostalgia sung beautifully by Jerry Garcia, with Bob Weir and Donna Godchaux singing backup. The Dead played this song only thirty-nine times, all from 1971 to 1973. Listen to this classic and powerful performance from the third set on August 27, 1972, at the famous Springfield Creamery benefit show in Veneta, Oregon: (Bonus Track #19). Watch it on the *Sunshine Daydream* documentary if you can.

20. "We Can Run, but We Can't Hide"

    This song, by Brent Mydland, with lyrics by John Perry Barlow, is the Dead's pro-environment anthem, which these days might be aimed at global warming. It's also a good finale for these bonus tracks. Brent puts his usual passion into the vocals. The Dead played this song only twenty-two times in 1989 and 1990. We think you'll like this version, from Pittsburgh on April 2, 1989: (Bonus Track #20).

Online Grateful Dead Resources

In writing this book, we've been helped immensely by the work of others that is available on the internet. This page lists many of those resources. To fully inform yourself about the Grateful Dead, these are recommended places to start. Of course, you can simply google "Grateful Dead," and you'll find more than 12,000,000 results!

All Grateful Dead Original Song Debuts

A wonderful Archive.org list of every debut live performance of original Dead tunes with direct links to the debut performances. (Resources #1)

Allmusic.com

Although it's not exclusively Grateful Dead, this site offers a thorough Dead discography and song list, among other items of interest. (Resources #2)

Annotated Grateful Dead Lyrics by David Dodd

Dodd's site has a terrific section on the Dead's song lyrics as well as discographies for the band and musicians. No cover songs at this site. (Resources #3)

Archive.org

Complete set lists for most every Dead show with reviews, highlights, and streaming. (Resources #4)

Azlyrics.com

A searchable site for lyrics of songs by the Dead and other artists. (Resources #5)

Compleat Grateful Dead Discography by Ihor Slabicky

An amazing amount of detailed information about Dead recordings, books, videos, and more, although its format is challenging. (Resources #6)

Deadessays.blogspot.com

This site offers an ongoing series of articles on songs and performances of the early Grateful Dead. (Resources #7)

Deadforayear.com

A remarkably comprehensive and user friendly site that offers streamable Dead music, reflections, lists of Dead official releases, books about the Dead, and more. (Resources #8)

Deadlists.org

Complete set lists with notes for every Dead show. The site is maintained by volunteers and provides multiple direct links to music on Archive.org. (Resources #9)

Dead.net

The official Grateful Dead site with loads of Dead-related news, music, pictures, posters, lyrics, merchandise, and much, much more. (Resources #10)

Grateful Dead Family Discography

Deaddisc.com is a user friendly, well-structured, searchable website with details about songs, albums, release dates, and more, updated through 2016. (Resources #11)

Greatest Stories Ever Told by David Dodd

Dodd's excellent blog on Dead.net, where he elaborates on song meanings and more. (Resources #12)

Headyversion.com

A searchable list of the "best" performances of Grateful Dead songs as voted by users, with comments and links to archive.org. (Resources #13)

Hooterollin' Blog by Corry Arnold

This blog offers insight and speculation from the dark corners of Grateful Dead research; an appendix to Lost Live Dead. (Resources #14)

Lostlivedead.blogspot.com

Author Corry Arnold is a Dead researcher beyond compare who digs deep into the Dead's history and writes about it in great detail. (Resources #15)

Relisten.net

At this site you can peruse the various Dead-related bands and listen to their live catalog. (Resources #16)

SetList Program

Grateful Dead set lists and listener experiences searchable by venue, city, etc. (Resources #17)

SongMeanings.com

The Grateful Dead section of this site offers song lyrics, album information, and more, but it isn't easy to navigate. (Resources #18)

Whitegum.com

Alex Allan's Grateful Dead lyric and song finder, with broad coverage of Dead-related information. (Resources #19)

Bibliography and Sources

For Further Reading

Beviglia, Jim. 2015. "Behind the Song: The Grateful Dead, 'Ripple.'" *American Songwriter: The Craft of Music.* September 29, 2015, http://americansongwriter.com/2015/09/behind -the-song-the-grateful-dead-ripple.

Browne, David. 2015. "Grateful Dead's Robert Hunter on Jerry's Final Days: 'We Were Brothers,' Part 2." *Rolling Stone.* March 11, 2015, www.rollingstone.com/music/features/ grateful-deads-robert-hunter-on-jerrys-final-days-we-were-brothers-20150311.

Carr, Revell. 2010. "Where All the Pages Are My Days: Metacantric Moments in Deadhead Lyrical Experience." In *The Grateful Dead in Concert: Essays on Live Improvisation*, ed. Jim Tuedio and Stan Spector, 107–17. Jefferson, NC: McFarland.

Dasaro, Daniel J., and Christian Crumlish. 2017. "The Dead's Three Decades of 'Dancin' in the Streets' (1966–1987)." March 24, 2018, http://deadessays.blogspot.com/2017/03/ dancin-in-streets-guest-post.html.

Dodd, David. 2005. *The Complete Annotated Grateful Dead Lyrics.* New York: Free Press.

Dowling, William C. 1997. "'Ripple': A Minor Excursus." Accessed September 11, 2017. http://artsites.ucsc.edu/GDead/agdl/dowling.html.

Fricke, David. July 10, 2014. "Branford Marsalis on His Unlikely Collaboration With the Grateful Dead." Accessed April 23, 2018. www.rollingstone.com/music/news/branford -marsalis-on-his-unlikely-collaboration-with-the-grateful-dead-20140710.

Gans, David. 2002. *Conversations with the Dead.* Cambridge, MA: Da Capo Press.

Greene, Elizabeth. 1988. "No Simple Highway." artsites.ucsc.edu, http://artsites.ucsc.edu/ GDead/agdl/greene.html

Hunter, Robert. 1990. *A Box of Rain: Collected Lyrics of Robert Hunter.* New York: Viking Penguin.

———. 2004. *All Good Things: Jerry Garcia Studio Sessions.* Booklet. Jerry Garcia Estate LLC and Warner Strategic Marketing, Warner Music Group.

Jackson, Blair. 1983. *Grateful Dead: The Music Never Stopped.* New York: Delilah Commu- nications.

———. 1988. "Robert Hunter: The Song Goes On." *The Golden Road*, Spring 1988.

Jackson, Blair, and David Gans. 2015. *This Is All a Dream We Dreamed: An Oral History of the Grateful Dead.* New York: Flat Iron Books.

Lesh, Phil. 2005. *Searching for the Sound: My Life with the Grateful Dead.* New York: Little Brown.

McNally Dennis, Ed. 2002. *A Long Strange Trip.* New York: Broadway Books.

———. 2015a. *Jerry on Jerry: The Unpublished Jerry Garcia Interviews.* New York: Black Dog and Leventhal Publishers.

———. 2015b. "Liner Notes." In *Dave's Picks, Volume 16,* pp. 3–9. Rhino Records.

McQuail, Josephine A. 1994. "Folk Songs and Allusions to Folk Songs in the Repertoire of the Grateful Dead." Accessed January 24, 2018. http://www2.iath.virginia.edu/sixties/HTML_docs/Texts/Scholarly/McQuail_Dead_01.html.

Meriwether, Nicholas. 2014. "Listening to Bobby Petersen." In *A Rare and Different Tune: The Seventeenth Grateful Dead Scholars Caucus,* ed. Nicholas G. Meriwether, 55–78. Albuquerque, NM: Dead Letters Press.

Metzger, John. "Terrapin Station Project." *The Music Box.* March 1998, www.musicbox-online.com/gd-ter.html#ixzz5GCHrquCF.

Myers, Marc. 2017. "How Cops, Pills and Parties Inspired the Grateful Dead's 'Truckin.'" *Wall Street Journal,* September 20, 2017, www.wsj.com/articles/how-cops-pills-and-parties-inspired-the-grateful-deads-truckin-1505922824.

Parrish, Michael.1999. "Drums and Space: The Evolution of Drumz and Space." Accessed January 24, 2018. http://deadessays.blogspot.com/2017/03/drums-and-space-guest-post.html.

Scott, John W., Michael Dolgushkin, and Stuart Nixon. 1995. *Deadbase IX: The Complete Guide to Grateful Dead Song Lists.* Hanover, NH: Deadbase.

Scott, John W., Stu Nixon, and Michael Dolgushkin. 2015. *DeadBase 50.* San Francisco: Watermark Press and Pacific Standard Print, RR Donnelley Companies.

Shenk, David, and Steve Silberman. 1994. *Skeleton Key: A Dictionary for Deadheads.* New York: Doubleday.

Trager, Oliver. 1997. *The American Book of the Dead: The Definitive Grateful Dead Encyclopedia.* New York: Simon and Schuster.

Trudeau, Robert H. 2012. "A Super-Metacantric Analysis of 'Playing in the Band.'" In *Reading the Dead,* ed. Nicholas G. Meriwether, 93–108. Lanham, MD: Scarecrow Press.

Wendel, Peter. 2016. "Dead Best: 7 Smoldering Versions of 'Black Peter.'" Accessed January 24, 2018. http://songmango.com/dead-best-7-smoldering-versions-of-black-peter.

Index

About the Authors

Barry Barnes, PhD, saw 194 Grateful Dead concerts between 1974 and 1995. He was a "taper" and recorded 189 of those performances, which he traded in the days before downloads. He owned a record store and was a DJ on a progressive FM rock station from 1974 to 1976. Barry is author of *Everything I Know about Business I Learned from the Grateful Dead: The Ten Most Innovative Lessons from a Long Strange Trip* as well as numerous book chapters, case studies, research articles, and concert reviews focused on the Grateful Dead.

Bob Trudeau, PhD, saw approximately fifty Grateful Dead shows between 1973 and 1994 while holding a day job as professor of political science at Providence College, where he specialized in Latin American politics and history. He is the author of one book and many conference papers and book chapters on Central America. In the field of Grateful Dead studies, Bob is the author of a detailed analysis of *Playing in the Band* and worked with Scott Deetz on a research project using Q methodology to study Deadhead responses to Grateful Dead music. He has been an avid listener of Grateful Dead music since 1971.

CPSIA information can be obtained
at www.ICGtesting.com
Printed in the USA
LVHW092305300419
616203LV00003B/36/P

9 781538 110577